DEALING WITH DEPRESSION NATURALLY

KEATS TITLES OF RELATED INTEREST

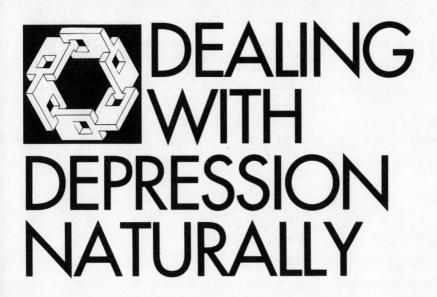

DEALING WITH DEPRESSION NATURALLY

Syd Baumel

Introductory comments by
ABRAM HOFFER, PH.D., M.D., HARVEY ROSS, M.D.,
and MELVYN R. WERBACH, M.D.

 KEATS PUBLISHING INC. ■ **New Canaan, Connecticut**

> *Dealing with Depression Naturally* is not intended as medical advice. Its intent is solely informational and educational. Please consult a health professional should the need for one be indicated.

DEALING WITH DEPRESSION NATURALLY

Copyright © 1995 by Syd Baumel

ISBN 0-87983-645-8

Printed in the United States of America

Published by Keats Publishing, Inc.
27 Pine Street (Box 876)
New Canaan, Connecticut 06840-0876

*For my mother Maria
and in memory of my father Paul,
with deepest love and gratitude.*

Table of Contents

Introductory Comments

There are very few good books which describe in any comprehensive detail the connection between depression and the host of environmental factors which impinge upon it. In my opinion, this book does it better than the others. The author writes well, he has a flair for description, and he covers the various types of depression fully. In addition, he has provided an excellent list of references to back up his conclusions.

The book is informative, easy to read and not dogmatic. I like the balanced approach—both conventional and natural treatments are discussed. If the medical profession would read it, they would find that the information is valid since it is taken from the medical literature and accurately referenced. All physicians ought to have it on their shelves.

Dealing With Depression Naturally contains valuable information for the general reader—with or without depression. It is also a useful textbook for medical and psychological students.

A. Hoffer, M.D., Ph.D.

I was quite impressed. Syd Baumel has done a superb job of digesting and summarizing a massive literature in a style light enough for enjoyable reading.

It has much to offer to both health professionals (psychiatrists in particular) and to the general public. The references make it possible for those who become interested in a specific approach to investigate it further.

Melvyn R. Werbach, M.D.

The great value of this book is in its bringing to the awareness of the reader the great number of different treatments of depression which have been studied and found to be useful. The bibliography is invaluable as a source for those who want to study a particular treatment in greater detail.

This book is an eye opener for those psychiatrists who are stuck in a narrow model of depression. However, they will probably not read it unless it is given to them by their patients! Any professional who does read it will be impressed.

The absolute variety of treatments offers great hope to those who are suffering from depression and to their friends and families, who often share the burden of directing the affected person to proper treatments.

Syd Baumel is to be congratulated for the work he has done in bringing this important information together. It can be of great benefit to those with depression, their families and friends, and to the professionals treating them.

Harvey M. Ross, M.D.

Preface

My interest in depression is more than academic. I've been there myself. I know what it's like to struggle with depression for years and feel that nothing can or will help. I also know what it's like to finally find things that do help (drugs, natural antidepressants), things that, in some cases, can turn depression off almost like a switch.

Not that this a book about "how I conquered my depression." What has worked for me won't necessarily work for you. Hence the diversity of alternatives you'll find on the following pages—the better to ensure we all find the solutions we need.

Some thanks are in order to the people who helped make this book a reality.

For responding to my letters, granting me interviews, providing me with resource materials, reading my drafts, or helping in other ways, my thanks to Jambur Ananth, M.D., Marion Baumel, Morris Baumel, Laure Branchey, M.D., MaryLynn Bryce, Todd Estroff, M.D., Alan Gelenberg, M.D., Abram Hoffer, M.D., Leo Hollister, M.D., David Horrobin, M.D., Joseph F. Lipinski, M.D., S. C. Man, M.D., Rudy Nowak, Sherman Paskov, Donald Rudin, M.D., Jonathan W. Stewart, M.D., John Varsamis, M.D., Bernard Weiss, M.D., Jose A. Yaryura-Tobias, M.D., Veronica Walsh, and Richard Zloty, M.D.

To friends, family, and acquaintances who casually shared experiences and opinions with me on the subject of depression, thanks for talking and listening.

For taking on this project, special thanks to Nathan Keats, the late founder and president of Keats Publishing, and my editors, Don Bensen and Jean Barilla.

Finally, for all the pep talks and manuscript critiques, for letting me devote all my time to the book during the last gruelling months, and for having been such a diverting natural antidepressant herself, I thank my friend and former partner, Anna Olson.

DEALING WITH DEPRESSION NATURALLY

ONE

A Character Sketch of Depression

DEPRESSION is a natural human response, a retreat from the front when we despair of having things the way they "must" be. So many things can bring us to this impasse—and so many can get us past it.

Antidepressant drugs dominate the conventional approach to treating depression. Yet they're just one of many choices we have. In this book we'll explore these alternatives and adjuncts to drugs, in particular the safer, more natural approaches, from nutrition to meditation, exercise to psychotherapy.

But first, in this chapter, I present a "character sketch" of depression, and in the next, a "model" that I hope will make it easier for us to understand our depressions and how they fit within the larger picture presented in the rest of this book.

THE COMMON COLD OF MENTAL ILLNESS

Depression is often described as "the common cold of mental illness." At any time, some 13 to 20 percent of us have at least a touch of it[1]—we at least feel a bit "scratchy in the psyche." About 2 to 3.5 percent of us are fully in the grips of what psychiatrists call a *major depression.* We are so depressed that we seem to be in exile from our comfortable, everyday selves—and, with that, from the rest of humanity, which can't begin to fathom our pain and desolation.

Another 2 to 3.5 percent of us are not so severely depressed,[1] but our mild depression (our *dysthymia*, as psychiatrists call it) has hung like a pall over our lives for years, eroding our confidence, smothering our initiative, diluting our joys and pleasures.

As for the rest of the depressed population, some are suffering from relatively mild, short-lived depressive reactions to distressing circumstances (*adjustment disorder, depressive type*). Others are weaving in and out of *recurrent brief depressions* that last no longer than a week or two. Still others are in the depressive phase of a *bipolar* or *cyclothymic disorder*. The approximately 1 percent of us with bipolar disorder (as psychiatrists now call manic-depression) suffer recurrently from major depression and its "polar" opposite, *mania*—a hyperactive, often euphoric state, marred by grandiosity and reckless bluster. Those with cyclothymia swing in a narrower arc from dysthymia (mild depression) to *hypomania* (lesser mania). Finally, there are those depressions with certain obvious biological or environmental precipitants: premenstrual, postnatal and menopausal depressions; and *seasonal affective* (mood) *disorders,* such as winter depression and summer mania.

Depression very often coexists with other disorders, physical and psychiatric. This comorbidity is highly interactive. Each disorder tends to feed the other(s). When depression (or mania) is the direct result of a physical cause, *organic depressive disorder* is diagnosed. More commonly, though, physical conditions merely *promote* depression.

People of all ages—even young children—get depressed. Among adults, depression favors both the young and the very old.

If you're a woman, the odds are about 20 to 25 percent that you'll be laid low at least once by major depression; if you're a man, 8 to 12 percent.[2] Other forms of depression also seem to hit women far more often than men. Only bipolar disorder is an equal opportunity mood disorder.

BEING DEPRESSED

Passive negativity—being stuck—is the hallmark of depression. In severe depression, the heart is a barren chamber, devoid of positive feelings and impulses. It may even feel like you've lost your soul. In *psychotic* major depression, the negativity becomes delusional. The rich believe they're bankrupt; the healthy that they're dying (or dead); the virtuous that they're guilty of unspeakable sins, even that they're the Devil himself.

Physically, the negativity of depression manifests itself in tiredness and fatigue, in an increased sensitivity to bodily aches and pains and in a neuropsychological dulling of the mind's edges (enough to make some elderly persons seem senile). The severely or psychotically depressed may think, say and do everything in extreme slow motion, and may even be catatonically "paralyzed."

Depression also is marked by "vegetative" disturbances: insomnia or hypersomnia (oversleeping), appetite loss or compulsive eating, gastrointestinal dysfunction (dry mouth, indigestion, constipation) and lowered sex drive.

Indeed, the subjectively disturbed state of being depressed seems to be mirrored objectively by disturbances in every organ and system of the body. When we're depressed, we're depressed through and through.

Often the symptoms of depression fall into a recognizable pattern. The most common one is called *typical, classic* or *endogenous depression.* Sleeplessness in the middle of the night or early in the morning, loss of appetite and weight and malignant self-reproach are its hallmarks. People with a severe form of typical depression called *melancholia* are enveloped by a gloom so impervious that nothing positive seems to reach them. Yet their mood, which characteristically is worst in the morning, tends to pick up spontaneously at night.

In contrast, *atypical depression* is characterized by insomnia at bedtime, oversleeping, overeating, a tendency to blame others rather than oneself, being easily affected by circumstances and feeling worst at night.

THE NATURAL HISTORY OF DEPRESSION ─────────────

Perhaps the best thing one can say about depression is that it usually comes to an end. Unfortunately, it often makes return visits, especially if recurrent major depression or bipolar disorder runs in the family. And sometimes it takes a chronic course.

Even without treatment, major depression usually lifts after several months to a year or two, though in some people a depressive aftertaste, a dysthymia, lingers for years.

Bipolar depressives are "between poles" most of the time, neither manic nor depressed. But *rapid cyclers* swing high or low at least a few times a year, and cyclothymics can really be on a roller-coaster.

As for dysthymia, by definition it persists for years. Indeed people with dysthymic temperaments are at least mildly depressed most or all of their lives.

A MULTITUDE OF CAUSES ─────────────────────

Until recently, the conventional wisdom has been that depression is simply an exaggerated reaction to one's problems. Today, depression is "nothing but a chemical imbalance."

Neither of these notions tells the whole story. The enlightened view in psychiatry today—the emerging consensus—is that depression is a *mind/body disorder* that is *multifactorial* (*bio-psycho-social*) in origin.[3] Everything seems to tell us that depression—like heart disease, cancer and other well-investigated diseases—arises from a multitude of interacting causes and risk factors that can originate in any segment of our lives, from chromosomes to broken homes. Loss or trauma can certainly depress us, but so, indirectly, can any physical disorder that saps our energy, impairs our creativity, dulls our sensitivity to pleasure or lowers our tolerance for pain. And, just as certain ingrained attitudes (defeatism, low self-esteem and perfectionism, for instance) can make us easy prey for depression, so can *genetically* ingrained metabolic quirks (chemical imbalances) that hamper our *biochemical* ability to cope.

TREATING DEPRESSION

Depression is very treatable—far more treatable than we think it is when we're under its influence. There are two major treatment approaches.

One is to identify and treat specific contributing causes. It isn't necessary to wipe out every single one. We humans have an instinct to rise above the stagnancy of depression, and so disposing of any contributing cause can be enough to spur us on to victory.

The other approach is to employ antidepressant therapies such as drugs, nutritional supplements, exercise and psychotherapy. Antidepressant therapies seem to address broad, generic causes of depression, such as low self-esteem and biochemical exhaustion, and to help normalize the disturbed psychology and physiology of depression.

Common sense dictates that the best chance we have for finding satisfactory, long-term relief from depression is to avail ourselves of the best of both therapeutic worlds. And that's what we'll be learning to do here.

NOTES

1. D. Blazer et al., "Depressive Symptoms and Depressive Diagnoses in a Community Population." *Arch Gen Psychiatry* 45(December 1988): 1078–1084.

2. E. A. Charney and M. M. Weissman, "Epidemiology of Depressive and Manic Syndromes." In: Anastasios Georgotas and Robert Cancro, eds., *Depression and Mania* (New York: Elsevier, 1988), pp. 26–52.

3. K. S. Kendler et al., "The Prediction of Major Depression in Women: Toward an Integrated Etiologic Model," *Am J Psychiatry* 150(August 1993):1139–1148.

TWO

A Model of Depression

In the years I've spent working on this book, I have, predictably, thought long and hard about depression. In that ferment, I have incubated and finally brought to term a model of depression that seems to explain how we become depressed and, by implication, how we become undepressed. The model is partially my own and partially an integration of other popular theories of depression. Try it on for size.

According to my model, depression is a "dysphoric" (emotionally unpleasant) retreat from engagement in life that happens whenever three ingredients or conditions are present within us:

The first ingredient is **discontent:** the perception that something is wrong. We can't become depressed unless there is something in our lives we wish were otherwise—a *problem.*

There are, I believe, three kinds of problems that can depress us: problems of *having* or *experiencing* (pain, loss: "I can't bear this"); problems of *doing* or *performance* (failure, guilt: "I can't support my family"); and problems of *being* or *identity* (negative self-image, shame: "I'm no good").

The second ingredient is **loss of hope** that this problem can be resolved. To become depressed we have to feel that our problem is a lost cause, that there's nothing we can do about it.

The third ingredient is **irreconciliation:** our inability (for now) either to live with the problem—to adjust to it—or to walk away, to detach from it. If having lost hope, we could just say "oh well" and get on with life, we wouldn't become depressed.

Whenever we get depressed, each of these mental conditions bears a piece of the responsibility. But because each is a *necessary condition,* without which the others would be insufficient to depress us, eliminating any *one* (or more) of them will extinguish the depression. That's what the antidepressant strategies in this book do. Thus:

- By alleviating underlying physical disorders—nutritional deficiencies, endocrine disorders, neurochemical imbalances—we can eliminate some of the most insidious collaborators in the creation or perpetuation of our seemingly hopeless problems: chronic low energy, impaired problem-solving ability, lowered responsiveness to pleasurable stimuli, heightened sensitivity to painful ones.
- By engaging in practices that nurture mind/body health and fitness—good nutrition, appropriate supplements, avoidance of toxins and allergens, physical activity, meditation—we can optimize our "problem-solving machinery" and bear stress more hardily and gracefully.

HOW TO USE THIS BOOK

In the following pages we're going to be discussing *dozens and dozens* of different antidepressant substances and strategies. By the time you get to the end of the book much of what seemed vivid and meaningful when you first read about it may be hazy or forgotten. So I encourage you to take notes (*stop that groaning!*), mark important passages, make marginal annotations—do whatever you can to simplify your encounter with this potential information overload. It doesn't have to be anything elaborate. Even a simple "thumbs up" or "thumbs down" (or "not sure") rating of each antidepressant strategy will make it much easier for you to narrow your options later. Better yet, you can rate each option—or at least the ones you think are worth rating—*twice* on a scale of −5 to +5: once for how likely you think it is the approach could work for you; second for how inclined you would be to try it.

- By becoming more mindful of the thoughts and feelings that nurture our discontent, our hopelessness and our rigidity, and by working on them (and through them) rationally, imaginatively and expressively, we can often work our way out of the depressing corners we've boxed ourselves into.
- By learning how to approach our "hopeless" problems more strategically and creatively, we sometimes can actually solve them.

Now let's get going.

THREE

Emotionally Depressed or Medically Ill?

The diagnosis of depression must include the search for other causes, as any illness can cause depression.

—SIGMUND FREUD[1]

Not too many years ago, researchers at the Texas University Medical Center decided to see if a novel medical approach could be of any help to 100 psychiatric patients who needed all the help they could get. Delivered under warrant to a Houston psychiatric center, most were on a fast track to a state mental hospital. The novel medical approach was really a very old-fashioned one: *a complete medical examination and workup.* It was only for the average psychiatric patient that it was a novelty.

But it was not, as it turned out, an extravagance. All but 20 of the 100 patients proved to have a previously unrecognized physical illness. And for nearly half of them—including 13 of the 30 depressed patients—the illness was deemed largely or entirely responsible for their *psychiatric condition.* "Twenty-eight of these 46 patients," psychiatrist Richard C. W. Hall and his associates reported, "evidenced dramatic and complete clearing of their psychiatric symptoms when medical treatment for the underlying physical disorder was instituted." The rest "were substantially improved."[2]

This was not the first, nor would it be the last time research would highlight how often patients labeled "psychiatric" suffer secretly from etiologic (causative) physical illnesses. Over a hundred physical conditions—often in their mild or subclinical stages—can cause or promote depression and other psychiatric syndromes, while producing few if any telltale physical symptoms.[3,4] Since early in the century, over a dozen investigations involving thousands of psychiatric patients have consistently demonstrated the scope of this problem—and just as consistently been ignored by most clinicians.[5,6]

It's not just severely disturbed psychiatric inpatients whose physical illnesses have been overlooked. When Hall and associates scrupulously examined 658 new admissions to a suburban psychiatric outpatient clinic, nearly 10 percent proved to have "a medical condition that was thought to be definitely or probably causal of their psychiatric symptoms."[7] The sickest group were the "neurotic" (dysthymic) depressives.

In a mammoth study from the Royal Ottawa Hospital, psychiatrist Erwin Koranyi meticulously screened 2090 psychiatric outpatients. Nearly half had at least one major physical illness. "The majority of these medical illnesses (69%)," Koranyi reported, "contributed considerably to the psychiatric state of the patients." Indeed, "in one in five instances (18%) the somatic pathologic condition alone was the cause of the psychiatric disorder."[8] Typically,[5] referring physicians had overlooked these conditions 30 to 50 percent of the time.

Authorities now estimate that as many as one-third to one-half of depressed patients have a physical disorder that is the primary cause of their depression, or a major contributing factor. Treating it will relieve the depression about 50 percent of the time.[9,10] Yet the sufferers are likely not to know they have it.[5,8]

Unfortunately, despite this evidence—despite textbook warnings that every psychiatric patient deserves a careful medical examination—many doctors continue to overlook the physical condition of their psychologically disturbed patients.[4,6] Even hospitalized psychiatric patients don't always receive this consideration.[6] And when examinations are done, too often they're cursory once-overs which, studies show, often yield a spuriously clean bill of health—"a false sense of security," Hall charges, which borders on medical malpractice.[2]

A COMPLETE MEDICAL EXAMINATION FOR DEPRESSION _____

The complete medical examination every depressed person needs has three elements: the history, physical examination and laboratory testing.

The History

"For every diagnosis based on physical examination and tests, ten are made first by a careful history-taking."[11] Your doctor should take at least 10 or 20 minutes to query you in detail about your symptoms, medical history, occupation, lifestyle and anything else that might shed light on the cause(s) of your depression.

The Physical Examination

When the history turns up nothing suspicious, many doctors don't bother to do a physical examination. This is a false expedient. When investigators at the University of Southern California physically examined 75 psychiatric inpatients, abnormal findings not suggested by the histories led them to diagnose causative physical illnesses in 19 percent of the patients.[12]

Cursory physicals present their own problems. In the Texas study described earlier, cursory examinations uncovered less than 20 percent of the illnesses detected by complete ones.[13] An adequate physical should take at least 15 to 20 minutes.[12]

Lab Tests

Lab tests can confirm suspicions raised by the history or physical, but they also can catch subtle disorders that would otherwise elude detection.[4,9]

Some studies have put a percentage value on the usefulness of standard lab tests. At the top of the list are the automated blood chemistry panels which measure blood levels of a dozen to several dozen important substances—minerals, hormones, antibodies and the like. In the Texas study,[13] the SMA-34 blood chemistry analysis alone detected more than half of the illnesses that caused or contributed to the patients' psychiatric disorders—more than four times the yield of the slightly cheaper, but much less thorough SMA-12. With the CBC (complete blood cell count) added, the yield rose to 77 percent. Smaller but worthwhile yields also came from urinalysis, the ECG (electrocardiogram), and the EEG (electroencephalogram) done after patients were deprived of sleep.

Hall and associates recommend the routine use of these tests for all psychiatric patients.[13] Others agree, but suggest that additional tests—most notably for mild or subclinical hypothyroidism (Chapter 5) and nutritional deficiencies (Chapter 12)—would add considerably to the yield.[3,4] Though expensive, brain scans can detect rare tumors that produce only psychiatric symptoms for years.[14] Other tests can be ordered if indicated, e.g., blood, urine, or hair tests for toxic chemicals, and blood levels of copper and ceruloplasmin to screen for Wilson's disease in depressed patients under 30.

What does it cost? In the Texas study,[13] over 90 percent of the illnesses were picked up by Hall and associates' protocol for about $400 (perhaps $1000 in today's currency). The most productive of these tests—the SMA-34 and the CBC—cost a small fraction of that. Expensive tests, like the EEG, can be deferred, if necessary.

WHO TO TURN TO

Not all doctors can be counted on to provide you with a careful and complete medical examination when you're depressed. Those best equipped and most inclined sometimes call themselves biologically or (ironically) medically oriented psychiatrists, or biopsychiatrists[15] or biobehavioral medical specialists.[3] You're also likely to get a fairly good workup in the psychiatric ward of a teaching hospital or from a psychiatrically oriented internist. When you book your appointment ask for a long one.

WHAT A COMPLETE MEDICAL EXAMINATION CAN REVEAL _____

I can only scratch the surface here of the information a complete medical examination can provide about the cause(s) of your depression. For much more detail, see *The Good News About Depression* by psychiatrist Mark Gold.[15] Gold is an outstanding expert in the field.

How old are you? (the doctor asks). The older you are, the more vulnerable you are to depressing physical illnesses. Indeed, "onset of psychiatric symptoms in a person over 40," one expert writes, "should be considered organic in origin until proven otherwise."[4]

How about your medical history? If you've recently had a stroke on the right side of your brain, you probably have an organic depression because of it. Even a bad bump on the head, especially if it knocked you out, can precipitate a depressive syndrome weeks or months later if a coagulated blood mass (a subdural hematoma) now presses against your brain.

Have you had any of your gastrointestinal tract removed? If so, malabsorption could be giving you depressing nutritional deficiencies.

Do any illnesses run in your family? Your depression could be an early symptom of diabetes, hypothyroidism, pernicious anemia, lupus, Huntington's chorea, celiac disease or porphyria, among others.

What about your symptoms? Are you feeling weak? This, more than mere fatigue, suggests physical illness. Even chronic fatigue syndrome (CFS)—a painful, depressing disorder—is accompanied by severe muscle weakness. CFS is commonly attributed to chronic, low-grade viral infection, especially infection with Epstein-Barr virus (EBV). But indistinguishable syndromes can also occur before or after any systemic infectious illness, including mononucleosis, brucellosis (contractable from unpasteurized milk), tuberculosis, infectious hepatitis and encephalitis, syphilis and AIDS. Chronic fatigue syndromes can also be noninfectious, the result of chemical intoxications, nutritional deficiencies, multiple allergies, endocrine disorders or other conditions.

Are you impotent? Maybe it's because you're depressed. But then maybe it's because you have a depressing physical disorder that causes impotence too, like multiple sclerosis, anemia, adverse reactions to certain drugs or dialysis and (especially) diabetes.[8]

Excessive thirst or high blood calcium may be the only sign that you have an uncommon endocrine disorder called hyperparathyroidism. It can depress or mentally derange you for years before it's recognized.[16]

Spontaneous tanning without benefit of sunlight or tanning parlors is a telltale sign of Addison's disease, an enervating failure of the adrenal glands with depressive symptoms. The tanning usually occurs in the creases of the palms, around the nipples, or wherever there is pressure from clothing or jewelry. Hiccoughs are another peculiar symptom.

A blimpy moon face, facial hair growth ((in a woman), an unusual fattening of the trunk and a "buffalo hump" on the back all signal the presence of a steroid-producing tumor—Cushing's syndrome. At first, Cushing's syndrome makes many people cocky, aggressive, even manic; but eventually up to a third tumble into a deep, sometimes suicidal depression.[16]

A butterfly-shaped rash across the nose and cheeks is a signature of *systemic lupus erythematosis,* or lupus, a rare autoimmune disease that usually strikes young women. It causes achey joints and psychiatric symptoms of every description.

Pain in the upper abdomen that feels like it's boring its way through to your back could be due to a rare, highly malignant tumor of the pancreas. Sufferers are usually 50- to 70-year-old men who just seem severely depressed. Other symptoms are substantial weight loss, intractable insomnia, a history of alcoholism or diabetes and, eerily, a gut fear that you have a life-threatening disease.[3]

Numbness, tingling or other queer sensations in your extremities suggest nerve damage from chemical toxins or vitamin deficiencies.

Hearing things may indeed be "all in your head," but if you're seeing, feeling or smelling things, the problem is almost certainly all in your brain.[4,7] A subtle form of epilepsy called *partial complex seizures* (PCS) is one cause. PCS (which includes temporal lobe epilepsy) is a remarkable condition. Instead of fits of movement, there are fits of *sensations, emotions, thoughts,* or *impulses*—smells that aren't there, disconnected feelings or impulses that come out of nowhere, even *déjà vu* or *jamais vu* (feeling like you *haven't* been here before) experiences.[3] Between fits, many people with PCS are driven in mystical, religious or philosophical directions, and many fit the profile of multiple personality disorder.[3] Extraordinarily suicidal, they often are misdiagnosed as depressives. In the Texas study by Hall and associates, three of the 30 depressed patients examined had PCS.[13] The best diagnostic test is an EEG with nasopharyngeal (up the nose) leads after a night without sleep.[3]

Tremors or loss of coordination in a young person could be an early sign of Wilson's disease, a genetic condition that causes copper to collect in the brain and other organs. Often the symptoms are mistaken as psychiatric. A diagnostic giveaway is a rusty-brown ring around the corneas of the eyes.

A depressed elderly person who shuffles as if he were "stuck to the floor" could have an operable brain disease called normal pressure hydrocephalus.

If the whites of your eyes have acquired a bluish cast, you could very likely have a depressing iron deficiency.[17]

Panic attacks—thumping heart, shakiness, sweatiness and the like—afflict many depressives. They can have a physical basis in such disorders as reactive hypoglycemia (Chapter 13), allergy (Chapter 14) and pheochromocytoma. Pheochromocytomas are tumors that flood the blood with adrenaline and other "fight or flight" hormones, often at the oddest moments, such as after you've sneezed, shaved, gargled, laughed or made love. They can also cause severe depression.[18]

NOTES

1. Siegfried Kra, *Aging Myths: Reversible Causes of Mind and Memory Loss* (New York: McGraw-Hill, 1986), p. 57.

2. R. C. W. Hall et al., "Unrecognized Physical Illness Prompting Psychiatric Admission: A Prospective Study," *Am J Psychiatry* 138(May 1981):629–635.

3. T. W. Estroff and M. S. Gold, "Psychiatric Misdiagnosis." In Gold et al., eds., *Advances in Psychopharmacology: Predicting and Improving Treatment Response* (Boca Raton, Fla:CRC Press, 1984), pp. 33–66.

4. D. E. Sternberg, "Testing for Physical Illness in Psychiatric Patients," *J Clin Psychiatry* 47(Suppl, January 1986):3–9.

5. E. K. Koranyi, "Somatic Illness in Psychiatric Patients," *Psychosomatics* 21(November 1980):887–891.

6. J. D. Chandler and J. E. Gerndt, "The Role of the Medical Evaluation in Psychiatric Inpatients," *Psychosomatics* 29(Fall 1988):410–416.

7. R. C. W. Hall et al., "Physical Illness Presenting as Psychiatric Disease," *Arch Gen Psychiatry* 35(November 1978):1315–1320.

8. E. K. Koranyi, "Morbidity and Rate of Undiagnosed Physical Illnesses in a Psychiatric Population," *Arch Gen Psychiatry* 36(April 1979):414–419.

9. R. C. Kathol, "Patient Evaluation." In R. A. Munoz, ed., *Therapeutic Potential of Mood Disorder Clinics* (San Francisco: Jossey-Bass, 1984), pp. 71–82.

10. M. S. Gold et al., "The Role of the Laboratory in Psychiatry." In Gold et al., *Advances in Psychopharmacology,* pp. 307–317.

11. Isadore Rosenfeld, *The Complete Medical Exam* (New York: Simon and Schuster, 1978).

12. W. K. Summers et al., "The Psychiatric Physical Examination—Part II: Findings in 75 Unselected Psychiatric Patients," *J Clin Psychiatry* 42(March 1981):99–102.

13. R. C. W. Hall, et al., "Physical Illness Manifesting as Psychiatric Disease," *Arch Gen Psychiatry* 37(September 1980): 989–995.

14. R. C. W. Hall, "Depression." In Hall, ed., *Psychiatric Presentations of Medical Illness* (New York: SP Medical & Scientific Books, 1980),pp. 37–63.

15. Mark S. Gold with Lois B. Morris, *The Good News About Depression* (New York: Bantam, 1987).

16. M. K. Popkin and T. B. Mackenzie, "Psychiatric Presentations of Endocrine Dysfunction." In Hall, pp. 139–156.

17. L. Kalra et al., "Blue Sclerae: A Common Sign of Iron Deficiency?" *Lancet* (Nov. 29, 1986):1267–1268.

18. James W. Jefferson and John R. Marshall, *Neuropsychiatric Features of Medical Disorders* (New York: Plenum, 1981).

FOUR

Mood Poisoning

"In this age of increasing accumulation of toxins in our environment, it is becoming more and more important to consider toxic conditions in the differential diagnosis of psychiatric disorders."[1]

IT'S not unusual, when you're depressed, to feel as if you've been drugged or poisoned—and *that's* why you're such a droopy, foot-dragging version of your usual self. *Ah, the tricks the depressed mind plays on itself* . . . but are they tricks?

Actually, some depressed people are being drugged or poisoned—by the pills in their medicine cabinets, the chemicals in their workplaces, or other toxic tormenters.

Our planet is so polluted that we're all chronically poisoned. But while we fret about the more vivid perils—the cancers, the birth defects—toxicologists warn of subtler dangers. "In the earliest form of chronic toxicity," authorities from the National Institute for Occupational Safety and Health point out, "mild mood disorders predominate as the patient's chief complaint."[2] These soft, psychobehavioral symptoms "may appear . . . at exposure levels *about one-tenth to one-hundredth* of those which produce overt symptoms of clinical poisoning, and in subjects who appear perfectly healthy by conventional medical criteria" (italics mine), other experts caution.[3] And because safety regulations are commonly set only with "overt symptoms of clinical poisoning" in mind, "acceptable" exposure levels still pose a threat to people's mental, if not physical, health. This is especially true for those few whom toxicologists call "outliers." Outliers' sensitivity to a given drug or chemical lies far "outside" the normal range.[4]

So what are these toxic depressants?

DRUGS

We begin by looking in the medicine cabinet. If you're depressed, take a close look here. "Approximately 200 drugs have been reported to cause depression, and others are believed to contribute to depressive reactions," authorities state.[5] In one study, nearly half of the depressed patients in a family practice setting were on depressing drugs.[6] In another study, eight out of 35 heavily medicated, elderly depressed patients were suffering from a depressive drug reaction.[7]

Doctors have a deplorable blind spot for this kind of devilry. In the latter study, 13 patients had become clinically *delirious* on "drugs of well-recognized psychotoxic potential."[7] Their doctors caught on in only three cases. Were it not for the researchers, the rest would have probably been given more drugs.

The drugs listed—prescription, over-the-counter and "recreational"—appear to be the most significant promoters of depression.[7,8,9,10] If you're taking a drug that isn't listed here, it's prudent to check it out in a good drug reference book anyway. I've listed most drugs by their *generic* names (brand names are capitalized) and, in some cases, simply by drug class (for example, "narcotics"). If that leaves you in the dark, again, consult a reference book or your doctor or pharmacist. Don't discontinue a prescribed drug without consulting a doctor—that can be dangerous.

actinomycin D
alcohol*
amantadine
most antipsychotic drugs (i.e.
    phenothiazines, like Thor-
    azine and Stelazine, and
    butyrophenones, like
    Haldol)
L-asparaginase

birth control pills
central nervous system stimu-
    lants (e.g. amphetamine,
    caffeine, cocaine, methy-
    phenidate, theophylline)*
chloroquin
clonidine
corticosteroids (e.g. cortisone,
    prednisone)*

*Depression may also occur when you *stop* taking high doses.

co-trimoxazole
cycloserine
o,p-DDD
digitalis
disulfiram
DTIC
ethambutol
ethchlovynol
Ftorafur
glutethimide
guanethidine
H2-receptor antagonists (e.g.
  cimetidine, ranitidine)
hexamethylenamine
hydralazine
hydroxychloroquine
ibuprofen
indomethacin
isonazid
levodopa (L-dopa)
marijuana
methyldopa
methyprylon
naproxen
narcotics (e.g. heroin, mor-
  phine, codeine,
  methadone)*

nitrogen mustard
PCP ("angel dust")
phenylbutazone
cis-platinum
procarbazine
propranolol (other beta-
  blocker drugs whose ge-
  neric names end in "-olol"
  are also suspect)
reserpine
sulfonamides ("sulfa drugs")
tamoxifen
toluene (in glue used for
  "sniffing")
tranquilizers and sedatives
  (i.e., benzodiazepines,
  like Valium and lorazepam;
  Miltown or Equanil; barbi-
  turates, like phenobarbital
  and other "-barbitals")*
vincristine
vinblastine
zompirac sodium

Recently, the following drugs have also come under suspicion: antihistamines, decongestants and diet pills (all if used long-term);[11,12] cholesterol-lowering drugs (lovastatin, pravastatin, simvastatin);[13] anticonvulsants;[14] and calcium-channel blockers such as nifedipine.[15]

Depression can also be promoted by very high doses of certain nutritional supplements: niacinamide, vitamin A, vitamin D, calcium (also found in antacids), magnesium (found in antacids and cathartics), zinc, iron, copper, choline and lecithin.[16]

SMOKING AND DEPRESSION

Need another reason to stop smoking? Smoking is strongly associated with neuroticism, depression and even suicidal behavior.[17] It's unclear which causes which, or if a common vulnerability simply predisposes some people both to depression and nicotine dependence. But clinical ecologists (unorthodox allergists who believe we're much more sensitive to foods and chemicals than we think) see smoking as an *addictive allergy* (see Chapter 14), like alcoholism and compulsive eating, that causes more mental dis-ease than it relieves.[18,19] Unfortunately, quitting can be particularly tough—even dangerous—for depressives.[17] So, if you try, fortify yourself with antidepressant/antiaddictive buffers like exercise, meditation, acupuncture and nutritional supplements (for example, vitamin C, amino acids).

METALS AND MINERALS

Most people today realize how destructive even minute doses of lead are to the brains of infants and children. But lead is poison to the brains of adults, too. "A high prevalence of nonspecific symptoms such as fatigue, irritability, insomnia, nervousness, headache, and weakness has been documented consistently in workers with moderate lead absorption," state two Yale psychiatrists.[20] When these investigators examined 31 hospital patients with mildly elevated blood levels of lead, nine were found to be depressed—four of them severely so.

As with lead, so with other metals and minerals. In mildly toxic doses, mercury, aluminum, organic tin compounds, arsenic, bismuth, boron, vanadium, selenium, calcium, magnesium, zinc, copper, iron and manganese can also promote depression.[2,21,10] The following metals appear to be the most significant culprits.

Lead

Approximately one million Americans are exposed occupationally to high levels of lead, usually in the form of fine dust or fumes from solder, ammunition, bearings, lead shielding, storage batteries, cables, leaded pigments, pottery glazes, leaded gasoline, bootleg whiskey, insecticides or processed metals.[2,20]

The rest of us are vulnerable to lead poisoning from other sources:

Lead-soldered food cans. A rough, smeared seam is the giveaway. Food in these cans typically contains *10* to *60* times as much lead as food in nonlead-soldered cans (smooth seam or round bottom).[22] Lead levels soar even higher when food is stored in opened cans.[23]

Eating utensils. *Underfired* glazed earthenware (beware of amateur-made and imported products), crystalware (50 percent lead), and possibly pewter cups and novelty glasses with lead enamel decals all can contaminate food and drink with lead.

Asian medications. Some traditionally prepared Asian medications contain toxic levels of lead as an ingredient.[24]

Bone meal and oyster shell calcium supplements. Many brands contain questionably high levels (see Chapter 12).

Lead-soldered water pipes. Run your tap for a few minutes before using water that has been standing for many hours in old pipes.

Lead water mains. Even after filtering, lead levels may still be unacceptably high.

Paint. Paint—especially old paint from the 1950s or earlier—can contain extremely high levels of lead. Removing it by sanding or scraping creates a fine, leaden paint dust that can contaminate your household unless elaborate precautions are taken.

Mercury

Toxic even in the tiniest amounts, mercury readily invades our bodies when we swallow, inhale or touch it. It not only promotes depression, but sometimes it produces a unique syndrome of extreme shyness, timidity and self-consciousness, often with sweating and blushing.[1,25]

It's essential to minimize our exposure to the following mercury sources:[2,25]

- Mercury amalgam ("silver") dental fillings (discussed in Chapter 6).
- Drugs and pharmaceuticals which contain thimerosal or sodium ethyl mercury, for example, various antiseptics, ointments, cosmetics, laxatives, eyedrops, contraceptive gels and douches.
- Broken fluorescent lights, thermometers and scientific instruments that contain mercury.
- These sometimes contain mercury: fabric softeners, floor polishes, wood preservatives, adhesives, fungicides, paints and dyes (including tattoos) and textiles.
- A diet high in fish and seafood could pose a mercury hazard, especially if lots of tuna, swordfish, shellfish, kelp and other seaweeds are on the menu. Sadly, these are otherwise very healthy foods.
- Occupational exposures: dentists and dental personnel (or anyone in a poorly ventilated building with a dental office); electroplaters; embalmers; farmers; gold and silver extractors; painters; photographers; taxidermists; makers/manufacturers of barometers, batteries, pressure gauges, switches, fireworks, explosive caps, fluorescent or neon light bulbs, fur, felt, ink, paint, paper or jewelry.

Aluminum

Aluminum is a depressing and (some research suggests) dementing mineral.[26] To avoid it, bear this in mind:

- Chronic dialysis increases aluminum in bones 9 to 50 times.[26]
- Many antacids are laden with aluminum. A postmortem study of peptic ulcer patients (heavy antacid users) found

aluminum deposits in their bones were midway between those of normal subjects and dialysis patients.[26]

- Other significant sources:[27] aluminum cookware (acidic liquids, especially with fluoridated water, leach aluminum avidly); tap water (in some cities); aluminum salts in foods and spices (e.g. baking powder, processed cheese); baby formulas and intravenous fluids; some drugs and pharmaceuticals (e.g. aluminum hydroxide gels, antiperspirants, deodorants); clay dust; the air from corroded air conditioners; water heaters with aluminum cores.

Copper

Some doctors implicate mild copper poisoning as a common cause of a multitude of ills, from hypertension and tinnitus to schizophrenia and depression.[28,29] At one orthomolecular psychiatric clinic (where, as we'll see in Chapter 7, nutritional prescriptions top the menu), about two-thirds of the female patients and one-third of the males were found in one year to have an overload of this essential nutrient.[29] Mainstream psychiatrists have also found high copper levels in depressives and other psychiatric patients.[29,30]

Water from copper pipes—especially soft water that's been standing for hours—or from reservoirs treated with copper sulfate may be "the most common route of copper intoxication."[29] Other culprits are vitamin-mineral supplements with 2 mg or more of copper, cigarettes, copper cookware and fungicides containing copper sulphate.[25,29]

Orthomolecular psychiatrists claim copper overload can gradually be relieved by copper-lowering supplements: manganese, molybdenum, calcium, magnesium, vitamin C, bioflavonoids and, especially, zinc.[28,29]

PETROCHEMICALS

Petrochemicals are everywhere, in the synthetic products of civilization, in paints and in fuels. Some toxicologists and physicians regard petrochemicals as our most ubiquitous toxic cause of mental-health problems.[18]

Volatile Organic Solvents and Fuels

The worst petrochemical offenders, it seems, are *volatile organic solvents and fuels* (VOSF).[21, 31] Most fuels (natural gas and oil included) are volatile organic fuels (VOF). Volatile organic solvents (VOS) are commonly found in paints, paint thinners, varnishes, fresh print and photocopies, oil-based correction fluids, permanent-ink pens and markers, glues, cleaning products, cheap perfumes and scented products, fumigants, disinfectants, pesticides, refrigerants, electrical insulators and furnace or air-conditioner filters sprayed with motor oil.[18,21,31]

Whether inhaled, absorbed through the skin or accidentally swallowed, VOSF easily cross the blood-brain barrier and provoke neurobehavioral symptoms.[18,21,31] At the Centers for Disease Control and elsewhere, researchers have repeatedly found an abnormal degree of depression, irritability, mental impairment and other symptoms of "painters' syndrome" in persons chronically exposed to "normal" occupational levels of VOS.[2] Rayon workers who chronically inhale "safe" levels of the VOS carbon disulfide are unusually suicide-prone.[21]

VOSF with confirmed depressant effects include carbon disulfide, creosol, toluene, methyl chloride and methyl n-butyl ketone.[1,21,32]

Of particular concern to clinical ecologists and experts on nontoxic living are natural gas and oil.[18,32,33] Their fumes, these experts claim, dull or depress sensitive persons.[18,33] Even the kitchen stove, one doctor reports, saddles some homemakers with an intractable depression that "often disappears when their gas range is replaced with an electric one."[33]

Formaldehyde

A volatile preservative, formaldehyde has been charged with provoking dozens of symptoms, including lethargy and depression.[33] You'll find it in a host of products, particularly urea formaldehyde foam insulation, "processed woods" (plywood, particle board, etc.) and the houses and furniture made from them, permanent press fabrics and cosmetics.[18,33]

Plastics

Plastics, particularly soft plastics, "leak" into air, food or water, especially when heated.[18] Even hot plastic lampshades "give off odors and fumes that can have a marked effect on mental and physical well-being."[18(p. 242)]

PESTICIDES

Most pesticides are nerve poisons. It is well-documented that in overexposed workers, pesticides induce depression and other neurologic symptoms.[21] But clinical ecologists maintain that even "safe" pesticide levels in sprayed apartments and on supermarket produce can depress sensitive people.[18]

CHEMICALIZED CARPETS AND OTHER MATERIALS

Ever wonder how modern carpets became so impregnable to spills, flames, mites, bugs and every other wicked thing known to man? The answer is *chemicals*—as many as 150 volatile chemical agents *we* may not be so impregnable to, say toxicologists and clinical ecologists.[34] "I've seen people change every single thing but their carpeting, and then find that the carpet was really the cause of it all," says Debra Lynn Dadd, an expert on nontoxic living.[35] "Broadloomitis" has even struck the Environmental Protection Agency (EPA). When the agency recarpeted its poorly ventilated headquarters, over 5 percent of the employees soon complained of fatigue, headaches or other ills.[34]

Stainproof upholstery, sunproof drapery, treated woods and other chemicalized space-age marvels may also subvert sensitive people's health.[36]

COSMETICS AND OTHER PERSONAL CARE PRODUCTS _____

Cosmetics, perfumes, soaps, lotions and other personal care products are a major hassle for many chemically sensitive people.[18] Not only are products with annoying scents suspect, but also those whose odors *you can't get enough of. Addictive allergy* (Chapter 14) could be at work. The least offensive products contain only natural, hypoallergenic ingredients.

TREATING AND PREVENTING TOXIC DEPRESSION _____

For every substance known to promote depression, many more await discovery. Ideally, we would purge all of these threatening chemicals from our midst. Realistically, we *can* strive to lead a *relatively* nontoxic, or "hypotoxic," life.

Basically, we can do this in three ways:

1) Completely avoid as many toxic materials as we can.
2) Use cleaning, ventilation, filtration or other means to keep them at bay.
3) Use nutritional or other means to enhance our antitoxic *defenses.*

Avoiding Toxic Materials

• Minimize exposure to smelly synthetic products (if you can smell it, you're ingesting it): paints, solvents, strong cleaning products, "off-gassing" construction materials. Experts in nontoxic living suggest inoffensive alternatives such as vinegar, salt, baking soda, borax, herbal scents and pesticides, chemically un-treated rugs, untreated wood, plaster, ceramic, terra cotta, ter-azzo, brick, marble, cement, low-temperature electric baseboard heaters, heat pumps, woodstoves (if they're airtight and meet other stringent specifications), passive solar heating systems.[32,33,36] "Green" stores and mail-order companies specialize in these products.

• Another way to eliminate toxins is to clear them from your body. Detoxifying regimes are commonly prescribed by naturo-paths and other alternative healers. Special diets or fasts, nutri-tional and herbal supplements, massage, exercise, baths, enemas and other measures are commonly employed to help the body purify and restore itself.

Keeping Toxins at Bay

• When you work with toxic materials, wear gloves, a face mask or other protective gear.

• Live and work in well-ventilated surroundings. Hermetically sealed and insulated buildings are "sick buildings" unless they have good ventilation systems.

• Consider using an air purifier. One with activated charcoal and alumina in its filter can dispatch most common pollutants.[37] Plants also help clean the air.

• Consider using bottled or distilled water, or filtering your tap water. Even an inexpensive, pitcher-type model with an activated charcoal filter will greatly diminish the organic solvent residues, pesticides, and other contaminants that can promote depres-sion.[38,39] A filter with an ion exchange resin will remove most heavy metals too.[38]

• Clean foods thoroughly. Nutritionist Ann Louise Gittleman rec-ommends using a Clorox bath (½ teaspoon of chlorine bleach per gallon of water) to eliminate microorganisms and chemical residues. Soak produce in it for 15 to 30 minutes (short soaks for delicate foods); rinse in clear water for 10 minutes; and dry. Not only does this make foods much less toxic/allergenic, it also doubles their shelf life, Gittleman claims.[38] No amount of cleaning can remove some residues (like the organochlorines on apples and cucumbers), so peeling sometimes is the only alternative.[27]

Improving Our Defenses

Anything that strengthens our systems tends to bolster our defenses against toxic materials.

• Take good nutrition (please!). A generous intake of mineral nutrients, such as calcium, magnesium, zinc, selenium and manganese, physiologically squeezes out toxic metals like lead, mercury, and aluminum.[27] In ample doses, other nutrients, like vitamins A (or beta-carotene), C and E, also give toxic substances a hard time. Vitamin C's antipathy for heavy metals, drugs, alcohol, tobacco, polychlorinated biphenyls (PCBs) and pesticides is especially well-documented.[40]

• *Allergic hypersensitivities* to extremely minute doses of chemicals may be amenable to neutralization therapy, suggestion or other system-boosting strategies discussed in Chapter 14 (page 00). The connection between *multiple chemical sensitivity* syndromes, or environmental illness, and psychological disease is a strong and probably two-way one, mediated by the mind's neurological linkage to the immune system.[41] Relief may come by addressing the problem from *either* end—chemical or psychological.

"ELECTROPOLLUTION" AND DEPRESSION _____

In 1981, when researchers reported that suicide victims were unusually likely to have lived near a high power transmission line,[42] it was easy to scoff. Not so easy today. The evidence may be conflicting,[43–46] but no one is scoffing now at the idea that "electromagnetic smog" or "electropollution" may promote cancer, birth defects, miscarriage and other health disasters. It stands to reason there may be subtler, neurobehavioral penalties too.

Two forms of electromagnetic smog are causing the most concern: the *nonionizing electromagnetic radiation* (NEMR) emitted primarily by broadcast towers, radar installations and microwave appliances, and the *magnetic fields* surrounding electrical appliances and power lines.

Even at low exposure levels, NEMR and magnetic fields can interfere with subtle electrobiochemical processes.[43,44] Magnetic fields, for instance, have been shown to induce depression-like abnormalities in neurotransmitter and endorphin levels[47] and body rhythms.[43,47] Less subtly, chronic overexposure to magnetic fields seems to promote brain cancer.[46]

In several studies, the possible link between magnetic fields, suicide and depression has been further explored. In one, the suicide rate among electric utility workers was normal.[48] The other studies have been less reassuring. In one survey, people living very near a transmission line right-of-way were nearly three times as likely to be depressed as people living far away.[48] In another study, apartment block residents already hospitalized for depression were significantly more likely than other residents to have lived near the block's main electrical supply cable.[49]

Cutting Through the Electromagnetic Smog

While it's impossible (or impractical) to escape the electronic smog of civilization, we *can* keep our distance.[43,44]

• Try not to live, work, or play within a few hundred yards of high-voltage towers, transmission lines, radio or television broadcasting towers or radar installations. Indoors, spend as little time as possible near where the main power line contacts or enters the building.

• Minimize prolonged exposure at close range to working electrical appliances, particularly those that use motors or heating elements (e.g. space heaters, electric clocks, arc welding equipment and possibly fluorescent lights). Only use electric blankets and heated waterbeds that have been wired to neutralize their powerful magnetic fields.

• Avoid liberal use of personal radio transmitters (e.g. CBs, cellular phones, cordless phones). They expose the brain to worrisomely high levels of NEMR and magnetic fields.

• Avoid rooms heated by electric cables. These rooms are permeated by magnetic fields strong enough, research suggests, even to promote miscarriage.

• Don't linger within an arm's length of the front, back or sides of a computer monitor even if there's a wall between you. Consider scrapping any monitor manufactured before 1983; it gives off much more NEMR. The newer, low-radiation monitors are the safest alternative. If possible, use a detached keyboard, because the computer's chassis also produces a magnetic field.

• Keep at least three or four feet away from the front, back or sides of small-screen TVs and up to eight to ten feet away from very large ones, again even if there's a wall between you.

• Avoid lingering within a few feet of a working microwave oven, especially a powerful commercial model. Have the oven inspected for microwave leakage any time there's damage to the door frame or gaskets. Beware of microwave heat-sealers. They're *extremely* leaky.

NOTES

1. G. E. Fagala and C. L. Wing, "Psychiatric Manifestations of Mercury Poisoning," *J Am Acad Child Adolescent Psychiatry* 31(March 1992):306–311.

2. E. L. Baker et al., "Environmentally Related Disorders of the Nervous System," *Medical Clinics of North America* 74(March 1990):325–345.

3. D. Bryce-Smith and R. Stephens, "Sources and Effects of Environmental Lead." In J. Rose, ed., *Trace Elements in Health* (Stoneham, Mass.: Butterworths, 1983), pp. 83–131.

4. B. Weiss, "Intersections of Psychiatry and Toxicology," *Int J Mental Health* 14(3, 1985):7–25.

5. J. T. Dietch and M. Zetin, "Diagnosis of Organic Depressive Disorders," *Psychosomatics* 24(November 1983):971–979.

6. D. A. Katerndahl, "Neuropsychiatric Disorders Associated with Depression," *J Fam Prac* 13(1981):619–624.

7. R. S. Hoffman, "Diagnostic Errors in the Evaluation of Behavioral Disorders," *J Am Med Assoc* 248(August 27, 1982):964–967.

8. D. E. Sternberg, "Testing for Physical Illness in Psychiatric Patients," *J Clin Psychiatry* 47(Suppl, January 1986):3–9.

9. R. C. W. Hall et al., "Behavioral Toxicity of Nonpsychiatric Drugs." In R. C. W. Hall, ed., *Psychiatric Presentations of Medical Illness: Somatopsychic Disorders* (Jamaica, NY: Spectrum Publications, 1980), pp. 337–349.

10. T. W. Estroff and M. S. Gold, "Psychiatric Misdiagnosis." In Mark S. Gold, et al., eds., *Advances in Psychopharmacology: Predicting and Improving Treatment Response* (Boca Raton, Fla: CRC Press, 1984), pp.33–66.

11. R. P. Climko, "Depression and Decongestants" (letter), *Am J Psychiatry* 144(October 1987):1376–1377.

12. B. Twerski, "Dr. Twerski Replies" (letter), *Am J Psychiatry* 144(October 1987):1377.

13. N. Duits and F. M. Bos, "Depressive Symptoms and Cholesterol-lowering Drugs" (letter), *Lancet* 341(January 9, 1993):114.

14. M. F. Mendez et al., "Depression in Epilepsy. Relationship to Seizures and Anticonvulsant Therapy," *J Nerv Ment Dis* 181(July 1983):444–447.

15. R. H. McAllister-Williams, "Calcium-channel Blockade and Depressive Illness" (letter), *Brit J Psychiatry* 157(October 1990):618–619.

16. F. A. Whitlock, *Symptomatic Affective Disorders* (New York: Academic Press, 1982).

17. A. H. Glassman, "Cigarette Smoking: Implications for Psychiatric Illness," *Am J Psychiatry* 150(April 1993):546–553.

18. Theron G. Randolph and Ralph W. Moss, *An Alternative Approach to Allergies,* rev. ed. (New York: Harper & Row, 1989).

19. William H. Philpott and Dwight K. Kalita, *Brain Allergies: The Psychonutrient Connection,* rev. ed. (New Canaan, Conn.: Keats Publishing, 1987).

20. R. S. Schottenfeld and M. R. Cullen, "Organic Affective Illness Associated with Lead Intoxication," *Am J Psychiatry* 141(November 1984):1423–1426.

21. B. Weiss, "Behavioral Toxicology and Environmental Health Science," *Am Psychologist* November 1983:1174–1187.

22. "Marketplace," CBC Television, December 19, 1989.

23. Arthur Winter and Ruth Winter, *Eat Right. Be Bright* (New York: St. Martin's Press, 1988).

24. P. F. D'Arcy, "Adverse Reactions and Interactions with Herbal Medicines. Part 1: Adverse Reactions," *Adverse Drug Reactions and Toxicol Rev* 10(4, 1992):189–208.

25. N. Edwards, "Mental Disturbances Related to Metals." In Hall, *Psychiatric Presentations* pp. 283–308.

26. Richard A. Passwater and Elmer M. Cranton, *Trace Elements, Hair Analysis and Nutrition* (New Canaan, Conn.: Keats Publishing, 1983).

27. Robert Buist, *Food Chemical Sensitivity* (San Leandro, Calif.: Prism Press, 1986).

28. K. R. Nolan, "Copper Toxicity Syndrome," *J Orthomol Psychiatry* 12(4, 1983):270.

29. C. C. Pfeiffer and R. Mailloux, "Excess Copper as a Factor in Human Diseases," *J Orthomol Med* 2(3, 1987):171–182.

30. R. L. Narang et al., "Levels of Copper and Zinc in Depression," *Ind J Physiol Pharmacol* 35(October 1991):272–274.

31. C. M. Ryan et al., "Cacosmia and Neurobehavioral Dysfunction Associated with Occupational Exposure to Mixtures of Organic Solvents," *Am J Psychiatry* 145(November 1988):1442–1445.

32. Debra Lynn Dadd, *The Nontoxic Home* (Los Angeles: Jeremy P. Tarcher, 1986).

33. Carol Venolia, *Healing Environments* (Berkeley, Calif.: Celestial Arts, 1988).

34. "Marketplace," CBC Television, January 9, 1990.

35. The Editors of *East West, Meetings with Remarkable Men and Women* (Brookline, Mass.: East West Health Books, 1989).

36. Natalie Golos and Frances Golos Golbitz, *Coping with Your Allergies* (New York: Simon & Schuster, 1986).

37. Sheldon Saul Hendler, *The Oxygen Breakthrough* (New York: William Morrow and Co., 1989).

38. Ann Louise Gittleman with J. Maxwell Desgrey, *Beyond Pritikin* (New York: Bantam, 1988).

39. David Steinman, *Diet for a Poisoned Planet* (New York: Harmony Books, 1990).

40. D. E. Holloway and F. J. Peterson, "Ascorbic Acid in Drug Me-

tabolism." In Daphne A. Roe and T. Colin Campbell, eds., *Drugs and Nutrients: The Interactive Effects* (New York: Marcel Dekker, 1984), pp. 225–295.

41. I. R. Bell et al., "An Olfactory-Limbic Model of Multiple Chemical Sensitivity Syndrome," *Biol Psychiatry* 32(1992):218–242.

42. F. S. Perry et al., "Environmental Power Frequency Magnetic Fields and Suicide," *Health Physics* 41(1981):267–277.

43. E. J. Lerner, "RF Radiation: Biological Effects," *IEEE Spectrum* December 1980, pp. 51–59.

44. Robert O. Becker, *Cross Currents* (Los Angeles: Jeremy P. Tarcher, 1990).

45. R. Stone, "Polarized Debate: EMFs and Cancer" (news), *Science* 258(December 11, 1992):1724–1725.

46. D. A. Savitz, "Overview of Epidemiologic Research on Electric and Magnetic Fields and Cancer," *Am Industrial Hygiene Assoc J* 54(April 1993):197–204.

47. M. Kavaliers and K–P. Ossenkopp, "Magnetic Fields and Stress: Day–Night Differences," *Prog Neuro-Psychopharmacol Biol Psychiatry* 11(1987):279–286.

48. C. Poole et al., "Depressive Symptoms and Headaches in Relation to Proximity of Residence to an Alternating-current Transmission Line Right-of-way," *Am J Epidem* 137(February 1, 1993):318–332.

49. S. Perry and L. Pearl, "Power Frequency Magnetic Field and Illness in Multi-storey Blocks," *Public Health* 102(1988):11–18.

FIVE

The Glandular Connection

ONE of the bleakest, most abject faces I've ever seen was in a textbook of endocrinology. A case study in myxedema (advanced hypothyroidism), this woman's harrowed mien testified to the psychological devastation a shortage of hormones can wreak.

Mental "dis-ease" is a common symptom of almost every disease or disorder of the endocrine glands: the testes and ovaries, the adrenals, the pancreas, the thyroid, the parathyroids and the pituitary.

It's no wonder. The hormones dispatched into the bloodstream by the endocrine glands are probably second only to the chemicals of the brain when it comes to shaping how we feel and behave. When an endocrine gland malfunctions, secreting either too few or too many of its hormones, depression is often a symptom.[1] And in any crowd of depressed people, a group with endocrine disorder can invariably be found.[2-5]

The most common depressing endocrine disorder, by far, is hypothyroidism or low thyroid function.

HYPOTHYROIDISM

The thyroid gland's hormones are spark plugs, firing the metabolism of every organ in the body and sensitizing our brain cells to the nervous system's natural stimulants.[6,7]

Deprived of thyroid hormones, we grow cold, dry, dull and depressed. If the deficiency is mild, we may seem to be "just depressed." Only sensitive blood tests will prove otherwise; yet doctors often fail to order them.

Around 1980, psychiatrist Mark Gold and his associates at Fair Oaks Hospital in New Jersey were the first to show how significant that omission can be. Their subjects were 250 patients admitted for depression or severe fatigue. While routine screening procedures uncovered two cases of clinically overt, Grade I hypothyroidism, the more sensitive blood tests revealed that 18 more patients suffered from mild (Grade II) or subclinical (Grade III) hypothyroidism.[3,4]

In studies since then of over a thousand patients, Gold's group and others have confirmed that mild or subclinical hypothyroidism afflicts some 10 to 15 percent of clinically depressed persons—mostly women[6,8–10]—and fully *half* of those depressives who don't respond to antidepressant drugs.[10] Thyroid hormone replacement therapy, sometimes with antidepressants on the side, is usually all it takes to end the long nightmare.[3,4,6,8,11]

Are You Hypothyroid?

Routine screening for hypothyroidism entails measuring blood levels of thyroid hormones and recognizing physical signs and symptoms of clinical hypothyroidism, such as cold intolerance; thinning hair and eyebrows; and drying, thickening and roughening of the skin. For every case of hypothyroidism that can be spotted this way, three or four more can be identified by finding low blood levels of thyroid stimulating hormone (TSH).[3,4] Yet another five or ten subclinical cases can only be uncovered by the costly TRH (thyrotropin releasing hormone) stimulation test[3,4] or by detecting high blood levels of thyroid antibodies.[6,8,10,11] These more sensitive tests are increasingly being used to screen depressed patients in sophisticated psychiatric clinics, but they're not yet routinely used elsewhere. Don't expect your GP to order them unless you ask.

Some doctors believe that the most sensitive test for hypothyroidism can be done cheaply at home with a thermometer.[12] Snuggle one into your armpit for ten minutes before you rise in the morning, and if your temperature is under 97.8—repeatedly on at least two or three days—your thyroid could be under par (barring other medical explanations). The inventor of this unorthodox technique, Broda Barnes, MD, advises menstruating women to take their temperatures on the second and third days of their period.[12]

Some things should raise your suspicion that you're hypothyroid:

• Taking lithium produces some degree of hypothyroidism in as many as 40 percent of users.[13] This may account for much of the fatigue, dullness, depression and rapid cycling many of them experience.[13]

• Rapid cyclers *usually* have some degree of hypothyroidism, especially if they're on lithium.[9,14-16] This probably explains why they often benefit dramatically from large doses of the thyroid hormone thyroxine.[14,16]

• You're also more likely to be hypothyroid if you're female,[9] if you have premenstrual[17] or postpartum depression,[9,18] if you're elderly, if you have a family history of hypothyroidism or if you've ever been treated for *hyperthyroidism* (overactive thyroid).

Treating Hypothyroidism

Most hypothyroid depressives recover on thyroid hormone alone, but some—usually subclinical cases—also require antidepressants.[10,11]

Most doctor's prescribe one of the purified thyroid hormones thyroxine (T4) or triiodothyronine (T3). Gold and associates, however, prefer whole, dessicated thyroid gland.[11] Closer to nature, and probably more body-friendly than T4 or T3, the whole gland may also be more reliable clinically. Some depressives on T4 have only recovered when T3 has been added[19]—the whole gland contains both. Orthomolecular psychiatrists also prefer dessicated thyroid.[20] So does Barnes. He prescribes just enough to raise each patient's underarm temperature back up to normal (97.8–98.2).[12]

It may also be possible to perk up your thyroid with kelp (a rich natural source of the iodine found in thyroid hormone), tyrosine (the antidepressant nutrient from which T3 and T4 are made), and a generous intake of riboflavin.[21]

Thyroid Hormone as an Antidepressant

Since the early 1970s the depression/thyroid connection has been explored from an entirely different direction, with equally significant results. In about a dozen clinical studies, depressed patients not responding to antidepressant drugs have had a small dose of thyroid hormone (usually T3) added to their regime. Usually 50 to 75 percent have improved or recovered within a few weeks.[16,22-24] In four out of five other placebo-controlled studies, T3 has been combined with antidepressant drugs right from the start. Female patients have responded much better and faster (in days rather than weeks) than patients on antidepressants alone.[16,22,23]

If you're sensing a connection here, you're probably right. Recent studies suggest most responders to T3 augmentation are actually mildly or subclinically hypothyroid.[7,10,25]

Very small doses of T3 are used to potentiate antidepressant drugs (usually 25 mcg per day; range: 5–50 mcg). They generally produce only mild and transient side effects, such as fine tremor, upset stomach, weakness and dizziness. There have been cases of mania, but overall there actually seem to be fewer side effects with T3 than without.[16,23]

Certain natural antidepressants may also combine synergistically with T3. Scientists suspect T3 boosts the effectiveness of antidepressant drugs by sensitizing brain cells to a neurotransmitter the antidepressants boost: norepinephrine (NE). NE is also boosted by many natural antidepressants, particularly the amino acids phenylalanine and tyrosine—it's *made* from them. Vitamins C and B6, folic acid, exercise, acupuncture, cold therapy and probably some herbal antidepressants also boost NE. So does sleep deprivation (Chapter 19); at least one person has already benefitted from combining it with thyroid supplements.[26]

OTHER ENDOCRINE DISORDERS, HORMONE THERAPIES AND DEPRESSION

For every person who owes his or her depression to hypothyroidism, another probably can blame some other endocrine disorder for the problem.[2,5] Even *hyperthyroidism* (thyroid hormone excess), which typically produces symptoms "opposite" to hypothyroidism (nervousness, restlessness, sweatiness), sometimes provokes a paradoxical depressive syndrome, especially in the elderly.[27]

A thorough medical examination can reveal if you have hyperthyroidism or any other depressing endocrine disorder: hyperparathyroidism, Cushing's syndrome, Addison's disease, diabetes, hypoglycemia, ovarian failure, testicular failure, hypopituitarism or hyperpituitarism. However, as with hypothyroidism, very mild or subclinical cases of some of these disorders may be common in depression, yet slip through the cracks of conservative diagnosis. Research suggests this is especially likely for hypogonadism.

In depressed men, testosterone levels tend to be low—the deeper the depression, the lower the testosterone.[28,29] Orthomolecular psychiatrist Herbert Newbold frequently gives depressed and other psychiatric patients with low testosterone levels injections of the hormone. Many, he reports, are dramatically improved.[20] In one clinical study, an oral, synthetic testosterone substitute improved the condition of 17 chronically depressed men slightly, but equally to an antidepressant drug.[30] Perhaps combining testosterone with other antidepressants would be synergistic for depressed men the way thyroid hormone and antidepressants so often are for women.

The evidence for a mood/sex-hormone link seems stronger for women. The ovarian hormone estrogen has antidepressant-like effects on brain tissue.[31] When estrogen levels fall—premenstrually, after childbirth, or during menopause—women are particularly depression-prone.[27,32] Estrogen supplements, some studies suggest, can be therapeutic.[32]

Can estrogen help other depressed women? Studies have been contradictory: sometimes yes, sometimes no. In some patients, depression has *worsened*.[28]

But estrogen alone is an unbalanced ovarian supplement; the ovaries also produce progesterone and a dash of testosterone. Progesterone (which may neutralize estrogen's carcinogenic potential) has antidepressant-like effects on neurotransmitters complementary to those of estrogen.[31] Testosterone has galvanized some of Newbold's meekest female patients. In clinical studies, surgically menopausal women (from hysterectomy) on estrogen or estrogen and testosterone combined were found to be significantly less depressed, "more composed, elated, and energetic," than controls on placebo or nothing at all. Significantly, the higher their blood levels of estrogen *and testosterone,* the better they felt.[28] In another report, two severely depressed women failed to recover until a balanced combination of estrogen and progesterone was added to their regime. Estrogen alone or with too little progesterone didn't work.[31] Indeed, there is evidence that not only estrogen alone,[33] but also progesterone alone,[34] can *promote* depression. Perhaps the safest, most effective gonadal antidepressant for women will prove, after all, to be *whole ovarian gland.*

NOTES

1. T. W. Estroff and M. S. Gold, "Psychiatric Misdiagnosis." In M. S. Gold et al., eds., *Advances in Psychopharmacology: Predicting and Improving Treatment Response* (Boca Raton, Fla: CRC Press, 1984), pp. 33–66.

2. E. K. Koranyi, "Morbidity and Rate of Undiagnosed Physical Illnesses in a Psychiatric Population," *Arch Gen Psychiatry* 36(April 1979):414–419.

3. M. S. Gold et al., "Hypothyroidism and Depression: Evidence from Complete Thyroid Function Evaluation," *J Am Med Assoc* 245(May 15, 1981):1919–1922.

4. M. S. Gold et al., "Grades of Thyroid Failure in 100 Depressed and Anergic Psychiatric Inpatients," *Am J Psychiatry* 138(February 1981): 253–255.

5. R. C. W. Hall et al., "Unrecognized Physical Illness Prompting Psychiatric Admission: A Prospective Study," *Am J Psychiatry* 138(May 1981):629–635.

6. M. S. Gold and J. S. Carman, "Thyroid Failure and Clinical Misdiagnosis." In M. S. Gold et al., eds., *Advances in Psychopharmacology*, pp. 67–81.

7. S. D. Targum et al., "The TRH Test and Thyroid Hormone in Refractory Depression" (letter) *Am J Psychiatry* 141(March 1984): 463.

8. C. B. Nemeroff, "Clinical Significance of Psychoneuroendocrinology in Psychiatry: Focus on the Thyroid and Adrenal," *J Clin Psychiatry* 50(Suppl, May 1989):13–22.

9. V. I. Reus, "Behavioral Aspects of Thyroid Disease in Women," *Psychiatric Clinics of North America* 12 (March 1989): 153–165.

10. R. H. Howland, "Thyroid Dysfunction in Refractory Depression," *J Clin Psychiatry* 54(February 1993):47–54.

11. P. Sinaikin and M. S. Gold, "Endocrinology and Depression II: Thyroid Function." In Oliver G. Cameron, ed., *Presentations of Depression: Depressive Symptoms in Medical and Other Psychiatric Disorders* (New York: John Wiley & Sons, 1987), pp. 275–290.

12. Broda Barnes, *Hypothyroidism: The Unsuspected Illness* (New York: Thomas Y. Crowell, 1976).

13. D. E. Sternberg, "Testing for Physical Illness in Psychiatric Patients," *J Clin Psychiatry* 47(Suppl, January 1986):3–9.

14. M. Kusalic, "Grade II and Grade III Hypothyroidism in Rapid-cycling Bipolar Patients," *Neuropsychobiology* 25(4, 1992):177–181.

15. M. S. Bauer et al., "Rapid Cycling Bipolar Affective Disorder: I. Association with Grade I Hypothyroidism," *Arch Gen Psychiatry* 47 (May 1990):427–432.

16. D. Stein and J. Avni, "Thyroid Hormones in the Treatment of Affective Disorders," *Acta Psychiatr Scand* 77(1988):623–636.

17. N. D. Brayshaw and D. D. Brayshaw, "Thyroid Hypofunction in Premenstrual Syndrome" (letter), *N Eng J Med* 315(December 4, 1986):1486–1487.

18. B. Harris et al., "Association Between Postpartum Thyroid Dysfunction and Thyroid Antibodies and Depression," *Brit Med J* 305(July 18, 1992):152–156.

19. R. G. Cooke et al., "T3 Augmentation of Antidepressant Treat-

ment in T4-replaced Thyroid Patients," *J Clin Psychiatry* 53(January 1992):16–18.

20. H. L. Newbold, *Mega-Nutrients for Your Nerves* (New York: Berkley Books, 1975).

21. I. R. Bell et al., "Low Thyroxine Levels in Female Psychiatric Inpatients with Riboflavin Deficiency," *Acta Psychiatr Scand* 85(May 1992):360–363.

22. F. K. Goodwin et al., "Potentiation of Antidepressant Effects of L-Triiodothyronine in Tricyclic Nonresponders," *Am J Psychiatry* 139(January 1982):34–38.

23. A. J. Prange, "Psychotropic Drugs and the Thyroid Axis: A Review of Interactions." In D. Kemali and G. Racagni, eds., *Chronic Treatments in Neuropsychiatry* (New York: Raven Press, 1985), pp. 103–110.

24. R. T. Joffe et al., "A Placebo-controlled Comparison of Lithium and Triiodothyronine Augmentation of Tricyclic Antidepressants in Unipolar Refractory Depression," *Arch Gen Psychiatry* 50(May 1993):387–393.

25. M. E. Thase et al., "Treatment of Imipramine-Resistant Recurrent Depression: I. An Open Clinical Trial of Adjunctive L-Triiodothyronine," *J Clin Psychiatry* 50(October 1989):385–388.

26. S. E. Southmayd et al., "Therapeutic Sleep Deprivation in a Depressed Patient: Prolongation of Response with Concurrent Thyroxine," *Acta Psychiatr Scand* 86(July 1992):84–85.

27. M. K. Popkin and T. B. Mackenzie, "Psychiatric Presentations of Endocrine Dysfunction." In Richard C. W. Hall, ed., *Psychiatric Presentations of Medical Illness* (New York: S P Medical & Scientific Books, 1980), pp. 139–156.

28. B. B. Sherwin, "Affective Changes with Estrogen and Androgen Replacement Therapy in Surgically Menopausal Women," *J Affect Dis* 14(1988):177–187.

29. R. Driscoll and C. Thompson, "Salivary Testosterone Levels and Major Depressive Illness in Men" (letter), *Brit J Psychiatry* 163(July 1993):122–123.

30. W. Vogel et al., "A Comparison of the Antidepressant Effects of a Synthetic Androgen (Mesterolone) and Amitriptyline in Depressed Men," *J Clin Psychiatry* 46(January 1985):6–8.

31. G. Chouinard et al., "Estrogen-Progesterone Combination: Another Mood Stabilizer?" (letter), *Am J Psychiatry* 144(June 1987):826.

32. J. Studd, "Oestrogens and Depression in Women" (editorial), *Brit J Hosp Med* 48(September 2–15, 1992):211–213.

33. L. A. Palinkas et al., "Estrogen Use and Depressive Symptoms in Postmenopausal Women," *Obstetrics and Gynecology* 80(July 1992):30–36.

34. D. W. Wardell and L. D. Littleton, "Depression May be Overlooked as a Progesterone Side Effect" (letter), *Nurse Practitioner* 17(May 1992):10, 18.

SIX

Alternative Diagnoses: Controversial Medical Conditions That May Promote Depression

Side by side with the textbook illnesses recognized by all doctors, there exists on the fringes of medicine a class of afflictions "believed in" by only a few. You've probably heard of some of these (environmental illness and the yeast syndrome, for instance) and the claims that they're commonly to blame for a host of ills, depression included.

In this chapter we'll take a look at three of these controversial conditions: the Candida or yeast syndrome, "dental depression" (from amalgam fillings), and weather sensitivity. We'll examine several more in later chapters.

THE CANDIDA SYNDROME

Candida albicans, the textbooks will tell you, is a strain of yeast that grows on the skin and mucous membranes of most of us. If it grows too much, there can be local infections, like thrush, diaper rash, and yeast vaginitis (candidiasis). More seriously (but rarely), in susceptible people there can be life-threatening infections of the internal organs.

Some doctors as well as many alternative or "holistic" health practitioners believe in another serious Candida problem. In as many as one in every three of us, they claim, the normal intestinal Candida population explodes. Sometimes it spreads throughout our bodies, invariably it upsets our health in any of innumerable ways, and typically it makes us fatigued and depressed. By following a special anti-Candida regimen, the "Candida doctors" (as we'll call them) maintain, most victims of the Candida syndrome (also known as the yeast syndrome) can find relief.[1-4]

Prominent orthomolecular psychiatrist Abram Hoffer describes how he became a believer in the Candida syndrome (CS). A patient of his had been depressed for years, unresponsive both to conventional and orthomolecular therapies. But she had many signs and symptoms of CS, so Hoffer decided to give the anti-CS approach a try. "One month later she was mentally and emotionally normal," he reports.[2(p. xii)] When the woman quit her anti-Candida medication a year later, she quickly relapsed. Back on the drug, she recovered and has remained well for years.

Richard Podell, a mainstream internist, also decided to investigate CS "with selected patients after carefully explaining my skepticism." "Four years later," he reported, "my experience is that about 50 percent of patients who score high on Dr. Crook's quiz [a questionnaire to identify CS sufferers, published in Crook's popular book[4]] and who adopt the Candida treatment program improve substantially . . . a better result than I would expect from a placebo."[5(p. 60)]

In one of just two formal reports on the anti-CS regimen to be published in medical journals, 70 out of 79 patients improved.[6] However in the other, a double-blind study, one important *component* of the regimen—the antifungal drug nystatin—was moderately effective, but no more than the placebo. There was weak evidence, though, that nystatin was better in the long run.[7]

An entirely different line of research complicates the issue. In preliminary studies, an anti-Candidal drug named ketoconazole, which anti-Candida doctors often prescribe, has performed well as an *antidepressant*.[8] Ironically, the researchers have prescribed it not to fight Candida, but to lower blood levels of *adrenal steroids*, which are high in many severely depressed persons.

Was the ketoconazole really effective because of its anti-Candidal effect (confirming that some depressed patients are suffering instead from yeast syndrome)? Or are anti-Candida doctors who prescribe ketoconazole really relieving depression by countering steroids, not Candida? And what are we to make of the poor fellow who developed obsessive suicidal ruminations while on the drug?[9]

So far, the medical establishment has found the case for CS wanting.[7,10] However, as one observer points out, CS "may well be without scientific 'proof,' but it certainly is not without scientific support."[11] Thus, mainstream medicine and research (1) agree with the Candida doctors that certain commonly prescribed drugs promote recurrent vaginal yeast infections[10] and Candida overgrowth in the gut;[12] (2) recognize that the Candida doctors' claim that refined carbohydrates encourage Candida growth "is not without some logic";[10] (3) suggest that Candida produces toxic byproducts,[13] including "canditoxin," a substance "reported to produce clear behavioral changes in experimental animals";[11] (4) note that intestinal infections can create a "leaky gut" that welcomes allergenic food molecules into the bloodstream,[14] paving the way for "brain allergies" (Chapter 14); and (5) confirm that most of the measures prescribed by Candida doctors are indeed effective yeast-busters.[2]

Do You Have Candida Syndrome?

There is no definitive way to diagnose CS; even blood tests for anti-Candida antibodies are merely "suggestive."[2(p. 114)] The diagnosis is therefore made *speculatively* if a person has more than a few CS symptoms and risk factors, such as these:

Common Symptoms: Depression; chronic fatigue, weakness or feeling "sick all over"; extreme mental dullness or fogginess; anxiety, irritability; feelings of unreality; headaches; multiple allergies; strong cravings for sweet or starchy foods (which may give you a lift) and/or for moldy, yeasty, fermented, pickled, smoked, or dried foods, including alcohol; feeling lousy or drained in moldy air (in mildewy basements, for instance); hyperactivity; premenstrual and menstrual disorders; postpartum depression; frequent urogenital inflammations/infections; constipation or diarrhea; abdominal pain, gas or bloating; chronic skin problems; loss of sexual interest.

Common Risk Factors: Yeast or fungal infections; heavy or long-term use of broad-spectrum antibiotics, steroid medications or birth control pills; many pregnancies; diabetes mellitus; immunosuppression (e.g., from AIDS or cancer chemotherapy); ulcers or gastrointestinal surgery.

Treating Candida Syndrome

The proof of the CS pudding is in the eating—in benefiting, that is, from the anti-CS regimen of diet, supplements and (often) antifungal medication. Though people on this austere program sometimes improve in days, more often it takes weeks, months or even years.[4] To remain well, they must continue on the regimen, albeit usually less restrictively.

The anti-CS regimen, in brief, goes as follows (self-help books on CS provide more detail along with lists of Candida doctors and CS support groups)[2-4]:

• Eliminate or lower your intake of foods, beverages and drugs that stimulate Candida growth: carbohydrate-rich foods, particularly sweets and other refined carbohydrates; yeasty/moldy, fermented, pickled and dried foods and beverages, including fruit juices (which tend to be yeasty and high in fruit sugars); broad-spectrum antibiotics, steroids and other immunosuppressant drugs.

• Use foods, natural supplements and/or drugs to suppress Candida. *Foods:* garlic, yogurt, onions, kale, turnips, cabbage, horseradish, broccoli. *Natural supplements:* garlic, caprylic acid, sorbic acid, olive oil, taheebo and mathake herbal tea, tea tree oil, certain homeopathic remedies. *Drugs:* nystatin, ketoconazole.

• Take large doses of "friendly bacteria" to crowd out and suppress Candida in the gastrointestinal tract. This usually means swallowing many capsules of *Lactobacillus* bacteria (available in health food stores) several times a day for a few weeks or more.

• Take nutritional supplements, either to correct CS-related deficiencies, to compensate for damage caused by Candida, or to stimulate the immune system. Favorites are vitamin B6, magnesium, biotin, linseed oil, fish oil and evening primrose oil.[2,13] Some doctors also prescribe very dilute, "desensitizing" doses of Candida or other molds,[1,2] and some recommend enemas or colon cleanses.[2]

DENTAL DEPRESSION: MERCURY POISONING BY MOUTH ____

A hundred and fifty years ago, dentists who dared to fill their patients' cavities with a new-fangled alloy of mercury, silver and tin called "amalgam" risked expulsion from the American Society of Dental Surgeons. Today, dentists who have a passion for getting the amalgam *out* of their patients' mouths are in hot water with *their* professional association.

The anti-amalgam dentists are convinced that the mercury in amalgam or "silver" fillings is a toxic waste site in people's mouths, the cause of many perplexing health problems—chronic fatigue and depression among them. Replace the amalgams with safer substitutes and the symptoms usually fade or disappear, the anti-amalgamists claim.[15] Hundreds of case histories filed with the FDA attest to that.[16]

There is some good scientific evidence for the anti-amalgam position. Studies show that people with amalgam fillings typically have enough mercury vapor on their breath to exceed EPA residential air standards.[17] *Chewing* usually puts them in violation of stricter workplace standards.[17] Ironically, if their mouths were dental offices they'd have to be closed down.[18]

Most of this inhaled mercury vapor goes straight into the bloodstream, boosting not only blood and urine levels of this heavy metal, but (autopsy studies show) *brain* levels too.[16] Indeed, the average person has far more to fear from dental mercury than from the mercury in food, the World Health Organization has concluded.[16] "A mouth with many fillings could release up to 560 mg of mercury over several years . . . a very toxic dose," observes physiologist Robert Siblerud.[17]

Some, but not all, research suggests this extra mercury is taking a toll. There are conflicting reports, for instance, that amalgams disturb[17,19–21] or don't disturb[21,22] the immune and cardiovascular systems.

A study of nearly 400 people by the Swedish Health Insurance Bureau found that replacing amalgams led, after two years, to a 33 percent reduction in sick leave.[16] People surveyed by Siblerud who had had their amalgams replaced typically reported major health improvements.[17,23] Yet large-scale studies from Sweden have found no positive association between symptoms of ill health, heart disease, cancer, diabetes or early death and the number of amalgams in women.[22]

On the psychological front, in a study by Siblerud, people with many amalgams had twice as many mental symptoms as people with none. Their most conspicuous symptoms were typical of mild mercury poisoning: angry outbursts, depression, fatigability and morning tiredness.[17] When Siblerud sent a questionnaire to nearly 300 people who had had their fillings removed, most of the 86 responders said their psychological symptoms had receded or remitted. Depression had improved in 32 out of 38, and "all 10 subjects who reported suicidal tendencies said that the condition was improved or eliminated."[17] (Of course, nonresponders may have been too depressed to answer the survey!) Similar benefits were later reported by people with multiple sclerosis who had ditched their amalgams.[23]

The American Dental Association (ADA) steadfastly defends amalgams. It insists they release so little mercury that only people who are allergic (less than 1 percent of the population, the ADA estimates; between 5 and 44 percent, studies cited by one critic[16] indicate) could be affected.[24] Some authorities are not so complacent. The German government advises dentists to keep amalgams out of the mouths of babes and pregnant women.[16] In Sweden, the Social Welfare and Health Administration has concluded that "amalgam is an unsuitable and toxic dental filling material." They've advised the government to ban amalgams for pregnant women and eventually for everyone.[16]

Are *Your* Fillings Getting You Down?

Anti-amalgamists attribute almost every conceivable symptom and ailment to amalgam fillings—and indeed mercury *is* toxic to most organs and tissues. However, "the most consistent sign of mercury intoxication" is low body temperature; the most typical is chronic fatigue (oversleeping, morning tiredness); and the most specific, perhaps, is a *metallic taste in the mouth*.[19] Apparently there is another surprisingly common symptom: a passive, "go with the flow" inclination to suicide. Hal Huggins, a leading anti-amalgam dentist, says suicidal patients are "the second largest section of our practice."[15(p. 122)]

Anti-amalgam dentists commonly use a variety of tests (none of them conclusive, some of uncertain validity) to help determine if, and to what extent, a patient has an amalgam problem. These include skin patch tests for mercury allergy, white blood cell counts and mercury levels in blood, urine and hair. Many anti-amalgam dentists also measure the minute electrical current generated by their patients' fillings. "The more fillings with negative current you have," claims Huggins, "the greater the probability that your symptoms are caused—at least in part—by mercury toxicity."[15(p. 52)]

Treatment

Treating amalgam toxicity is not as straightforward as one might expect. "Just removing fillings with no other form of therapy is probably not going to help very many people with mercury toxicity," says anti-amalgam dentist Joyal Taylor.[19(p.128)] Anti-amalgam therapy, as detailed in popular books by Taylor, Huggins and others,[15,16,25] is more complex. In a nutshell:

• While amalgam fillings are being drilled out, stringent precautions must be taken to prevent further poisoning from the abraded mercury.[19]

• Amalgams with the strongest negative electrical current must be removed first, Huggins warns. When positives are removed first, the improvement rate plummets from 80 percent to 10 percent, he claims.[15] Some anti-amalgamists are skeptical.[25] One reports that in over 50 patients whose amalgams were removed in no particular order, the results were just fine.[26]

• Huggins also insists that if patients don't follow his peculiar, high-fat detoxification diet and use his proprietary nutritional supplements, their symptoms can flare up during and after amalgam removal, and their "chances for improvement are slight."[15] Again, some colleagues are skeptical.[25]

• Replacement materials for amalgams must not themselves be toxic. Gold (if relatively pure), real porcelain and (less assuredly) composite are considered the safest.[15,19] As for cements, bases and other adjunctive materials, dropsin and glass ionomer are recommended.[15,19]

"Witches' Winds," Natural and Manmade

There are places in this world where the "witches' wind" blows, bringing sickness and malaise, mishaps and mayhem.

At least that's what the locals believe. And they have the records, it seems, to prove it. When the *foehn* blows in Europe, for instance, or the *sharav* in Israel, a significant increase in the suicide, homicide and accident rates occurs.[27]

Doctors and biometeorologists who have studied the phenomenon tell us that these and other ill winds (like the *mistral* in France, the Santa Ana in California, the summer winds of the Arizona/Mexico desert and the Chinook of the Rockies) can be a major irritant for "weather-sensitive" people. The winds can agitate or *enervate* them, triggering insomnia, panic attacks, lethargic depression, suicide attempts or other disturbances, and they can aggravate chronic conditions like asthma, arthritis and depression.[27-29]

In 1901, scientists discovered the secret of the witches' winds: They're full of positively charged air particles.[29]

Every time we breathe, we inhale thousands, sometimes millions, of positively and negatively charged air particles, or air ions.

These microscopic particles are as essential to our health as vitamins, but only in the right balance.[27] Scientists have found that if they pump up the volume of positive air ions, animals and human subjects typically behave as though they've been caught in a witches' wind.[27,29-31] Pump up the negative air-ion count, and people either feel nothing or, more often, they feel, think and perform better than usual or they find relief from symptoms of positive air-ion excess.[27,29,30,32]

The ion effect may be of special relevance to people with mood disorders; some 50 percent of them are weather sensitive, according to air-ion authority Felix Sulman, M.D.[28] Depressives who wilt in the summer heat are especially likely to benefit from negative ion replacement therapy, Sulman claims. Moreover, a controlled study suggests negative ions are a speedy tranquilizer for manics.[33]

Weather-sensitive individuals have more to fear than just witches' winds. Weather fronts (especially warm ones), thunderstorms and sunspots "are notorious for producing positive ionization."[28] Interestingly, because the ionization comes first, weather-sensitive depressives can "feel" them coming. Positive air-ion excesses and negative air-ion deficiencies also develop where the air is thick with combustion byproducts (from automobile exhaust, heating systems, cigarettes, etc.); in big buildings where air passes through hundreds of feet of metal ductwork; in the electromagnetic fields near power lines and electrical appliances (Chapter 4); and near synthetic clothing, carpets or other textiles under friction.[27-29,31]

Relief can be found in unpolluted country air, where negative air-ion counts typically are high, or near splashing or falling water—a fountain or waterfall, a rocky shore, even a bathroom shower—where they're sky high.[27,28] More accessible are the electronic negative-ion generators or ionizers routinely used in clinical studies and prescribed by some doctors.[28,29] These small, inexpensive appliances also serve as air purifiers and often are sold as such.

Doctors advise weather sensitives to keep at least two meters away from their ionizers, while avoiding close contact with synthetic fabrics. If relief doesn't come quickly (in minutes or hours), positive-ion overload probably isn't the problem.[28]

NOTES

1. C. O. Truss, "The Role of Candida Albicans in Human Illness," *J Orthomol Psychiatry* 10(4, 1981):228–238.

2. John Parks Trowbridge and Morton Walker, *The Yeast Syndrome* (New York: Bantam, 1986).

3. Shirley Lorenzani, *Candida: A Twentieth Century Disease* (New Canaan, Conn.: Keats Publishing, 1986).

4. William G. Crook, *The Yeast Connection: A Medical Breakthrough* (New York: Vintage, 1986).

5. Richard N. Podell, *Doctor, Why Am I So Tired?* (New York: Pharos Books, 1987).

6. M. H. Zwerling et al., " 'Think Yeast'—the Expanding Spectrum of Candidiasis," *J South Carolina Med Assoc* 9(September 1984):454–456.

7. W. E. Dismukes et al., "A Randomized, Double-Blind Trial of Nystatin Therapy for the Candidiasis Hypersensitivity Syndrome," *N Eng J Med* 323(December 20,1990):1717–1723.

8. O. M. Wolkowitz et al., "Ketoconazole Administration in Hypercortisolemic Depression," *Am J Psychiatry* 150(May 1993):810–812.

9. R. Z. Fisch and A. Lahad, "Drug Induced Suicidal Ideation," *Israeli Journal of Psychiatry and Related Sciences* 28(1, 1991):41–43.

10. E. R. Blonz, "Is There an Epidemic of Chronic Candidiasis in Our Midst?" *J Am Med Assoc* 256(December 12, 1986):3138–3139.

11. D. A. Edwards, "Depression and *Candida*" (letter) *J Am Med Assoc* 253(June 21, 1985):3400.

12. B. Zimmerman and E. Weber, "*Candida* and '20th-Century Disease,' " *Can Med Assoc J* 133(November 15, 1985):965–966.

13. L. Galland, "Nutrition and Candidiasis," *J Orthomolecular Psychiatry* 14(1, 1985):50–60.

14. American Academy of Allergy and Immunology Committee on Adverse Reactions to Foods, National Institute of Allergy and Infectious Diseases, *Adverse Reactions to Foods* ((NIH Publication No. 84-2442, July 1984).

15. Hal A. Huggins and S. A. Huggins, *It's All in Your Head: Diseases*

Caused by Silver-Mercury Fillings (P.O. Box 2589, Colorado Springs, CO 80901, 1985).

16. C. A. Strong, "Health Risks Associated with Mercury from Dental Amalgams" (letter), *Nurse Practitioner* 18(June 1993): 14–15, 21.

17. R. L. Siblerud, "The Relationship Between Mercury from Dental Amalgam and Mental Health," *Am J Psychotherapy* 43(October 1989): 575–587.

18. D. H. Rosen, "Are 'Silver' Fillings Safe?" *Medical Self-Care* (Fall, 1983), pp. 22–25.

19. Joyal Taylor, *The Complete Guide to Mercury Toxicity from Dental Fillings* (San Diego, Calif.: Scripps Publishing, 1988).

20. R. L. Siblerud, "The Relationship Between Mercury from Dental Amalgam and the Cardiovascular System," *Science of the Total Environment* 99(December 1, 1990):23–35.

21. M. Wilhelm et al., "Failure to Detect any Effect of Amalgam Restorations on Peripheral Blood Lymphocyte Populations," *Clinical Investigation* 70 (September 1992): 728–734.

22. M. Ahlqwist et al., "Number of Amalgam Fillings in Relation to Cardiovascular Disease, Diabetes, Cancer and Early Death in Swedish Women," *Community Dentistry and Oral Epidemiology* 21(February 1993):40–44.

23. R. L. Siblerud, "A Comparison of Mental Health of Multiple Sclerosis Patients with Silver/Mercury Dental Fillings and Those with Fillings Removed," *Psych Rep* 70(June 1992):1139–1151.

24. P. K. Friedman, "Safety of Dental Amalgam," *J Am Med Assoc* 260(October 21, 1988):2295.

25. Guy S. Fasciana, *Are Your Dental Fillings Poisoning You?* (New Canaan, Conn.: Keats Publishing, 1986).

26. A. V. Zamm, "Candida Albicans Therapy," *J Orthomolecular Med* 1(4, 1986):261–266.

27. Fred Soyka and Alan Edmunds, *The Ion Effect* (Toronto: Lester and Orpen, 1977).

28. Felix G. Sulman, *Short and Long-Term Changes in Climate, Volumes I and II* (Boca Raton, Fla.: CRC Press, 1982).

29. A. J. Giannini et al., "The Serotonin Irritation Syndrome—A New Clinical Entity," *J Clin Psychiatry* 47(January 1986):22–25.

30. J. M. Charry, "Biological Effects of Small Air Ions: A Review of Findings and Methods," *Environmental Research* 34(August 1984): 351–389.

31. A. J. Giannini et al., "Anxiogenic Effects of Generated Ambient

Cations—A Preliminary Study," *Int J Psychiatry Med* 16(3, 1986–87): 243–248.

32. A. Hedge and M. D. Collis, "Do Negative Air Ions Affect Human Mood and Performance?" *Ann Occ Hygiene* 31(3, 1987):291–298.

33. J. Misiaszek et al., "The Calming Effect of Negative Air Ions on Manic Patients," *Biol Psychiatry* 22(January 1986):107–110.

Of all the influences in our lives, nothing affects us quite so intimately, tangibly and continually as food. Our "umbilical cord to Mother Earth," food supplies all the energy and raw materials (except oxygen) we need to continually repair and rebuild ourselves, brains and all.

In the next nine chapters, we'll see how the good things in food (the vitamins and other nutrients) can make us more vulnerable to depression if we don't get enough of them. We'll also see how "extra helpings" of certain nutrients can probably relieve depression. Finally, we'll see how too much of certain foods or food elements—or other questionable eating habits—also can depress us, and how we may be able to put things right by returning to a healthier, more balanced way of eating.

SEVEN

Nutritional Supplements: The Orthomolecular Approach to Depression

You won't find nutritional supplements in the little black bags of most psychiatrists. Yet some psychiatrists' satchels contain little else. These orthomolecular psychiatrists, as they often call themselves, believe (along with Nobel Laureate Linus Pauling[1]) that the best way to treat mental illness is to supply the brain with an optimal ("ortho") concentration of the nutrients or other natural substances ("molecular") it needs.

Formerly known as megavitamin therapy, orthomolecular psychiatry evolved in the 1950s and 1960s in a skeptical, even hostile, medical climate. A withering task force report from the American Psychiatric Association (APA) in 1973[2] all but relegated the movement to leper status. Later, as research sympathetic to orthomolecular psychiatry accumulated, the distinguished chairman of the APA task force, Morris Lipton, tempered his earlier judgments. "[I]t appears that small subpopulations who respond favorably to the addition of vitamins in large quantities or the elimination of additives from the diet may exist, particularly among children," he wrote.[3] And: "The possibility that there is a subgroup of schizophrenics who require megavitamin therapy must not be ignored."[4] But by then most psychiatrists were convinced that their good reputations depended precisely *on* ignoring such possibilities.

In the next few chapters we'll be examining many other possibilities—this time regarding the nutritional treatment of *depression*—which, unfortunately, most psychiatrists also ignore. But before we get down to specifics, let me address in a basic way the reasons we stand to benefit from nutritional supplements when we're depressed.

Many depressed persons have subclinical nutritional deficiencies. When someone has laboratory signs of nutritional deficiency but no specific clinical (i.e. physical) signs or symptoms, he has a *subclinical* deficiency. Researchers have consistently found subclinical nutritional deficiencies known to promote depression in an abnormally high percentage of depressed patients. Even non-orthomolecular experts suspect these deficiencies are a commonly overlooked cause of depression.[9-11]

Some depressives may need certain nutrients in quantities much greater than any diet can provide. It's medically recognized that some people have genetic defects that grossly exaggerate their need for certain nutrients.[5] Typically, these *vitamin dependencies* announce themselves in infancy through severe neurological symptoms which can only be allayed by megadoses of the appropriate vitamin.[5] Orthomolecular psychiatrists suspect that milder vitamin dependencies underlie the mental disorders of many adults. Some mainstream research supports their suspicion of a vitamin C dependency in schizophrenia.[8]

Some depressed people, despite having adequate diets and normal test results for nutritional deficiencies, may have hidden *deficiencies.* It's possible to have normal nutrient levels in your food and even in your blood, yet still be suffering from a depressing nutritional deficiency if the levels in your brain are low. The nutrients in our food have to run a gauntlet of hoops and hurdles before they get to our brains:

• First they must be absorbed from the digestive tract. Disturbed digestion, parasites and certain drugs, microorganisms and genetic diseases can prevent us from absorbing all the nutrients we need.

• Once absorbed, many nutrients must attach themselves to special "carrier molecules" that take them to the tissues. Sometimes in vitamin dependency diseases these carrier molecules are genetically defective or deficient in number; megadoses of the vitamins they carry are therapeutic.[5] Orthomolecular psychiatrists suspect that such defects account for many of their own patients' responses to megadoses.[1]

• Many nutrients are useless until they've been converted in the body into their metabolically active form(s). Such inadequate bioconversion is another cause of vitamin dependency disease, and again, huge doses of the unconverted vitamin sometimes are therapeutic.[5] Bioconversion defects also show up in many psychiatric patients examined by orthomolecular[12] *and* mainstream researchers alike.[13]

• The brain is very fussy about what it picks up from the bloodstream; its blood-brain barrier (BBB) ensures that even nutrients have a hard time getting through *en masse* without a lift from special carrier molecules. In 1968, in his seminal paper on orthomolecular psychiatry, Linus Pauling hypothesized that faulty transport of nutrients across the BBB could result in "localized cerebral [brain] deficiencies."[1] Such deficiencies, Pauling wrote, could be a cryptic cause of mental illness. Megadoses of the missing nutrients could possibly overcome the bottleneck. Mainstream psychiatrists condescendingly reminded Pauling he'd won his Nobel prize in chemistry, not medicine. But subsequent research has been more supportive of Pauling's ideas. Low nutrient levels in the cerebrospinal fluid despite normal levels in the blood have been reported in people with Alzheimer's disease,[14-16] AIDS,[17] postpartum and toxic depression[14] and several other conditions.[18,19] Large doses of the missing nutrients have, according to preliminary reports, seemed beneficial.[14-16,18] Other research suggests "restricted central hypothyroidism" (a localized brain deficiency of thyroid hormones) may be a common cause of refractory depression.[20] Pauling was later joined in his speculations by mainstream psychiatrists from Columbia University,[20] Harvard Medical School,[21] and the University of Iowa,[18] among others.[14-16]

In large doses, some nutrients combat depressing chemicals (Chapter 4) *or mitigate depressing allergic reactions* (Chapter 15).

Nutritional supplements can make up for heavy nutrient losses brought on by extreme depression-related distress. The distinguished British psychiatrist Alec Coppen and his associate M. T. Abou-Saleh have proposed "a nutritional deficiency model for the psychoses."[22] With a respectful nod to orthomolecular pioneers, they suggest that stressed-out people may deplete themselves of adaptive neurochemicals and the nutrients they need to make them. These deficiencies may then "predispose, provoke, promote or aggravate psychiatric illness such as depression."[22]

Nutritional supplements may improve the function of defective or deficient enzymes. Every one of our body processes is catalyzed by enzymes. We have about 50,000 of these complex, genetically encoded chemicals. Increasingly, scientists are discovering that gene-enzyme defects or deficiencies are a major contributing cause of many, perhaps all, human maladies. There's a nutritional connection here: Most enzymes are useless until they've hooked up with specific vitamins or minerals. This has enormous clinical potential. As the vitamin dependency diseases have shown, large doses of these co-enzyme nutrients can enhance the performance of faulty enzymes. Similarly, it is believed that some enzyme flaws can be compensated for by providing a surplus of the nutrients these enzymes normally convert into other biochemicals. Some amino acids, for example, are enzymatically converted to mood-regulating neurotransmitters. Faulty versions of these enzymes are suspected by biological psychiatrists of being responsible for the chemical imbalance of depression. Vitamins, amino acids and other nutrients that can potentially compensate for these defects are some of the most important natural antidepressants.

Megadoses of some nutrients could have drug-like *antidepressant effects, above and beyond their normal physiological effects.* Megadoses of niacinamide (vitamin B3), for instance, have Valium-like effects.[23] And megadoses of vitamin B1, one study indicates, behave like a popular class of antidepressant drugs (page 68).

NOTES

1. L. Pauling, "Orthomolecular Psychiatry," *Science* 160(April 19, 1968): 265–271.

2. *American Psychiatric Association Task Force Report #7: Megavitamin and Orthomolecular Therapy in Psychiatry* (Washington: American Psychiatric Association, 1973).

3. M. A. Lipton and J. C. Wheless, "Diet as Therapy." In Sanford Miller, ed., *Nutrition & Behavior* (Philadelphia: Franklin Institute Press, 1981), pp. 213–233.

4. M. A. Lipton and G. Burnett, "Pharmacological Treatment of Schizophrenia." In Leopold Bellak, ed., *Disorders of the Schizophrenic Syndrome* (New York: Basic Books, 1979), pp. 320–352.

5. S. H. Mudd, "Vitamin-Responsive Genetic Abnormalities." In Harold H. Draper, ed., *Advances in Nutritional Research,* Vol. 4 (New York: Plenum, 1982), pp. 1–34.

6. C. M. Reading, "Relatively Speaking: Family Tree Way to Better Health: Orthomolecular Genetics," *J Orthomolecular Med* (2, 1986): 113–119.

7. David R. Hawkins and Linus Pauling, eds., *Orthomolecular Psychiatry* (San Francisco: W. H. Freeman and Co., 1973).

8. K. Suboticanec et al., "Vitamin C Status in Chronic Schizophrenia," *Biol Psychiatry* 28(1959):956–959.

9. M. W. P. Carney, "Thiamine and Pyridoxine Lack in Newly-Admitted Psychiatric Inpatients," *Brit J Psychiatry* 135(1979):239–254.

10. T. W. Estroff and M. S. Gold, "Psychiatric Misdiagnosis." In Mark S. Gold et al., eds., *Advances in Psychopharmacology: Predicting and Improving Treatment Response* (Boca Raton, Fla.: CRC Press, 1984), pp. 33–66.

11. R. Crellin et al., "Folates and Psychiatric Disorders. Clinical Potential," *Drugs* 45(May 1993):623–636.

12. L. C. Abbey, "Agoraphobia," *J Orthomolecular Psychiatry* 11(4, 1982):243–259.

13. J. R. Smithies et al., "Abnormalities of One-Carbon Metabolism in Psychiatric Disorders," *Biol Psychiatry* 21(1986):1391–1398.

14. C. J. M. van Tiggelen et al., "Vitamin B12 Levels of Cerebrospinal Fluid in Patients with Organic Mental Disorder," *J Orthomolecular Psychiatry* 12(4, 1983):305–311.

15. C. J. M. van Tiggelen et al., "Assessment of Vitamin B12 Status in CSF" (letter), *Am J Psychiatry* 141(January 1984):136–137.

16. T. Ikeda et al., "Treatment of Alzheimer-type Dementia with Intravenous Mecobalamin," *Clinical Therapeutics* 14(May–June 1992): 426–437.

17. I. Smith et al., "Folate Deficiency and Demyelinization in AIDS," *Lancet* (July 25, 1987):215.

18. E. P. Frenkel et al., "Cerebrospinal Fluid Folate, and Vitamin B12 in Anti-Convulsant-Induced Megaloblastosis," *J Lab Clin Med* 81(1973): 105–115.

19. R. Spector et al., "Is Idiopathic Dementia a Regional Vitamin Deficiency State?" *Medical Hypotheses* 5(1979):763–767.

20. Julie A. Hatterer et al., "CSF Transthyretin in Patients with Depression," *Am J Psychiatry* 150(May 1993):813–815.

21. I. R. Bell et al., "Vitamin B12 and Folate Status in Acute Geropsychiatric Inpatients," *Biol Psychiatry* 27(January 15, 1990):125–137.

22. M. T. Abou-Saleh and A. Coppen, "The Biology of Folate in Depression: Implications for Nutritional Hypotheses of the Psychoses," *J Psychiatric Res* 20(2, 1986):91–101.

23. H. Mohler et al., "Nicotinamide Is a Brain Constituent with Benzodiazepine-like Actions," *Nature* 278(April 5, 1979):563–565.

EIGHT

Vitamin Power

VITAMINS make up only a tiny portion of our food. Even on the most festive holidays we probably swallow no more than a gram of them. But take any one of these essential nutrients away (essential because we can't make them ourselves) and we would sicken and die a slow and painful death.

We need vitamins primarily for the catalytic functions they fulfill in all our bodily processes, including everything that goes on in our brains. The vitamins discussed in this chapter bear a more apparent relationship to depression than others.

VITAMIN B1 (THIAMINE)

The simple sugar glucose is the brain's main fuel, but without vitamin B1 the brain can't "burn" it. People who are deficient in B1 (and some studies,[1,2] but not all,[3] suggest about a third of depressed persons are at least mildly so) typically become nervous wrecks: They feel anxious, irritable, run down, depressed, even suicidal.[4,5] In one study, when psychiatric patients with mild B1 deficiencies were given B1 supplements and told to cut down on refined carbohydrates (a major drain on B1 reserves), their neuroses quickly faded.[4]

For information on using vitamins and other nutritional supplements, please see Chapter 12.

In megadoses, vitamin B1 is regarded by orthomolecular psychiatrists[5-7] as a stimulant that can help some people—B1-deficient or not—"raise themselves out of the valley of depression."[6] Interestingly, megadoses of B1 also seem to inhibit an enzyme called *monoamine oxidase* (MAO).[8] So does a major class of antidepressant drugs, boosting brain levels of mood-lifting neurotransmitters in the process.

VITAMIN B3 (NIACIN, NIACINAMIDE)* _____

Mainstream physicians often prescribe megadoses of niacin to lower blood cholesterol. Orthomolecular psychiatrists frequently prescribe it to counter depression.[6]

Most, but not all, studies of niacin as an antidepressant have been favorable. In one of several reports in the early 1950s, 14 out of 15 young, withdrawn, "retarded" (very slowed down) depressives improved within days—dramatically, in most cases—on megadoses of the vitamin. Eleven responded again to niacin the next time they got depressed.[9] A decade later, megadoses of B3 dramatically reduced the long-term suicide rate in schizophrenics.[10] Finally, a double-blind study commissioned by the National Institute of Mental Health seemed to echo these findings: Megadoses of niacin were markedly superior to placebos in young, depressively retarded schizophrenics.[11]

Orthomolecular psychiatrists claim that niacin can be especially beneficial for elderly[12] and alcoholic depressives.[13]

VITAMIN B6 (PYRIDOXINE) _____

Most of the neurochemicals that help keep us undepressed depend on vitamin B6 for their synthesis.[14] Not coincidentally, perhaps, low blood levels of B6 are commonly found in depressed persons.[1-3,15,16]

*Formerly known as nicotinic acid and nicotinamide, respectively.

When one researcher briefly gave B6 supplements to two B6-deficient depressives, neither improved.[17] However another investigator reported that B6 (with zinc) relieved depression and anxiety in depressives within four weeks.[18] (Tryptophan [Chapter 11] enhanced the response even more.) In a placebo-controlled study, B6 proved highly effective for severely depressed women who had become B6-deficient on oral contraceptives.[19] And in another double-blind trial, a modest dose of vitamins B6, B1 and B2 appeared to enhance the response of elderly depressives to antidepressant drugs.[20]

Vitamin B6 is best known as a treatment for premenstrual depression (and PMS in general). At one major London hospital it helped 70 to 80 percent of 630 women with PMS.[21] Clinical studies—including five out of seven double-blind, placebo-controlled trials—have usually supported the B6 prescription for PMS.[22,23]

Schizoaffective disorder is a very hard-to-treat cross between schizophrenia and depression. Many schizoaffectives, according to orthomolecular psychiatrists, have a metabolic defect that washes most of their B6 and zinc away in the urine.[24] These "pyrollurics" typically have china doll complexions, white spots on their fingernails and a hard time remembering their dreams. Super megadoses of B6 and zinc supplements usually help them.[24]

FOLIC ACID (FOLATE, FOLACIN)

Like vitamin B6, folic acid helps catalyse the synthesis of most of our mood-regulating neurochemicals.[25,26] In over a dozen studies, blood levels of this B vitamin have usually been abnormally low in about one in every three or four depressed persons[3,25-27]—the more severe or "typical" the depression, the lower the levels have been.[25,26] Supplements of folic acid have often proven therapeutic.[25,26]

Just as low folate levels promote depression, high levels seem to deter it.[26] Some studies,[26,27] but not all,[28] indicate that recovered depressives who have very high folate levels from diet or supplements are much less vulnerable to relapse. And in three recent

clinical trials, megadoses of *methylfolate* (5-methyltetrahydrofo-
late)—a more potent, bioconverted form of the vitamin—have dis-
played significant antidepressant effects.[26,29] In one double-blind
study, methylfolate performed as well as a popular antidepressant drug.[26]

This will come as no surprise to orthomolecular psychiatrists.
For years they've claimed megadoses of folate can be a mood-
lifting stimulant.[6]

VITAMIN B12 (COBALAMIN, HYDROXOCOBALAMIN, CYANOCOBALAMIN)

You don't have to have low blood levels of vitamin B12 (perhaps 10 to 30 percent of depressives do)[3,30] to benefit from megadose injections or oral supplements.* So some psychiatrists[31,32]—
especially orthomolecular ones[6,33]—believe. Most doctors, however, dismiss B12 injections as placebo medicine.

Controlled research suggests otherwise. In a double-blind
study, B12 shots boosted energy and lifted mood in chronically
fatigued patients better than placebo shots of sterile water.[34] In a
single-blind trial, the effect was replicated for psychiatric
patients.[33]

Interestingly, researchers have successfully used *oral* megadoses of B12 to treat chronic sleep-wake rhythm disorders—being
sleepy when you should be awake and vice versa.[35] Such rhythm
disorders are part and parcel of many depressions (Chapter 20).
Allaying them may account for much of B12's antidepressant
effect.

People with normal blood levels of B12 who benefit from B12
therapy may, in some cases, have a localized brain deficiency of
B12. Studies suggest such deficiencies occur frequently in postpartum depression,[36] Alzheimer's disease,[36,37] and toxic depressions or other toxic neuropsychiatric disorders (Chapter 4).[36]

---

*B12 injections are preferred because large oral doses are poorly absorbed.

VITAMIN C (ASCORBIC ACID, ASCORBATE)

Under heavy stress, most animals produce within their bodies a special coping elixir: megadoses of vitamin C. We can't. Nor can any but the most exotic diets accommodate us. So our coping abilities probably suffer, and we may become depressed more easily for it. Unless, perhaps, we obtain our megadoses of vitamin C from a bottle.

In one double-blind study, a single megadose of vitamin C (3 grams) outperformed placebo in 11 manic and 12 depressed patients, cutting depression 40 percent after four hours.[38] In a longer trial, vitamin C (together with a drug called EDTA) equalled an antidepressant drug.[39]

The researchers had prescribed C to neutralize a depressing trace mineral called vanadium. Vanadium tends to be high in people with affective disorders.[38] But vitamin C also combats many other depressing metals and chemicals.[40] And in its spare time it helps the immune system fight infections and cancer, while moderating the immune system's allergic and autoimmune tendencies.[41] So vitamin C can probably fight depressions arising from many different causes: stress-induced, toxic, infectious, allergic and autoimmune. No wonder it's the "chicken soup" of orthomolecular psychiatry.[5,6]

CHOLINE

Choline is a vitaminlike, "nonessential" nutrient (we can make it ourselves) from which an important neurotransmitter, acetylcholine, is made. Acetylcholine enjoys a see-saw relationship with mood. Lower its activity with drugs (including most antidepressant drugs) and some people become euphoric or manic. Boost its activity with drugs or large doses of choline or lecithin (a choline-rich foodstuff) and some people become depressed, but many manic persons become calm and grounded.[42] In a placebo-controlled trial from Harvard, lecithin rapidly grounded five out of six high-flying manics.[43] Some doctors use choline and lecithin supplements to help keep their biopolar patients earthbound.[5,44]

L-CARNITINE

Like choline, L-carnitine is a vitaminlike nutrient we can manufacture ourselves—but perhaps not always as much as we need. In Europe, where L-*acetyl*carnitine (a close relative) is being investigated as a treatment for senile dementia, it has also proven helpful for elderly depressives in three placebo-controlled trials.[45,46]

L-carnitine is supplied mainly by muscle meat, so vegetarian depressives may need it the most.

NOTES

1. M. W. P. Carney, et al., "Thiamine and Pyridoxine Lack in Newly-Admitted Psychiatric Inpatients," *Brit J Psychiatry* 135(1979):239–254.

2. M. W. P. Carney et al., "Thiamine, Riboflavin and Pyridoxine Deficiency in Psychiatric Inpatients," *Brit J Psychiatry* 141(1982):271–272.

3. I. R. Bell et al., "B Complex Vitamin Patterns in Geriatric and Young Adult Inpatients with Major Depression," *J Am Geriatr Soc* 39(March 1991):252–257.

4. D. Lonsdale and R. J. Shamberger, "Red Cell Transketolase as an Indicator of Nutritional Deficiency," *Am J Clin Nutr* 33(February 1980):205–211.

5. Priscilla Slagle, *The Way Up from Down* (New York: Random House, 1987).

6. H. L. Newbold, *Mega-Nutrients for Your Nerves* (New York: Berkley Books, 1975).

7. Abram Hoffer, *Common Questions on Schizophrenia and Their Answers* (New Canaan, Conn.: Keats Publishing, 1987).

8. D. J. Connor, "Thiamine Intake and Monoamine Oxidase Activity," *Biol Psychiatry* 16(September 1981):869–872.

9. A. C. Washburne, "'Nicotinic Acid in the Treatment of Certain De-

pressed States: A Preliminary Report," *Ann Int Med* 32(February 1950):261–269.

10. H. Osmond and A. Hoffer, "Massive Niacin Treatment in Schizophrenia: Review of a Nine-Year Study," *Lancet* i(1962):316–320.

11. J. R. Wittenborn, "A Search for Responders to Niacin Supplementation," *Arch Gen Psychiatry* 31(1974):547–552.

12. Abram Hoffer and Morton Walker, *Nutrients to Age Without Senility* (New Canaan, Conn.: Keats Publishing, 1980).

13. J. P. Cleary, "The NAD Deficiency Diseases," *J Orthomolecular Med* 1(3, 1986):149–157.

14. K. Dakshinamurti, "Neurobiology of Pyridoxine." In Harold H. Draper, ed., *Adv Nutr Res, Vol. 4* (New York: Plenum, 1982), pp. 143–179.

15. C. S. Russ et al., "Vitamin B-6 Status of Depressed and Obsessive-Compulsive Patients," *Nutrition Reports International* 27(April 1983): 867–873.

16. J. W. Stewart, et al., "Low B6 Levels in Depressed Outpatients," *Biol Psychiatry* 19(4, 1984):613–616.

17. Jonathan W. Stewart, letter to author, April 16, 1986.

18. M. J. Hoes, "L-Tryptophan in Depression and Strain," *J Orthomolecular Psychiatry* 11(4, 1982):231–242.

19. V. Wynn et al., "Tryptophan, Depression and Steroidal Contraception," *Journal of Steroid Biochemistry* 6(1975):965–970.

20. I. R. Bell et al., "Brief Communication: Vitamin B1, B2, and B6 Augmentation of Tricyclic Antidepressant Treatment in Geriatric Depression with Cognitive Dysfunction," *J Am Coll Nutr* 11(April 1992):159–163.

21. M. G. Brush and M. Perry, "Pyridoxine and the Premenstrual Syndrome," *Lancet* (June 15, 1985):1399.

22. K. E. Kendall and P. P. Schnurr, "The Effects of Vitamin B6 Supplementation on Premenstrual Syndrome," *Ob Gyn* 70(August 1987):145–149.

23. H. Doll et al., "Pyridoxine (Vitamin B6) and the Premenstrual Syndrome: A Randomized Crossover Trial," *J Royal Coll Gen Practitioners* 39(September 1989):364–368.

24. Carl C. Pfeiffer, *Mental and Elemental Nutrients* (New Canaan, Conn.: Keats Publishing, 1975).

25. M. T. Abou-Saleh and A. Coppen, "The Biology of Folate in Depression: Implications for Nutritional Hypotheses of the Psychoses," *J Psychiatric Res* 20(2, 1986): 91–101.

26. R. Crellin et al., "Folates and Psychiatric Disorders: Clinical Potential," *Drugs* 45(May 1993): 623–636.

27. Sing Lee et al., "Folate Concentration in Chinese Psychiatric Outpatients on Long-Term Lithium Treatment," *J Affect Dis* 24(April 1992):265–270.

28. P. McKeon et al., "Serum and Red Cell Folate and Affective Morbidity in Lithium Prophylaxis," *Acta Psychiatr Scand* 83(March 1991): 199–201.

29. G. P. Guaraldi et al., "An Open Trial of Methyltetrahydrofolate in Elderly Depressed Patients," *Ann Clin Psychiatry* 5(June 1993):101–105.

30. M. W. P. Carney and B. F. Sheffield, "Serum Folic Acid and B12 in 272 Psychiatric In-Patients," *Psychological Med* 8(1978):139–144.

31. K. Geagea and J. Ananth, "Response of a Psychiatric Patient to Vitamin B12 Therapy," *Dis Nerv Sys* 36(June 1975):343–344.

32. J. Dommisse, "Subtle Vitamin-B12 Deficiency and Psychiatry: A Largely Unnoticed but Devastating Relationship?" *Medical Hypotheses* 34(February 1991):131–140.

33. H. L. Newbold, "Vitamin B-12: Placebo or Neglected Therapeutic Tool," *Medical Hypotheses* 28(1989):155–164.

34. F. R. Ellis and S. Nasser, "A Pilot Study of Vitamin B12 in the Treatment of Tiredness," *Brit J Nutr* 30(1973):277–283.

35. T. Ohta et al., "Daily Activity and Persistent Sleep-Wake Schedule Disorders," *Prog Neuro-Psychopharmacol Biol Psychiatry* 16(July 1992):529–537.

36. C. J. M. van Tiggelen et al., "Vitamin B12 Levels of Cerebrospinal Fluid in Patients with Organic Mental Disorder," *J Orthomolecular Psychiatry* 12(4, 1983):305–311.

37. T. Ikeda et al., "'Treatment of Alzheimer-Type Dementia with Intravenous Mecobalamin," *Clinical Therapeutics* 14(May–June 1992): 426–437.

38. G. J. Naylor and A. H. W. Smith, "Vanadium: A Possible Aetiological Factor in Manic Depressive Illness," *Psychological Med* 11 (1981):257–263.

39. D. S. G. Kay et al., "The Therapeutic Effect of Ascorbic Acid and EDTA in Manic-Depressive Psychosis: Double-Blind Comparisons with Standard Treatments," *Psychological Med* 14(August 1984):533–539.

40. D. E. Holloway and F. J. Peterson, "Ascorbic Acid in Drug Metabolism." In Daphne A. Roe and T. Colin Campbell, eds., *Drugs and Nutrients* (New York: Marcel Dekker, 1984), pp. 225–295.

41. R. Anderson, "The Immunostimulatory, Anti-Inflammatory, and Anti-Allergic Properties of Ascorbate." In Harold H. Draper, ed., *Advances in Nutritional Research, Volume 6* (New York: Plenum, 1984), pp. 19–45.

42. S. C. Risch and D. S. Janowsky, "Cholinergic-Adrenergic Balance in Affective Illness." In Robert M. Post and James C. Ballenger, eds., *Neurobiology of Mood Disorders* (Baltimore: Williams & Wilkins, 1984), pp. 652–663.

43. B. M. Cohen et al., "Lecithin in the Treatment of Mania: Double-blind, Placebo-Controlled Trials," *Am J Psychiatry* 139(September 1982):1162–1164.

44. Sheldon Saul Hendler, *The Oxygen Breakthrough: Thirty Days to an Illness-Free Life* (New York: William Morrow, 1989).

45. R. Bella et al., "Effect of Acetyl-L-Carnitine on Geriatric Patients Suffering from Dysthymic Disorders," *Int J Clin Pharmacol Res* 10(6, 1990):355–360.

46. G. Garzya et al., "Evaluation of the Effects of L-Acetylcarnitine on Senile Patients Suffering from Depression," *Drugs Under Experimental and Clinical Research* 16(2, 1990):101–106.

NINE

Balancing Minerals to Balance Emotions

IRON, copper, calcium, magnesium, chromium, zinc, manganese—there's a mine of minerals in our food and water, and inside of us. At least 15 of them are as essential to our health as vitamins.

- They help catalyze most physiological processes.
- They're key components of important biochemicals like hemoglobin and thyroid hormone.
- The electric charge some of them carry sparks the flow of electrochemical "messages" from brain cell to brain cell.
- Deficiencies or imbalances of most of them can make us depressed.

SODIUM AND POTASSIUM

Too much sodium, too little potassium. That's probably the most glaring mineral imbalance in our modern diets. A by-product of our overindulgence in salted, processed, packaged foods, this imbalance is a medically well-recognized cause of high blood pressure. But it may also promote affective (mood) illness.

Most studies indicate that the dietary sodium/potassium imbalance is exaggerated in the body fluids of depressives.[1] In particular, studies have usually found depressed "sodium pumps" (enzymes) in depressives' cellular membranes.[2-4] These enzyme pumps keep cells from overloading with sodium and starving for potassium. When they falter, nervous transmission in the brain can suffer.

A diet rich in fresh, whole food (Chapter 15) is naturally low in sodium and high in potassium. It's a healthy antidote to this (possibly) mood-disturbing mineral imbalance. Although there is no research on such a diet's effect on depression, people with high blood pressure (whose sodium pumps also tend to be depressed) reportedly feel happier and less depressed on a low-sodium diet.[5] Sodium restriction is also a popular, if unproven, antidote for premenstrual syndrome, another depressing condition involving sodium retention. So, as one psychiatrist suggests: "Take no added salt and you may be rewarded by improvement in your mood."[6]

But don't overdo it. Sodium *deficiency* can also be depressing.[7] Only an extremely sodium-restricted diet would put you at risk, though. More likely causes are overmedication with diuretics, excessive water intake, and certain medical conditions such as edema and dehydration.

MAGNESIUM

Magnesium helps catalyze all of the body's energy reactions. Deficiencies and excesses can be mentally disturbing or depressing.[8] Some studies indicate magnesium levels are low in the blood and cells of depressives,[8-10] that their "magnesium pumps" are depressed,[3] and that it's largely by raising magnesium levels that lithium (see below) relieves depression (and mania).[8,12] Other studies find magnesium is *high* in depression.[1,8]

Nonetheless, deficiency is more likely to be the problem than excess. Our diets are low in magnesium-rich foods: beans, greens, whole grains, and hard water. And the stress of depression may further deplete what little magnesium we have.[10] Thus orthomolecular practitioners claim,[6,11] and academic researchers suspect,[8,12] that depressives (including manic-depressives) need more, not less, magnesium.

Clinical research concurs. In a preliminary trial from the University of Southern California, magnesium shots promptly relieved the aches, pains, weakness and lethargy of depressed patients.[13] In another pilot study, magnesium aspartate tablets helped stabilize rapid-cycling manic-depressives who had responded poorly to previous treatments.[14] Similar benefits had been reported generations earlier.[14] In another investigation, people with chronic fatigue syndrome were found to have low magnesium levels. Shots of magnesium relieved their physical and psychological symptoms much better than a placebo.[15] Subsequent reports, however, have not all been supportive.[16,17]

A whole-food, plant-based diet (Chapter 15) is itself a modest magnesium supplement. It can't hurt to try it.

Your chances of being magnesium-deficient are increased if you have high blood pressure, coronary heart disease, rapid heartbeat, tremors, spasms, seizures, malabsorption or chronic fluid loss (e.g., vomiting, diarrhea).

CALCIUM

The relationship between calcium and mood disorder is complex and confusing. Deficiencies and excesses can both cause depression.[18] Depressed people, however, usually have high calcium levels which return to normal on recovery.[3,12] Bipolar depressives are particularly apt to have calcium-loaded cells, both when depressed and when manic.[19] In fact, lowering calcium—whether with lithium,[12] calcium-channel blocking drugs[19] or a calcium-restricted diet[20]—"lowers" their mania. Calcium supplements heighten it.[20]

Then what are we to make of the fact that in preliminary controlled trials, depression ("ordinary"[21] and premenstrual[22]) has been relieved by ample *supplements* of calcium?

Perhaps the following guidelines can help:

• If you suspect your calcium levels are low, increasing your intake might be worth a try, as long as you keep your magnesium intake up. Magnesium balances calcium physiologically, as potassium does sodium. But proceed with caution if you have a bipolar illness.

• If your calcium intake is very high, relief from depression or mania may come from consuming less calcium, and/or from consuming more magnesium, especially if you have a bipolar disorder.

ZINC

Acrodermatitis enteropathica is a rare genetic disease that drastically interferes with zinc absorption. Half of its victims have just one symptom: "periodic, typical, disabling depressions."[18]

Ordinary depressives often suffer from zinc deficiency too. In one study, 8 of 21 depressed women and one of nine depressed men did. The most severely depressed were zinc deficient in *two cases out of three*.[23] Other studies confirm that depressed women, but seldom men, tend to be low in zinc.[24]

Interestingly, zinc deficiency, which tends to distort taste, smell, and appetite, seems to be common in people with eating disorders, most of whom are female, many of whom are depressed. Zinc supplements reportedly are therapeutic in these cases.[25,26]

A small, preliminary report[25] indicates that zinc does indeed help zinc-deficient depressives. Orthomolecular psychiatrists concur.[6,27]

You may be zinc-deficient if you avoid zinc-rich foods (organ meats, shellfish, legumes, red meat, whole grains). If you are deficient, your sense of taste or smell may be weak or distorted; you may have stretch marks on your skin, white spots on brittle fingernails or an eating disorder. Other conditions associated with zinc deficiency include high estrogen levels (e.g., premenstrually, or from oral contraceptives or pregnancy), diabetes, lung cancer, hemolytic anemia, cirrhosis of the liver, a recent history of infection or surgery, or high intakes of calcium, iron, copper or alcohol.

Stunted growth or retarded sexual development in a child also suggests zinc deficiency.[6,18,23,25]

LITHIUM

Someday nutritionists may confirm their suspicions that lithium, a mineral found in food and water, is an essential nutrient. This will mean that one of psychiatry's most potent "drugs" is actually an orthomolecular medication.

Popularly perceived as a kind of "magic bullet" for manic-depression, lithium is actually considerably less and more than that—less, because while it helps many people with bipolar disorders, it's a magic bullet for only a few of them; and more, because lithium allays other conditions too, such as compulsive aggression and unipolar depression. Not only does lithium act as an antidepressant in acute cases (though probably rather a weak one),[28] but it may even outdo antidepressant drugs in preventing recurrent unipolar depression.[28,29] Finally, with lithium, the high suicide rate of manic-depressive patients plummets.[29]

Lithium's most popular role today in the treatment of depression is as an adjunct to antidepressant drugs. Studies have shown that when lithium is added to the regimen of depressives who aren't responding to antidepressant medication, about 50 to 70 percent improve or recover within days or weeks.[30,31] And one of two preliminary studies suggests lithium can accelerate the normally slow response to antidepressant drugs.[32]

Lithium probably can augment natural antidepressants too. Abram Hoffer finds low doses useful in his orthomolecular approach to depression.[33] In preliminary reports, lithium has augmented the amino acid tryptophan[34] and sleep deprivation therapy (Chapter 19).

Lithium has traditionally been prescribed in megadoses that would give even an orthomolecular psychiatrist pause. But recently the trend has been toward "lithium lite" because some studies suggest lower doses lessen side effects without compromising clinical efficacy (see page 116). Could doses much lower yet—doses obtainable by drinking lithium-rich mineral waters such as Knazmilos, Vichy St. Yorre Royal and Original Saratoga Geiser[35,36]—also have antidepressant value? Such waters have been prescribed since antiquity for mania and melancholy. In a contemporary study from the University of Texas, higher lithium levels in drinking water were associated with lower homicide, suicide and mental hospitalization rates.[37,38] But then perhaps some of the credit should go to the other mood-regulating minerals that often abound in lithium-rich waters: magnesium, calcium and rubidium.[37]

RUBIDIUM

Rubidium has a lot in common with its sister element lithium. Suspected, like lithium, of being an essential nutrient,[38] it too appears to be a potent, mood-modifying mineral. But again it's taking a long time for doctors to catch on.

Lithium's antimanic effects were first reported in 1949, but it wasn't until the early 1970s that this unpatentable "orphan drug" gained entry into North American pharmacies. Ironically, this was when American psychiatrists published the first evidence of rubidium's antidepressant effect, an effect which has since been confirmed by half a dozen major university research teams in Italy[37] and in a collaborative Italian/American study.[39] Yet rubidium is still an "orphan" in America, unavailable outside of a few research clinics.

If lithium is a tranquilizing antidepressant, just the ticket for those inclined toward manic-depression, rubidium (it seems) is its complement: a stimulating antidepressant, ideal for depressives who are very slowed down and apathetic.[37,39] Indeed, just as some people become dull or depressed on lithium, on rubidium some become manic.[37]

Would people on mineral water just become balanced?

Perhaps the real magic bullet for affective illness ought to be less like a drug, more like a beverage—say, a bottle or two a day of condensed mineral water.

NOTES

1. J. Widmer et al., "Evolution of Blood Magnesium, Sodium and Potassium in Depressed Patients Followed for Three Months," *Neuropsychobiology* 26(4, 1992):173–179.

2. J. D. R. Rose, "Disturbed Hypothalamic Control of Na,K-ATPase: A Cause of Somatic Symptoms of Depression," *Medical Hypotheses* 19(1986):179–183.

3. J. H. Thakar et al., "Erythrocyte Membrane Sodium-Potassium and Magnesium ATPase in Primary Affective Disorder," *Biol Psychiatry* 20 (July 1985):734–740.

4. P. L. Reddy et al., "Erythrocyte Membrane Sodium-Potassium Adenosine Triphosphatase Activity in Affective Disorders," *Journal of Neural Transmission—General Section* 89(3, 1992):183–209.

5. T. C. Beard et al., "Randomised Controlled Trial of No-Added-Sodium Diet for Mild Hypertension," *Lancet* (August 28, 1982): 455–458.

6. Michael Lesser, *Nutrition and Vitamin Therapy* (New York: Grove Press, 1980).

7. H. Ohsawa et al., "An Epidemiological Study on Hyponatremia in Psychiatric Patients in Mental Hospitals in Nara Prefecture," *Jap J Psychiatry Neurol* 46(December 1992):883–889.

8. J. Ananth and R. Yassa, "Magnesium in Mental Illness," *Comprehensive Psychiatry* 20(September/October 1979):475–482.

9. B. Berube, "Depression, Virus Link," *Medical Post* 23(June 2, 1987):1,12.

10. G. K. Kirov and K. N. Tsachev, "Magnesium, Schizophrenia and Manic-Depressive Disease," *Neuropsychobiology* 23(2, 1990):79–81.

11. Lendon Smith, *Feed Yourself Right* (New York: McGraw Hill, 1983).

12. D. Pavlinac et al., "Magnesium in Affective Disorders," *Biol Psychiatry* 14(4, 1979):657–661.

13. I. M. Cox et al., "Red Blood Cell Magnesium and Chronic Fatigue Syndrome," *Lancet* 337(March 30, 1991):757–760.

14. G. Chouinard et al., "A Pilot Study of Magnesium Aspartate Hydrochloride (Magnesiocard) as a Mood Stabilizer for Rapid Cycling Bipolar Affective Disorder Patients," *Prog Neuro-Psychopharmacol Biol Psychiatry* 14(2, 1990):171–180.

15. I. M. Cox et al., "'Red Blood Cell Magnesium and Chronic Fatigue Syndrome," *Lancet* 337(March 30, 1991):757–760.

16. J. E. Clague et al., "Intravenous Magnesium Loading in Chronic Fatigue Syndrome," *Lancet* 340(July 11, 1992):124–125.

17. J. Durlach, "Chronic Fatigue Syndrome and Chronic Primary Magnesium Deficiency (CFS and CPMD)," *Magnesium Research* 5(March 1992):68.

18. N. Edwards, "Mental Disturbances Related to Metals." In Richard C. W. Hall, ed., *Psychiatric Presentations of Medical Illness* (Jamaica, N.Y.: Spectrum Publications, 1980), pp. 283–308.

19. S. L. Dubovsky et al., "Elevated Platelet Intracellular Calcium Concentration in Bipolar Depression," *Biol Psychiatry* 29(March 1, 1991):441–450.

20. J. S. Carman et al., "Calcium and Calcitonin in Bipolar Affective Disorder." In Robert M. Post and James C. Ballenger, eds., *Neurobiology of Mood Disorders* (Baltimore: Williams & Wilkins, 1984), pp. 340–355.

21. Arthur Winter and Ruth Winter, *Eat Right, Be Bright* (New York: St. Martin's Press, 1988).

22. J. M. Alvir and S. Thys-Jacobs, "Premenstrual and Menstrual Symptom Clusters and Response to Calcium Treatment," *Psychopharmacol Bull* 27(2, 1991):145–148.

23. K. Y. Little et al., "Altered Zinc Metabolism in Mood Disorder Patients," *Biol Psychiatry* 26(October 1989): 646–648.

24. I. J. McLoughlin and J. S. Hodge, "'Zinc in Depressive Disorder," *Acta Psychiatr Scand* 82(December 1990):451–453.

25. D. Bryce-Smith and R. I. D. Simpson, "Anorexia, Depression, and Zinc Deficiency," *Lancet* (Nov. 17, 1984):1162.

26. L. Humphries et al., "Zinc Deficiency and Eating Disorders," *J Clin Psychiatry* 50(December 1989): 456–459.

27. Priscilla Slagle, *The Way Up from Down* (New York: Random House, 1987).

28. F. G. Souza and G. M. Goodwin, "Lithium Treatment and Prophylaxis in Unipolar Depression: A Meta-Analysis," *Brit J Psychiatry* 158(May 1991):666–675.

29. I. Glen, "Practical Aspects of Long-Term Treatment with Lithium," *J Psychopharmacol* 6(Suppl., 1992):330–333.

30. M. P. Austin et al., "'Lithium Augmentation in Antidepressant-Resistant Patients: A Quantitative Analysis," *Brit J Psychiatry* 159(October 1991):510–514.

31. R. T. Joffe et al., "A Placebo-Controlled Comparison of Lithium and Triiodothyronine Augmentation of Tricyclic Antidepressants in Unipolar Refractory Depression," *Arch Gen Psychiatry* 50 (May 1993):387–393.

32. H. V. Jensen et al., "Combining Nortriptyline and Lithium in Eld-

erly Depressed Patients: A Double-Blind, Placebo-Controlled Study," *Lithium* 3(November 1992):259–262.

33. Abram Hoffer and Morton Walker, *Orthomolecular Nutrition* (New Canaan, Conn.: Keats Publishing, 1978).

34. A. S. Hale et al., "Clomipramine, Tryptophan and Lithium in Combination for Resistant Endogenous Depression: Seven Case Studies," *Brit J Psychiatry* 151(August 1987):213–217.

35. H. E. Allan et al., "Chemical Composition of Bottled Mineral Water," *Archives of Environmental Health* 44(March/April 1989):102–116.

36. R. Papaioannou and C. C. Pfeiffer, "Pure Water For Drinking," *J Orthomolecular Med* 1(3, 1986):184–198.

37. Ronald Fieve, *Moodswing,* rev. ed. (New York: Morrow, 1989).

38. P. Malek-Ahmadi and J. A. Williams, "Rubidium in Psychiatry: Research Implications," *Pharmacol Biochem Behav* 21(Suppl 1, 1984):49–50.

39. Gianfranco Placidi et al., "Exploration of the Clinical Profile of Rubidium Chloride in Depression: A Systematic Open Trial," *J Clin Psychopharmacol* 8(June 1988):184–188.

TEN

Separating the Good Fats From the Bad

There's more to the connection between fat (the edible kind) and health than bacon grease clogging arteries or fish oil preventing heart attacks. Fat, research suggests, may also have a lot to do with feelings.

At the forefront of the fat/mood connection is an important class of hormonelike substances called the prostaglandins. We produce prostaglandins from essential fatty acids, the key nutrients in fats and oils.

Prostaglandins come in three complementary varieties, or series. The 2-series, for example, tends to provoke inflammation and the 1- and 3-series tend to be anti-inflammatory. We need a balance of these series; yet we seem to lack it when we're depressed.

Soaring levels of 2-series prostaglandins—up to 8 to 18 times normal[1]—have repeatedly been found in the body fluids of depressed patients.[1-4] The deeper the depression, the higher the levels.[4] Other studies have noted signs of a generalized inflammatory process in depression.[5] This, too, suggests 2-series overactivity.

Research also suggests depression is associated with a complementary deficiency of 1-series prostaglandins, specifically, prostaglandin E1 (PGE1). In contrast, excesses of PGE1 are associated with euphoria and mania.[1,6]

Some investigators have reasons to believe that these prostaglandin abnormalities help cause depression or exacerbate it:[1,3,4,6,7]

- The 2-series prostaglandin prostacyclin has caused depression in rats and humans. A person may become depressed on prostacyclin but not on PGE1.[8]
- Antidepressant drugs suppress 2-series prostaglandins.[1] One psychiatrist has also found other 2-series suppressors, like aspirin and ibuprofen, useful for some severely depressed patients.[7]
- Alcohol acutely inhibits 2-series prostaglandins while increasing PGE1; but eventually it depletes PGE1. This pattern could help account for both the pleasant acute effects of alcohol and the unpleasant delayed effects, including the chronic depression of many alcoholics.[6]

If a glut of 2-series and a deficiency of 1-series prostaglandins really does contribute to depression, then correcting the imbalance should help. There's evidence it does.

EVENING PRIMROSE OIL

Evening primrose oil is an exceptionally rich source of gamma-linolenic acid (GLA), a potent fatty acid precursor to the 1-series of prostaglandins.

The body can actually produce its own GLA from linoleic acid (LA), an essential fatty acid that abounds in vegetable oils. But in people with certain disorders, including premenstrual syndrome (PMS), chronic viral infections[9] and perhaps depression, a bottleneck in the conversion of LA to GLA may exist.[10] This could account for the 1-series deficiency in depression. Evening primrose oil—or other good GLA sources like borage oil and black currant seed oil—would be a remedy.[10,11]

In practice, evening primrose oil has proven highly effective for PMS, particularly the depression, in several placebo-controlled trials.[10,11] Combined with fish-oil fatty acids, it has also dramatically outperformed placebos in assuaging the fatigue, depression and other symptoms of postviral chronic fatigue syndrome.[9]

There have been no trials of evening primrose oil for depression itself. However some doctors find it useful as an adjunct to antidepressant drugs,[11] and one authority notes that mood elevation has been a consistent side effect of the oil in clinical trials.[12]

LINSEED OIL

In many cultures, linseed oil, the oil of flax seeds, is a time-honored "health food."[13] It's also an exceptionally rich source of alpha-linolenic acid (ALA), the essential fatty acid grandfather of the 3-series of prostaglandins. Linseed oil also contains lots of LA (all vegetable oils do), the source of the 1- and 2-series prostaglandins. But its net metabolic effect is to reduce 2-series prostaglandins while increasing the 3-series and possibly the 1-series.

Linseed oil is therefore often prescribed by orthomolecular psychiatrists. Donald Rudin, who pioneered the practice, claims linseed oil has eased the depression and manic-depression of some of his toughest cases. This doesn't seem to be a placebo effect. Some patients have become manic on the oil; others, after quitting prematurely or being switched to a placebo oil, like corn or safflower oil, have soon relapsed.[14-16]

People who benefit psychiatrically from linseed oil, Rudin finds, tend to have other symptoms which also abate: chronic fatigue, dermatosis (e.g., dandruff; dry, rough, flaky skin), tinnitus (chronic buzzing or ringing in the ears), cold intolerance and inflammatory bowel disorders.[14,16] Theoretically, any conditions brought on or worsened by cold (winter depression?) might respond to linseed oil, or to fish oil.

FISH OIL

Fish oil is exceptionally rich in eicosapentaenoic acid (EPA). Derived from alpha-linolenic acid (ALA), EPA is the direct precursor to the 3-series prostaglandins. It's probably better, therefore, than ALA at curbing the excess of 2-series prostaglandins in depression.[17] So it may, as Dr. Rudin speculates, work better for some people than ALA-rich linseed oil.[15]

Psychiatrist Richard Kunin finds fish oil helpful for PMS.[18] Fish oil might also check the depression and dementia of AIDS. EPA and DHA (a related fatty acid found in fish oil) are important "brain foods"; in a recent study, they were found to be strikingly low in AIDS patients.[19]

A DIET WITH THE RIGHT KIND OF FAT _____

The prostaglandin imbalance found in depression is similar, if not identical, to the one found in many other diseases of civilization, including cancer, heart disease, arthritis and multiple sclerosis.[20,21] This should come as no surprise. The modern Western diet promotes the imbalance. Switching to a more wholesome and natural diet, abundant evidence suggests, can treat or prevent these diseases. Could this also be therapeutic for depression?

What's wrong with the fat in our diets? To begin with, there's all the saturated fat. Even our most carnivorous ancestors hunted and bred animals which were far leaner than today's factory-farmed specimens, and what fat these animals had was mostly unsaturated and rich in essential fatty acids.[13,20] Livestock today is marbled with saturated fat, which is full of saturated fatty acids that crowd out essential fatty acids in the body. As a result, cell membranes deteriorate, cholesterol rises, 1- and 3- series prostaglandins fall, and 2-series prostaglandins soar (their precursor, arachidonic acid, abounds in modern *grain*-fed livestock).[20]

Then there are the refined vegetable oils: clear, odorless, flavorless (usually) and "purified" of the nutrients our bodies need to handle them safely.[13] Taking their place are traces of toxic solvents and hordes of mutant essential fatty acids—innocent nutrients turned subversive, toxic and possibly carcinogenic by the searing heat of processing.[20]

So how *should* we eat? Here are some guidelines:

• Minimize your consumption of the following: the flesh or whole-fat dairy products of grain-fed, factory-farmed animals; processed vegetable oils, shortenings and hydrogenated (artificially satu-rated) margarines; and foods made with these fats and oils. Don't use polyunsaturated oils for *high temperature* frying or baking—it's probably healthier to use small amounts of butter, clarified butter, lard or tropical oil. Don't reuse heated oils.[13]

• Try to eat more foods that are indigenous to your climate. Plants and animals produce fatty acids that are adaptively balanced to the climate they live in. Eating them helps us adapt. Thus, North Americans who live in temperate regions (as most of us do) should eat more whole wheat, soybeans and other beans, wal-nuts, hazelnuts, flax seeds, pumpkin seeds, dark green vegetables and (for non-vegetarians) cold-water fish and seafood, regional game and traditionally-reared local farm animals (e.g., barnyard chickens, grazing cattle).

• Use oils that are minimally processed and as fresh and well preserved as possible. The most healthful oils are sold in health food stores. The "perfect oil" has been mechanically or "expeller" pressed (not chemically extracted) from organically grown nuts or seeds, is crude or unrefined (no bleaching, deodorizing, etc.), has a "best before" date if it's highly polyunsaturated (which makes it very perishable), is refrigerated in an opaque container and may be preserved with vitamin E or other antioxidants.[13]

NOTES

1. J. Lieb et al., "Elevated Levels of Prostaglandin E2 and Thrombox-ane B2 in Depression," *Prostaglandins, Leukotrienes and Medicine* 10(1983):361–367.

2. M. Linnoila et al., "CSF Prostaglandin Levels in Depressed and Schizophrenic Patients," *Arch Gen Psychiatry* 40(1983): 405–406.

3. J. R. Calabrese et al., "Depression, Immunocompetence, and Pros-taglandins of the E Series," *Psychiatry Res* 17(1985): 41–47.

4. S. Nishino et al., "Salivary Prostaglandin Concentrations: Possible State Indicators for Major Depression," *Am J Psychiatry* 146(March 1989):365–368.

5. M. Maes et al., "Leukocytosis, Monocytosis and Neutrophilia: Hallmarks of Severe Depression," *J Psychiatric Res* 26(April 1992):125–134.

6. D. F. Horrobin and M. S. Manku, "Possible Role of Prostaglandin E1 in the Affective Disorders and in Alcoholism," *Brit Med J* 280(June 17, 1980):1363–1366.

7. P. Lowinger, "Prostaglandins and Organic Affective Syndrome" (letter), *Am J Psychiatry* 146(December 1989):1646–1647.

8. D. Ansell et al., "Depression and Prostacyclin Infusion," *Lancet* (August 30, 1986):509.

9. P. O. Behan et al., "Effect of High Doses of Essential Fatty Acids on the Postviral Fatigue Syndrome," *Acta Neurol Scand* 82(September 1990): 209–216.

10. D. F. Horrobin, "The Role of Essential Fatty Acids and Prostaglandins in the Premenstrual Syndrome," *J Reproductive Med* 28(July 1983):465–468.

11. Ann Nazzaro and Donald Lombard, with David Horrobin, *The PMS Solution: The Nutritional Approach* (Montreal: Eden Press, 1985).

12. David Horrobin, letter to author, May 1986.

13. Udo Erasmus, *Fats and Oils: The Complete Guide to Fats and Oils in Health and Nutrition* (Vancouver: alive, 1986).

14. D. O. Rudin, "The Major Psychoses and Neuroses as Omega-3 Essential Fatty Acid Deficiency Syndrome: Substrate Pellagra," *Biol Psychiatry* 16(September 1981):837–850.

15. Donald O. Rudin, letter to author, May 7, 1986.

16. Donald O. Rudin and Clare Felix, *The Omega-3 Phenomenon: The Nutrition Breakthrough of the '80s* (New York: Rawson Associates, 1987).

17. D. F. Horrobin and Y-S Huang, "Schizophrenia: The Role of Essential Fatty Acid and Prostaglandin Metabolism," *Medical Hypotheses* 10(1983):329–336.

18. Richard Kunin, *Mega-Nutrition for Women* (New York: McGraw Hill, 1983).

19. M. E. Begin et al., "Plasma Fatty Acid Levels in Patients with Acquired Immune Deficiency Syndrome and in Controls," *Prostaglandins, Leukotrienes and Essential Fatty Acids* 37(1989):135–137.

20. H. M. Sinclair, "Essential Fatty Acids in Perspective," *Human Nutr: Clin Nutr* 38C(1984):245–260.

21. A. P. Simopoulos, "Summary of the NATO Advanced Research Workshop on Dietary w3 and w6 Fatty Acids: Biological Effects and Nutritional Essentiality," *J Nutr* 119(1989):521–528.

ELEVEN

Amino Acids: The Stuff Natural Antidepressants Are Made of

OF all the nutrients, none fit the profile of "natural antidepressant" as well as the *amino acids.*

Amino acids are the building blocks from which all proteins are made. They're also the precursors for most of the body's known antidepressant substances—the hormones, neurotransmitters, endorphins and other mood-regulating compounds that tend to be lacking in depression. Some amino acids are neurotransmitters themselves.

And there is an impressive body of clinical evidence that amino acids can relieve depression.

PHENYLALANINE AND TYROSINE

Phenylalanine and tyrosine are two closely related, nutritionally essential amino acids; the latter is made from the former. In the body, these amino acids are converted into the activating hormones of the adrenal medulla and thyroid gland.

In the brain, they are converted into two important neurotransmitters, dopamine and norepinephrine. Dopamine deficiency is what immobilizes people who have Parkinson's disease, and it may also depress them. Norepinephrine (NE) may be our most important coping neurotransmitter. It presses the "go" button in our pleasure centers. A lack of NE or of NE activity is generally thought to be a major cause or mediator of depression. Most anti-depressant drugs counteract this deficit.

When laboratory rats are heavily stressed, the NE levels in their brains soon dwindle and they become "depressed"—unless they're given tyrosine supplements.[1] In a study of human subjects stressed by cold and high altitude, tyrosine supplements reduced their physical and psychological symptoms.[2] "Dietary supplementation with TYR [tyrosine]," an army scientist speculates, ". . . may prove to be a simple, safe, and inexpensive way to help troops cope with stress."[3]

Phenylalanine is also the precursor to *phenylethylamine* (PEA). A near dead-ringer structurally for amphetamine,[4] PEA has been likened to the brain's home-brewed "speed,"[5] the neurochemical that intoxicates people when they fall in love or win a lottery.[6] Psychiatrists who subscribe to the PEA hypothesis of affective disorder suspect PEA deficiency is the primary cause or mediator of depression.[4,5]

Phenylalanine and tyrosine ought to be antidepressants, and there is clinical evidence that they are.

Tyrosine as an Antidepressant

Tyrosine's first trial as an antidepressant in 1972 was unsuccessful. But a decade later, psychiatrists from Harvard, MIT and elsewhere had better luck. Under double-blind conditions, their chronically depressed subjects recovered completely on large doses of tyrosine, only to relapse on placebo, and then recover again on tyrosine.[8] In a double-blind, placebo-controlled follow-up study, four of six patients on tyrosine improved within four weeks, compared to three of eight on placebo. Three of the five placebo-nonresponders then responded to tyrosine.[9] Finally, the researchers conducted an expanded double-blind study with 65 patients.[10] By the end of the short four-week trial, tyrosine had cut depression about 45 percent; imipramine (a popular antidepressant drug) by 50 percent; and placebo by about 35 percent. Statistically, tyrosine was neither significantly better than placebo nor worse than imipramine. But fewer people on tyrosine had quit because of side effects or clinical deterioration.

Other trials of tyrosine have been more positive. Researchers have successfully used it to wean depressives off amphetamines,[11] to enhance the antidepressant effect of 5-hydroxytryptophan[12] (an amino acid derivative we'll discuss later) and to relieve depression in people with sleep-EEG patterns like those found in Parkinson's disease.[13]

Phenylalanine as an Antidepressant

Studies of phenylalanine as an antidepressant have been inspired mainly by the PEA hypothesis of depression. Because D-phenylalanine (DPA) is more readily converted to PEA than L-phenylalanine (LPA),[14] most of these studies have used either DPA or DLPA (a cheaper, 50:50 mixture of DPA and LPA). The dosages have been high enough to increase PEA, but probably too low to significantly increase NE. Hundreds of patients suffering from mild to severe depression have participated. In all but one of these half-a-dozen-plus studies, most patients have enjoyed complete recovery or marked improvement within one or two months. A majority have recovered in one or two weeks.[14-17] In the two controlled trials, phenylalanine has equaled or slightly bettered the antidepressant imipramine, prescribed at a fixed, low-moderate dosage.[17] Unfortunately all of the positive studies appear to have emanated from the same research group. The only clearly independent investigation was negative. Just two of the 11 patients responded to DPA. Two others deteriorated.[16]

L-phenylalanine's antidepressant effect first became apparent in 1966 when intravenous infusions induced euphoria in patients with Parkinson's disease.[18] Nearly 20 years later, low doses of LPA were added to the regimen of 155 depressed patients unresponsive to an antidepressant drug. Sixty-nine percent recovered; 15 percent improved.[19] That same year, at a major Chicago medical center, large doses of LPA were administered to 40 mostly "refractory" (treatment resistant) depressives. Eleven recovered; 20 improved.[4,18] Shortly thereafter, a psychiatrist reported that half of the depressed bipolar patients he treated with a low dose of LPA recovered rapidly.[20] Later, another psychiatrist gave stiffer doses of LPA to ten refractory bipolar depressives, along with an antidepressant drug. Nine felt better immediately and "6 viewed their episodes of depression as terminated within 2 to 3 days."[21]

Tyrosine and phenylalanine have become popular antidepressants in orthomolecular circles. DLPA is the centerpiece of physician Arnold Fox's natural antidepressant program. It can work in even the severest cases, he claims.[22] Tyrosine, writes Sheldon Saul Hendler, M.D., of the University of California at San Diego, has been particularly effective for his patients who have premenstrual syndrome or chronic fatigue.[23] Psychiatrist Priscilla Slagle of the University of Southern California uses tyrosine and phenylalanine in an orthomolecular regimen she claims works for most of her depressed patients.[24] Orthomolecular psychiatrists Eric Braverman and Carl Pfeiffer have seen tyrosine and phenylalanine heal some of their most difficult cases.[25]

Is Tyrosine or Phenylalanine for You?

Consider yourself a better than average candidate for tyrosine or phenylalanine if:

• Lab tests suggest you have a deficiency. Women on birth control pills or with postpartum depression may be tyrosine-deficient.[26]

• Your depression is associated with severe mental or physical stress (including, perhaps, summer *heat* depression—see Chapter 18). This could be draining your brain's NE reserves.[1,2]

• You're hypothyroid. Tyrosine or LPA might increase your thyroid hormone levels.[24,25]

• You have Parkinson's disease. As the precursor to L-dopa, the principal treatment for Parkinson's, tyrosine may be a useful adjunct or alternative to it.[1,7,25] (Oddly, phenylalanine appears to aggravate Parkinson's.)[27]

• You're dysfunctionally addicted to the highs of romance, applause or winning (rejection or losing sends you reeling). By boosting PEA, phenylalanine (especially DPA or DLPA) could ease your dependency.[6]

• You enjoy (or are addicted to) stimulants like cocaine, amphetamines,[21] chocolate, nicotine or caffeine. Stimulants tend to work by releasing the brain's natural stimulants, PEA and NE. But eventually they can deplete these neurochemicals, promoting lethargy and depression. Supplementary phenylalanine or tyrosine will replenish the missing PEA and NE; they may even reduce the craving for artificial stimulants in the first place.[9,25]

• You have chronic pain. Studies suggest DPA and DLPA, which preserve the body's painkillers (the endorphins), can help relieve it.[22,25]

METHIONINE AND "SAM"

Psychiatrists from Harvard Medical School, the University of California and major research centers in Europe are enthusiastic about an orthomolecular substance named SAM: "a safe, effective antidepressant with remarkably few side effects"[28] . . . "a rapid and effective treatment for major depression"[29] . . . "if truly efficacious, would be a major contribution to the antidepressant pharmacopoeia."[30]

We make SAM (S-adenosylmethionine) in our own bodies from the essential amino acid methionine. SAM, in turn, helps metabolize a wide range of biochemicals, including the mood-mediating neurotransmitters norepinephrine, dopamine and serotonin.[29] The conversion of methionine to SAM may be sluggish in depressed persons.[31] A little extra SAM, studies suggest, can be therapeutic in 70 to 80 percent of cases.

In over a dozen controlled clinical trials, mostly in Europe, a parenteral (injectable) form of SAM has been studied. Investigators report that when SAM was pitted double-blind against other antidepressant treatments (mainly drugs), it "was generally noted to be equally or more effective and to produce an earlier response (often within 3 to 7 days) with fewer side effects. Similarly . . . parenteral SAM was generally more effective than placebo."[30] Subsequent American trials have done nothing to spoil this report card.[29,32] Nor has a large, double-blind study from Mexico. In it, parenteral SAM accelerated the response to an antidepressant drug.[33]

A newer, oral form of SAM is also being studied. In small uncontrolled trials from England and the US, it has brought somewhat slower recovery to 12 of 26 mostly chronic depressives.[30,34] In controlled studies from Italy, it has nearly equalled an antidepressant drug[31] and significantly bettered a placebo in 80 postmenopausally depressed and dysthymic women.[35] Back in the US, in a UCLA study, six of nine hospitalized depressives responded to SAM; only one of six responded to placebo.[28] In another American trial, however, SAM was only slightly, and not significantly, better than placebo.[36] But a newer and, as it turned out, less bioavailable form of SAM had been used. The researchers suspect this was the problem.[36]

If SAM—which is available in Europe but not yet available in the US—can really relieve depression, so probably can its precursor, methionine, which is available in health food stores (except in Canada). When blood levels of methionine rise, so do brain levels of SAM.[37] Indeed, according to orthomolecular psychiatrists Eric Braverman and Carl Pfeiffer, research indicates that methionine supplements raise brain levels of SAM even better than SAM.[25] Braverman and Pfeiffer have seen quite a few depressed patients—including some very severe cases—improve or recover on methionine supplements.[25]

Is SAM or Methionine for You?

People whose depressions are marked by lethargy, apathy, guilt and suicidal feelings seem to respond best to SAM.[38] People who don't respond to antidepressant drugs may be poor responders.[34]

According to orthomolecular psychiatrists, methionine is often very helpful for schizoaffective persons who are strongly obsessive, suicidal and allergic.[25] (Also helpful: the anticonvulsant drug dilantin, vitamin B12, calcium, zinc and manganese.)[39]

SAM and methionine may also be useful for several depression-related conditions: premenstrual syndrome, chronic pain, fibromyalgia, allergy, heavy metal poisoning, Parkinson's disease, liver disease and drug dependency.[1, 23, 25, 30, 40]

TRYPTOPHAN

When psychiatrists talk about a chemical imbalance causing depression, what they're usually thinking about is a deficiency of norepinephrine and/or of another neurotransmitter, *serotonin*. They have ample reason to be suspicious:

- Depressed persons tend to have low blood levels of tryptophan,[41] the amino acid from which serotonin is made, and low levels of tryptophan relative to other amino acids that compete with it for passage across the blood-brain barrier.[42] More importantly, abundant laboratory research suggests there is a deficiency of serotonin or serotonin activity in the brains of most depressed (and bipolar) persons,[41] especially those who are (or were) violently suicidal.[41, 42]

- Most antidepressant drugs stimulate serotonin activity in the brain.[41] Depriving depressives of tryptophan after they've recovered on a serotonin-stimulating antidepressant usually provokes a relapse.[44]

- Depriving anyone of tryptophan usually makes them fretful and depressed within hours.[44]

And there is one more piece of evidence: Studies suggest that tryptophan (as well as the more immediate precursor to serotonin, 5-hydroxytryptophan [5-HTP]) is an antidepressant.

In six out of seven clinical trials, tryptophan has performed about equally with antidepressant drugs against major depression.[45,46] It has even been more effective than electroconvulsive ("shock") therapy in two out of four studies.[45] In other placebo-controlled trials, tryptophan has usually boosted the effectiveness of antidepressant drugs,[45,47] leading to widespread textbook endorsements of it for this purpose.

In eight or nine placebo-controlled trials, tryptophan has often failed to outperform placebo, but almost always only when it has been prescribed at high dosages.[7,45,47] When this trend was first noticed in the early 1980s, experts speculated that tryptophan might have a therapeutic window, that too much might be as useless as too little. Studies have since confirmed that at low to moderate dosages (1.5 to 3 grams a day), tryptophan is indeed superior to placebo.[46,48,49]

Interestingly, as dosages rise and tryptophan's antidepressant effect fades, a complementary mood-regulating effect emerges. At very high dosages, tryptophan is antimanic.[50] Experts recommend it as an adjunct or alternative to lithium (which also boosts serotonin).[50]

In the body, tryptophan is converted to 5-hydroxytryptophan (5-HTP). 5-HTP is then converted to serotonin. As one would expect, 5-HTP is a more potent precursor to serotonin.[7] It also somehow increases the activity of norepinephrine.[12] This may explain why 5-HTP has proven superior to tryptophan in one study and to placebo in most of over half a dozen others, and why it has held its own against antidepressant drugs or enhanced their effectiveness in most other investigations.[12,45]

Like tryptophan, 5-HTP has been marketed as an antidepressant in Europe,[12] but in North America it's an "orphan drug," available only to researchers or physicians by special request to the FDA.

That's not the worst of it. In 1989, a sudden outbreak among tryptophan users of a serious, sometimes deadly, eosinophilia-myalgia syndrome (EMS) led to tryptophan's removal from the market. Soon thereafter, virtually all cases of EMS were traced to tryptophan contaminated during manufacture with genetically engineered bacteria.[51] But there were a few exceptions, including at least two cases of EMS in users of 5-HTP.[51] It also seems that certain metabolites of *uncontaminated* tryptophan can cause EMS or EMS-type symptoms in animals.[52]

In the end, it may prove that EMS results either from preventable contamination of tryptophan[52] or from tryptophan metabolites that accumulate to toxic levels only when the body is short of the nutrients needed to handle tryptophan safely,[53] which is also a preventable problem. But until the safety of tryptophan and 5-HTP can be assured, the FDA has restricted their availability to doctors who apply for an Investigational New Drug Application.[51] (In Canada tryptophan is still available by prescription.)

Is Tryptophan or 5-HTP for You?

When and if tryptophan and 5-HTP become more freely available, some depressed persons will be more likely than others to benefit. Major indications for using tryptophan or 5-HTP will include: low blood levels of tryptophan, especially relative to other large, neutral amino acids; violent suicidal impulses or attempts;[41,43] melancholic depression;[42] poor impulse control (e.g., violent or criminal impulses,[43] or compulsive eating, drinking, shopping or gambling)[54]; obsessiveness[55] or obsessive-compulsive disorder;[54] postpartum depression;[26] premenstrual syndrome;[56] Tourette's syndrome;[57] attention deficit disorder/hyperactivity;[57] alcoholism since youth;[58] insomnia;[49] anxiety;[55] depersonalization;[55] paranoia;[55] chronic pain[59] or fibromyalgia;[40] carbohydrate craving;[60] fall/winter depression[48]; bipolar disorder;[50] Parkinson's disease treated with L-dopa;[7] migraine;[59] perceptual illusions or hallucinations[61] and senile dementia.[62]

In the meantime, there are other ways to increase brain levels of serotonin. A high-carbohydrate, low-protein, low-fat diet maximizes tryptophan's passage into the brain.[59,60] Certain supplements (vitamins B3, B6 and C) facilitate serotonin synthesis. Aerobic exercise (Chapter 21) may raise blood tryptophan levels.[37] Lithium boosts serotonin and so do many antidepressant drugs (Chapter 32).

OTHER AMINO ACIDS AND DEPRESSION _____

There are other amino acids that have some bearing on the treatment of depression.

• Considerable evidence suggests depression is often promoted by low levels or underactivity of an amino acid neurotransmitter named GABA (gamma-aminobutyric acid), and that drugs which stimulate GABA—*or perhaps GABA itself*—can be therapeutic.[63] GABA also has anti-anxiety and anticonvulsant effects; however, too much of it can *promote* depression.[64]

• Orthomolecular psychiatrists sometimes find low blood levels of glutamine, threonine, glycine, taurine or aspartic acid in their depressed patients. Supplementing these amino acids, they say, often is therapeutic.[23, 25]

• L-dopa is a medically established orthomolecular treatment for Parkinson's disease. Taken in low doses with a "decarboxylase inhibitor,"[65] L-dopa may also be useful for depressives who, like people with Parkinson's, are extremely slowed down,[66] or for suicidal depressives.[67]

• Investigators report that threonine may be "a useful adjunct therapy in agitated depression and manic depression."[25 (p.239)]

• In very large doses (15 to 30 grams) glycine has rapidly calmed high-flying manics."[25]

NOTES _____

1. R. J. Wurtman, "Effects of Dietary Amino Acids, Carbohydrates, and Choline on Neurotransmitter Synthesis," *Mount Sinai J Med* 55(January 1988):75–86.

2. L. E. Banderet and H. R. Lieberman, "Treatment with Tyrosine, a Neurotransmitter Precursor, Reduces Environmental Stress in Humans," *Brain Res Bull* 22(1989):759–762.

3. C. A. Salter, "Dietary Tyrosine as an Aid to Stress Resistance Among Troops," *Military Med* 154(March 1989):144–146.

4. H. C. Sabelli et al., "Clinical Studies on the Phenylalanine Hypothesis of Affective Disorder: Urine and Blood Phenylacetic Acid and Phenylalanine Dietary Supplements," *J Clin Psychiatry* 47(February 1986):66–70.

5. M. E. Wolf and A. D. Mosnaim, "Phenylethylamine in Neuropsychiatric Disorders," *Gen Pharmacol* 14(4, 1983):385–390.

6. Michael R. Liebowitz, *The Chemistry of Love* (New York: Little, Brown, 1983).

7. A. J. Gelenberg et al., "Neurotransmitter Precursors for the Treatment of Depression," *Psychopharmacol Bull* 18(1, 1982):7–18.

8. A. J. Gelenberg et al., "Tyrosine for the Treatment of Depression," *Am J Psychiatry* 137(1980):622–623.

9. A. J. Gelenberg et al., "Tyrosine for Depression," *J Psychiatric Res* 17(2, 1982/83):175–180.

10. A. J. Gelenberg et al., "Tyrosine for Depression: A Double-blind Trial," *J Affect Dis* 19(June 1990):125–132.

11. I. K. Goldberg, "L-Tyrosine in Depression," *Lancet* 2(August 16, 1980):364–365.

12. H. M. van Praag, "Studies in the Mechanism of Action of Serotonin Precursors in Depression," *Psychopharmacol Bull* 20(3, 1984):599–602.

13. J. Mouret et al., "Treatment of Narcolepsy with L-Tyrosine," *Lancet* (December 24/31, 1988): 1458–1459.

14. J. A. Yaryura-Tobias et al., "Phenylalanine for Endogenous Depression," *Orthomolecular Psychiatry* 3(2,1974): 80–81.

15. J. A. Yaryura-Tobias and F. Neziroglu, "Phenylethylamine and Glucose in True Depression," *J Orthomolecular Psychiatry* 5(3, 1976):199–202.

16. J. Mann, "D-Phenylalanine in Endogenous Depression," *Am J Psychiatry* 137(December 1980):1611.

17. H. Beckmann, "Phenylalanine in Affective Disorders," *Adv Biol Psychiatry* 10(1983):137–147.

18. H. M. Kravitz et al., "Dietary Supplements of Phenylalanine and Other Amino Acid Precursors of Brain Neuroamines in the Treatment of Depressive Disorders," *J Am Osteopathic Org* 84(Suppl., September 1984):119–123.

19. W. Birkmayer et al., "L-Deprenyl Plus L-Phenylalanine in the Treatment of Depression," *Journal of Neural Transmission* 59(January 1984):81–87.

20. M. Simonson, "L-Phenylalanine" (letter), *J Clin Psychiatry* 46(August 1985):355.

21. H. Sabelli, "Rapid Treatment of Depression with Selegiline-Phenylalanine combination" (letter), *J Clin Psychiatry* 52(March 1991):137.

22. Arnold Fox and Barry Fox, *DLPA to End Chronic Pain and Depression* (New York: Pocket Books, 1985).

23. Sheldon Saul Hendler, *The Oxygen Breakthrough: Thirty Days to an Illness-Free Life* (New York: William Morrow, 1989).

24. Priscilla Slagle, *The Way Up from Down* (New York: Random House, 1987).

25. Eric R. Braverman and Carl C. Pfeiffer, *The Healing Nutrients Within: Facts, Findings and New Research on Amino Acids* (New Canaan, Conn.: Keats Publishing, 1987).

26. M. Maes et al., "Disturbances in Dexamethasone Suppression Test and Lower Availability of L-Tryptophan and Tyrosine in Early Puerperium and in Women Under Contraceptive Therapy," *J Psychosom Res* 36(February 1992):191–197.

27. G. C. Cotzias, "Aromatic Amino Acids and Modification of Parkinsonism," *N Eng J Med* 276(1967):374–379.

28. B. L. Kagan, "Oral S-Adenosylmethionine in Depression: A Randomized, Double-Blind, Placebo-Controlled Trial," *Am J Psychiatry* 147(May 1990):591–595.

29. K. M. Bell et al., "S-Adenosylmethionine Treatment of Depression: A Controlled Clinical Trial," *Am J Psychiatry* 145(September 1988): 1110–1114.

30. J. F. Rosenbaum et al., "An Open-Label Pilot Study of Oral S-Adenosyl-L-Methionine in Major Depression: Interim Results," *Psychopharmacol Bull* 24(1, 1988):189–194.

31. M. de Vanna and R. Rigamonti, "Oral S-Adenosyl-L-Methionine in Depression," *Current Therapeutic Research* 52(September 1992): 478–485.

32. J. P. Lipinski et al., "Open Trial of S-Adenosylmethionine for Treatment of Depression," *Am J Psychiatry* 141(March 1984):448–450.

33. C. Berlanga et al., "Efficacy of S-adenosyl-L-Methionine in Speeding the Onset of Action of Imipramine," *Psychiatry Res* 44(December 1992):257–262.

34. J. F. Rosenbaum et al., "The Antidepressant Potential of Oral S-Adenosyl-L-Methionine," *Acta Psychiatr Scand* 81(May 1990):432–436.

35. P. Salmaggi et al., "Double-Blind, Placebo-Controlled Study of

S-Adenosyl-L-Methionine in Depressed Postmenopausal Women," *Psychother Psychosom* 59(1, 1993):34–40.

36. M. Fava et al., "The Thyrotropin Response to Thyrotropin-Releasing Hormone as a Predictor of Response to Treatment in Depressed Outpatients," *Acta Psychiatr Scand* 86(July 1992):42–45.

37. L. A. Conlay et al., "Effects of Running the Boston Marathon on Plasma Concentrations of Large Neutral Amino Acids," *Journal of Neural Transmission* 76(1989):65–71.

38. E. H. Reynolds et al., "Methylation and Mood," *Lancet* (July 28, 1984):196–198.

39. Carlton Fredericks, *Carlton Fredericks' Nutrition Guide for the Prevention & Cure of Common Ailments & Diseases* (New York: Simon and Schuster, 1982).

40. P. J. Goodnick and R. Sandoval, "Psychotropic Treatment of Chronic Fatigue Syndrome and Related Disorders," *J Clin Psychiatry* 54(January 1993):13–20.

41. A. J. Coppen and D. P. Doogan, "Serotonin and Its Place in the Pathogenesis of Depression," *J Clin Psychiatry* 49(Suppl., August 1988):4–11.

42. M. Maes et al., "Clinical Subtypes of Unipolar Depression: Part I. A Validation of the Vital and Nonvital Clusters," *Psychiatry Res* 34(October, 1990C):29–41.

43. V. M. Linnoila and M. Virkkunen, "Aggression, Suicidality, and Serotonin," *J Clinical Psychiatry* 53(Suppl., October 1992): 46–51.

44. H. L. Miller et al., "Acute Tryptophan Depletion: A Method of Studying Antidepressant Action," *J Clin Psychiatry* 53(Suppl., October 1992): 28–35.

45. H. M. van Praag, "Management of Depression with Serotonin Precursors," *Biol Psychiatry* 16(3, 1981): 291–310.

46. J. Thomson et al., "The Treatment of Depression in General Practice: A Comparison of L-Tryptophan, Amitriptyline, and a Combination of L-Tryptophan and Amitriptyline with Placebo," *Psychol Med* 12(November 1982):741–751.

47. S. N. Young, "The Potential for the Use of Tryptophan and Other Amine Precursors in the Treatment of Affective Disorders," *Adv Biol Psychiatry* 7(1981):113–125.

48. R. E. McGrath et al., "The Effect of L-Tryptophan on Seasonal Affective Disorder," *J Clin Psychiatry* 51(April 1990):162–163.

49. R. Asheychick et al., "The Efficacy of L-tryptophan in the Reduc-

tion of Sleep Disturbance and Depressive State in Alcoholic Patients," *Journal of Studies on Alcohol* 50(November 1989):525–532.

50. G. S. Sachs, "Adjuncts and Alternatives to Lithium Therapy for Bipolar Affective Disorder," *J Clin Psychiatry* 50(Suppl., December 1989):31–39.

51. MaryLynn D. Bryce, letter to the author on behalf of David Kessler, Commissioner of the FDA, January 1992.

52. A. Blauvelt and V. Falanga, "Idiopathic and L-Tryptophan-Associated Eosinophilic Fasciitis Before and After L-Tryptophan Contamination," *Arch Derm* 127(August 1991):1159–1166.

53. W. E. Catterall, "Tryptophan and Bladder Cancer" (letter), *Bio Psychiatry* 24(October 1988):733–734.

54. J. J. Lopez-Ibor, Jr., "Serotonin and Psychiatric Disorders," *Internat Clin Psychopharmacol* 7(Suppl. 2, October 1992):5–11.

55. M. Maes et al., "Symptom Profiles of Biological Markers in Depression: A Multivariate Study," *Psychoneuroendocrinology* 15(1, 1990): 29–37.

56. U. Halbreich and H. Tworek, "Altered Serotonergic Activity in Women with Dysphoric Premenstrual Syndromes," *Internat J Psychiatry Med* 23(1, 1993):1–27.

57. D. E. Comings, "Blood Serotonin and Tryptophan in Tourette Syndrome," *Am J Med Genetics* 36 (August, 1990):418–430.

58. L. Buydens-Branchey et al., "Age of Alcoholism Onset. II. Relationship to Susceptibility to Serotonin Precursor Availability," *Arch Gen Psychiatry* 46(March 1989):231–236.

59. Robert L. Pollock et al., *The Pain-Free Tryptophan Diet* (New York: Warner Books, 1986).

60. R. J. Wurtman and J. J. Wurtman, "Carbohydrates and Depression," *Scientific American* (January, 1989):68–75.

61. J. A. Yaryura-Tobias and F. Neziroglu, "Tryptophan and Perceptual Schizophrenias," *J Orthomolecular Psychiatry* 6(2, 1977):193–194.

62. D. E. Thomas et al., "Tryptophan and Nutritional Status of Patients with Senile Dementia," *Psychol Med* 16(May, 1986):297–303.

63. K. G. Lloyd et al., "The Gabaergic Hypothesis of Depression," *Prog Neuro-Psychopharmacol Biol Psychiatry* 13(3–4, 1989):341–351.

64. H. A. Ring et al., "Vigabatrin and Depression," *J Neurol Neurosurg Psychiatr* 56(August 1993):925–928.

65. J. Mendels et al., "Amine Precursors and Depression," *Arch Gen Psychiatry* 32(January 1975):22–30.

66. A. S. Brown and S. Gershon, "Dopamine and Depression," *Journal of Neural Transmission—General Section* 91(2–3, 1993):75–109.

67. A. Roy et al., "Marked Reduction in Indexes of Dopamine Metabolism Among Patients with Depression Who Attempt Suicide," *Arch Gen Psychiatry* 49(June 1992):447–450.

TWELVE

Using Nutritional Supplements

WHILE it's possible to use nutritional supplements to self-treat depression, it can be easier, safer and more reliable to seek expert help. Two organizations that can assist you in finding such help are the American Association of Orthomolecular Medicine's public-outreach wing, the Huxley Institute (900 N. Federal Highway, Suite 160, Boca Raton, FL 33432, 1–800–847–3802) and the American Holistic Medical Association (4101 Lake Boone Tr., Ste. 201, Raleigh, NC 27607, (919) 787–5146).

TESTING FOR NUTRITIONAL DEFICIENCIES

You don't need to be tested for nutritional deficiencies in order to use supplements effectively. But lab tests can help you zero in on the supplements most likely to succeed. Unfortunately, few doctors other than orthomolecular ones and some biologically oriented psychiatrists are inclined (or even able) to accommodate you here, unless perhaps you have some blatant clinical signs, symptoms or risk factors. The more of the following generic ones you have (or of the more specific ones mentioned earlier), the more suspicious you and your doctor should be:

Signs and Symptoms: depression and any of its symptoms; lesions in and around the mouth (e.g., swollen, inflamed tongue; bleeding gums; cracks around the mouth); skin disorders (oily, dry, rough or flaky skin; easy bruising; dandruff); hair loss; severe mental impairment; strange sensations, particularly in the extremities (e.g., numbness, tingling, burning); weak legs; dizziness, uncoordination.

Risk Factors: poor diet; chronic emotional distress; immoderate use of alcohol or caffeine; smoking; exposure to toxic chemicals and pollutants; pregnancy and nursing; use of certain drugs (e.g., birth control pills, MAO inhibitors, dilantin, cholestyramine); surgery/injury; dialysis; infection; chronic gastrointestinal disorders; rapid growth spurts; old age.

The following tests for nutritional deficiencies are considered the most sensitive, but are not infallible. They can't, for example, detect a localized brain deficiency. This is why some practitioners prescribe supplements even when tests are "negative."

Tests for Vitamin Deficiencies

B1: Erythrocyte transketolase.

B2: Erythrocyte glutathione reductase.

B3: N-methylnicotinamide.

B6: Pyridoxal-5-phosphate, erythrocyte glutamic-pyruvic transaminase, kynurenic acid and/or xanthurenic acid.

Folic acid: FIGLU (forminoglutamic acid) and/or RBC (red blood cell) folate.

B12: Serum B12 (*microbiological* assay only) or (preferably) serum or urinary MMA (methylmalonic acid) or homocysteine, and/or the deoxyuridine suppression test.

Vitamin C: White blood cell ascorbate.

Carnitine: Serum carnitine or (preferably) muscle or liver carnitine.

Tests for Mineral Deficiencies

Magnesium: RBC magnesium or (preferably) muscle magnesium or a magnesium loading test.

Calcium: Ionized calcium.

Iron: Serum ferritin.

Zinc: Blood and urine tests are standard, but some investigators claim that a simple taste test is more reliable.[1] Five to 10 ml of a zinc solution (1 gram zinc sulphate heptahydrate [sold in drugstores] in 1 liter of distilled water) is held in the mouth for 10 seconds. People who are *not* zinc deficient notice a strong, usually unpleasant, metallic taste. People who *are* deficient taste little or nothing. The taste test is sold in health food stores.

Tests for Fatty Acid Deficiencies or Imbalances

Measures of the *balance* in the blood or blood-cell membranes of important fatty acids, like alpha-linolenic acid, linoleic acid, dihomogamma-linolenic acid, gamma-linolenic acid, arachidonic acid and eicosapentanoic acid.

Tests for Amino Acid Deficiencies

Probably the most revealing test, some research suggests,[2,3] is the ratio in the blood plasma of tyrosine, phenylalanine, tryptophan and methionine to each other and to the other amino acids that compete with them for passage across the blood-brain barrier. Low ratios suggest brain deficiency. So may poor erythrocyte membrane transport of the amino acids.[4] Another indirect gauge is low blood or urinary levels of metabolites of the neurotransmitters made from tyrosine, phenylalanine and tryptophan, i.e., low 5-HIAA, MHPG, HVA or PAA.[5-7] Low blood levels of the following amino acids have also been associated with depression: GABA, threonine, histamine, glycine, glutamic acid, taurine and aspartic acid.[6,7]

USING NUTRITIONAL SUPPLEMENTS _____

Clinical Response

Some nutritional supplements—vitamin C, thiamine, niacin and linseed oil, for instance—can bring noticeable relief from depression within hours or days. But usually it takes weeks for supplements to do their stuff. Fast-acting antidepressant treatments such as thyroid hormone and sleep deprivation (Chapter 19) may help accelerate recovery.

After you've recovered from a serious mood disorder on nutritional supplements, wait at least a few months before venturing to cut down, very gradually, to a maintenance dosage or to quit.[7] Rapid discontinuation encourages relapse.[8] Indeed, research with antidepressant drugs suggests it may be advisable not to cut down at all if you have a severe recurrent disorder—unless perhaps you've found an effective alternative. (However, as noted below, sometimes the dosage of certain supplements needs to be lowered to maintain clinical response.)

Dosage and Administration

The dose ranges listed below are those commonly employed in research and practice. To find a dosage that's right for you, it's best to start low and increase gradually, while watching for improvements or adverse reactions. Going slowly is especially important if a nutrient has a "therapeutic window" (it's only effective within a narrow dose range) of if it worsens depression at too high a dosage.

Most supplements are absorbed and utilized best when taken in capsule or powder form after a meal and—if the dosage is high—divided into two or more doses daily. (Exceptions are noted below.) Sometimes doctors will *inject* supplements, usually because of poor absorption (common in the elderly) or because the oral supplements don't seem to be working.

Balanced Supplementation

It's important to take supplements in a balanced way. Too much of one nutrient can shut out others or be a burden on the body if nutrients that help metabolize it aren't supplemented too. The best insurance against nutritional imbalance is a well-balanced diet (Chapter 15), a medium- to high-potency multivitamin and mineral supplement and following the recommendations below (or those of a knowledgeable health practitioner).

Safety and Side Effects

If you're used to thinking of nutritional supplements as nature's boundlessly benevolent bounty, the cautions and adverse effects listed below may give you a start. The tryptophan disaster (Chapter 11) has been a deadly object lesson in the fallacy of such romanticism. Nevertheless, the side effects of nutritional supplements, used knowledgeably (as discussed below), typically are mild and infrequent. Severe effects are rare. Drugs really *are* much pricklier. For the smoothest ride, orthomolecular experts recommend using the purest hypoallergenic supplements.

Although some supplements can benefit pregnant women or their fetuses (e.g., folic acid), not enough is known about the effects of megadoses of nutrients during pregnancy to assure their safety.[7]

I've tried to be thorough in my presentation of the side effects, cautions, contraindications, and so on, below. But space prevents me from being exhaustive. If you'd like more detail, Patricia Hausman's *The Right Dose* is an outstanding reference.[9]

Where to Buy Supplements

Except where noted, all of the following supplements are available wherever supplements are sold. An important exception is the amino acids. These are not available over-the-counter in Canada. Canadians, however, can legally obtain personal supplies from the United States, in person or from mail-order companies such as:

Vitamin Research Products, 2044 Old Middlefield Way, Mountain View, CA 94043. 1–800–877–2447. Sells all major amino acids. Bronson Pharmaceuticals, P.O. Box 1632, Windsor, Ontario N9A 7C9. 1–800–235–3200. Sells tyrosine and L-phenylalanine.

NUTRITIONAL SUPPLEMENTS FOR DEPRESSION _____

Multivitamin and Mineral Supplement

A well-balanced, medium- to high-potency multivitamin and mineral supplement is the backbone of any supplement program. It may even be all you need to correct most depression-related nutritional deficiencies. Look for one that includes all the obscure nutrients (e.g., chromium, manganese), not just the superstars like zinc and vitamin C. A daily dose probably should provide at least 15–20 mg of vitamins B1, B2, B3, B5 and B6.

Vitamins

VITAMIN B1 (THIAMINE)

RDA (recommended daily allowance)*:1–1.5 mg.

Dosage: 200–2000 mg/day.

Side effects: May raise blood pressure.[6]

VITAMIN B3 (NIACIN)

RDA: 13–19 mg.

Dosage: 500 mg to 40 grams/day; usually 3–6 grams/day.[10-12] (Slow-release forms are effective at one-half to one-third the dosage, but risk of liver damage is much greater.)[13] Experts caution against using over 500 mg/day without medical supervision.[10]

Side effects: Doses over 100–200 mg produce dramatic but harmless flushing, which abates or disappears with regular use. The flushing can be diminished by taking niacin with meals or cold liquids or by using slow-release niacin, inositol niacinate or xanthene niacinate.[12] Enjoying the flush augurs well clinically.[11] Other side effects: nausea, vomiting, abdominal pain, frontal headaches, overstimulation/restlessness, darkening of the skin, itchiness, im-

* The RDAs listed here are the *range* for adults, which varies primarily according to weight. RDAs during pregnancy and lactation usually are somewhat higher.

paired vision, swollen ankles, cardiac arrythmias, liver dysfunction, hyperglycemia and gouty arthritis.[10, 14-17]

Cautions and contraindications: May be contraindicated (consult your doctor) if you have peptic ulcers, diabetes, high blood pressure, gout, porphyria, gall bladder disease or liver disease.[10,14,18] Because megadoses (especially of the slow-release forms)[13] may cause hepatitis[13] or liver damage, liver function tests should be done regularly, perhaps every six months. According to orthomolecular medical authority Abram Hoffer,[12] about 1 in 2,000 patients develops a mild liver disease (obstructive jaundice) which soon clears when B3 is stopped. (The natural antidepressant SAM protects the liver and might prevent it.) Hoffer, who disputes the existence of some of the above side effects and contraindications, also argues that concerns about megadoses being potentially able to cause birth defects[14,18] are based on spurious evidence.[12]

VITAMIN B6 (PYRIDOXINE)

RDA: 1.4–2 mg.

Dosage: Usually 50–500 mg/day. Pyridoxal-5-phosphate is more biopotent and, perhaps, more effective than pyridoxine hydrochloride.[7]

Side effects: Mild memory impairment.[19] Some people—usually on super-megadoses (1 gram or more)—have developed neurologic symptoms, such as numbness and staggering, and sometimes skin disorders.[19] Experts who never see these reactions[7,12,20] attribute them to overdose or failure to balance B6 with other B vitamins and magnesium.

Cautions: B6 supplements neutralize the effectiveness of L-dopa therapy (and possibly tyrosine),[21] unless carbidopa is prescribed too.[19]

FOLIC ACID (FOLATE, FOLACIN)

RDA: 150–200 mcg.

Dosage: Folic acid: Usually 5 to 20 mg/day.[10] Maximum benefits can take months to accrue.[22] There appears to be a therapeutic window, so it may be necessary to lower dosage after a while to maintain the response.[10] In the form of methylfolate, dosage would be 15–50 mg/day.[22]

Side effects: Folic acid: Allergic reactions (pain, hives, hot flushing, itching, fever), gastrointestinal upsets, taste distortions, weight loss, insomnia, anxiety, poor concentration, hyperactivity or rambunctiousness (usually after weeks or months on a high dosage).[22,23] Methylfolate: probably similar.

Cautions and contraindications: Large doses are poorly tolerated by people with allergies,[6] including "china doll" schizoaffectives described on page 69. May provoke seizures in some epileptics; [22,24] will invalidate *crude* screening tests for vitamin B12 deficiency (warn your doctor); and may promote mild zinc deficiency if zinc intake is low.[24] Methylfolate: probably similar.

VITAMIN B12 (COBALAMIN, CYANOCOBALAMIN. HYDROXOCOBALAMIN)

RDA: 2 mcg.

Dosage: Parenteral (injection): from 1000 mcg every few days up to 10,000 to 26,000 mcg/day.[10] Oral (including sublingual) and nasal gel: probably 500–5000 mcg/day.

Side effects, cautions, contraindications: None reported.

VITAMIN C (ASCORBIC ACID, ASCORBATE)

RDA: 60 mg.

Dosage: From 1 or 2 grams/day up to 50–200 grams/day or the "bowel tolerance" dosage recommended by orthomolecular physicians—i.e., as much as you can take without getting loose stools.[12]

Side effects and hazards: Aside from loose stools, side effects are rare. They include dry nose and nosebleeds, abdominal cramps, nausea, vomiting, heartburn, flushing, headache, fatigue and insomnia.[9] There is disputed [12,25] evidence that gram dosages can adversely lower blood levels of copper, [9,14] and that they may temporarily lower fertility.[9,14] Some even claim (paradoxically, in light of other evidence) that megadose C impedes the detoxification of some substances, promotes cancer and shortens lifespan![14] (This didn't deter Linus Pauling from megadosing well into his ninth decade.)[26]

Cautions and contraindications: High dosages (over 20 grams/day) of buffered *mineral* ascorbates might cause mineral excesses or imbalances. High blood or urinary levels of vitamin C can interfere with certain lab tests[9] (warn your doctor). There is disputed[12,25] evidence that megadoses may increase iron absorption to a dangerous degree for people at risk for or suffering from hemochromatosis (iron overload);[9,14] aggravate sickle cell anemia and G-6PD deficiency (conditions not uncommon among Blacks);[9,14] interfere with certain drugs (warfarin, tricyclic antidepressants);[9] and create an exaggerated need (probably temporary) for vitamin C in the newborns of mothers who took megadoses during pregnancy.[14] Evidence that megadoses can promote calcium-oxalate kidney stones and even serious kidney damage in vulnerable (though probably rare) individuals[9] is hotly disputed.[12,27] If mega-C does promote kidney stones, taking extra vitamin B6 (probably less than 100 mg a day) or using *buffered* ascorbate can be preventive, orthomolecular experts claim.[28] Ascorbic acid may leach calcium and magnesium from the body, so make sure your intake of these minerals is adequate.[28]

CHOLINE

RDA: None.

Dosage: For acute antimanic effect, usually 250–2000 mg of choline, 10–100 grams of lecithin, or 2–20 grams of phosphatidylcholine per day.[7,29] Much lower doses may suffice if large or megadoses of niacinamide are also taken.[30]

Caution: Large doses can worsen depression.

L-CARNITINE

RDA: None.

Dosage: L-carnitine: 2–3.5 grams/day. L-acetylcarnitine: 1.5–3 grams/day.

Side effects: Mild diarrhea.[6]

Contraindications: Possibly uremia.[6]

Minerals

A good diet (Chapter 15) can go a long way—if not all the way—toward providing the minerals you need in the right balance. When mineral supplements are taken, it's important not to take too much of one without getting enough of the others.

MAGNESIUM

RDA: 280–350 mg.

Dosage: Generally around 400–1200 mg of inorganic magnesium (e.g., magnesium oxide) or about half to a quarter as much amino-acid-chelated magnesium (e.g., aspartate or orotate) per day.[7,10]

Side effects: Dizziness or faintness from lowered blood pressure. Excess may cause sluggishness, mental impairment and increased depression.[31.]

Cautions and contraindications: May be contraindicated if you have kidney failure, myasthenia gravis or Addison's disease.[7] May induce calcium deficiency if calcium intake is low.

CALCIUM

RDA: 800–1200 mg.

Dosage: 500–2000 mg/day of inorganic calcium (e.g., calcium carbonate or citrate). Most bone meal and oyster shell calcium supplements have questionably high lead levels.[32]

Side effects: Large doses may worsen depression or mania.

ZINC

RDA: 12–15 mg.

Dosage: 15–60 mg/day.[10,12]

Side effects: Nausea, drowsiness.

Cautions: Dosages above 50 mg/day can reduce blood levels of "good" HDL (high density lipoprotein) cholesterol, probably by inducing mild copper deficiency. To prevent a depressing manganese deficiency, supplemental manganese gluconate—perhaps 5 mg per 10 mg of zinc—is recommended.[33]

Lithium (available by prescription only)

RDA: None.

Dosage: Traditionally, 900–1200 mg lithium carbonate/day (lower in the elderly). The trend today is toward much lower doses (and blood levels), because this greatly reduces side effects and, some studies suggest, enhances clinical response (other studies suggest the opposite, though).[34] Lithium-rich mineral waters, such as Knazmilos, Vichy St. Yorre Royal and Original Saratoga Geiser, provide much lower doses.

Major side effects: Weight gain, tremor, thirst, diarrhea, frequent urination, and possibly kidney damage and hyperparathyroidism. Lithium promotes autoimmune disorders—especially hypothyroidism, which may affect nearly *half* of long-term users (usually in mild or subclinical form), provoking lethargy, dullness, depressive relapses and rapid-cycling.

Cautions and contraindications: Contraindicated for hypothyroid depressives. May worsen rapid-cycling bipolar disorder. Not recommended if you have personal or family history of autoimmune disorders.[35] Combining lithium with other antidepressants, especially "serotonergic" ones (e.g., tryptophan, SSRIs and MAOIs page 254), has triggered (rarely, it seems) severely adverse reactions, including two fatalities.[36]

Fatty Acids

GAMMA-LINOLENIC ACID (GLA)

RDA: None determined.

Dosage: Usually four to eight 500-ml capsules of evening primrose oil per day, providing 160–320 mg of GLA. The oils of borage, black currant and gooseberry also contain GLA, but it may not be as biopotent. Your body may need extra magnesium, zinc and vitamins B3, B6 and C to fully utilize the extra GLA.[37]

Cautions: May aggravate epilepsy or (ironically) worsen psychiatric disorder.[38] May disagree with people genetically adapted to diets very low in plant food (e.g., Inuit).

ALPHA-LINOLENIC ACID (ALA)

RDA: None determined.

Dosage: Usually 1 tsp to 2–4 tbsp of fresh, unrefined linseed oil per day. Freshly ground or cooked flax seeds (about 50 percent linseed oil) can also be used. (Whole, uncooked seeds are poorly digested.) Take the minimal effective dosage; more can worsen your symptoms. Usually after several months to a year or two, symptoms of overload (e.g., sleepiness, skin problems, achey muscles, depressive relapse) will occur unless you cut down or quit.

Side effects: Although usually calming, linseed oil often triggers "racing thoughts." Occasionally it provokes euphoria, hyperactivity or mania, and it appears to have triggered rapid cycling in one bipolar depressive.[39,40]

Cautions: "Dosages should be carefully monitored by a qualified professional whenever symptoms of any seriousness are apparent," expert Donald Rudin warns. Rudin[40(p.79)] also recommends backing it up with a good diet (see Chapter 15) and a multivitamin and mineral supplement, with extra vitamin C and selenium to ensure the oil is safely and efficiently metabolized. Extra magnesium (which abounds in ALA-rich whole foods, such as flax seeds) may also help prevent mood destabilization and other side effects. So may GLA. Megadoses of certain nutrients—notably vitamins A, E, B3 and B6—may have to be reduced, for their potency can be exaggerated by linseed oil.[39]

EICOSAPENTANOIC ACID (EPA)

RDA: None determined.

Dosage: 1 tsp to several tbsp (5–40 ml) of fish liver oil or MaxEPA per day. EPA-rich food sources: cold-acclimatized game, fish or seafood, such as anchovies, salmon, herring, mackerel, sardines, trout, eel, cod or carp.

Cautions: Has upset blood-sugar control in insulin-dependent diabetics. May lower tolerance for anticoagulant medications (including aspirin) and be contraindicated before surgery. Long-term use of very large doses of fish liver oil (but not MaxEPA) may cause overdoses of vitamin A or D.

Amino Acids

GENERAL SAFETY CONSIDERATIONS

Except for the mysterious outbreak of EMS among tryptophan users (see below), amino acids have enjoyed a good safety record. *"In all the years I have been treating depression with amino acids, I have never had to discontinue the treatment because of side effects,"* avers psychiatrist Priscilla Slagle.[7(p.56)] However, large doses may be contraindicated if you have severe liver or kidney disease, Slagle warns. She also advises long-term users who are on low-protein diets and juvenile users to take a balanced amino acid supplement also, the kind that is dissolved and taken with meals. This is to prevent induced deficiencies of other amino acids.

L-TYROSINE AND L-PHENYLALANINE

RDA: None established; however the estimated requirement for L-tyrosine and L-phenylalanine combined is 14 mg/kg body weight, or about 1 gram/day for a 150-pound person.

Dosage: Tyrosine: 1–8 grams/day.[6,7,21] L-phenylalanine: 500 mg to 6 grams/day.[6,7] Relatively low doses suffice when taken on a protein-free stomach, i.e., at least 45 minutes before or three hours after eating protein. Blood levels of other amino acids that compete for passage across the blood-brain barrier are low then.

Side effects: Irritability, aggression, feeling tense or "wired," headache (if chocolate gives you headaches, phenylalanine may too), constipation, nausea or upset stomach, difficulty falling asleep if taken at night, mania or hypomania.[6,21] Other side effects have been attributed to aspartame, which is 40 percent phenylalanine, though these effects—which include dizziness, blurred vision, hives, epileptic seizures, mental confusion, and (paradoxically) depression—could be due to aspartame's other ingredients, aspartic acid and methanol. Some side effects could be attributable to induced deficiencies of serotonin, in which case extra tryptophan or a high complex-carbohydrate diet could help.

Cautions and contraindications: Use with caution (especially phenylalanine), or avoid, if you have a history of aggressive behavior, mania (these amino acids may retrigger it), hallucinations, delusions, schizophrenia, migraines, heart rhythm irregularity, high blood pressure or mitral valve prolapse.[6,7,41] May raise blood pressure if combined with older, nonreversible MAOI antidepressants (Chapter 32).[6] Theoretically, large doses may promote an involuntary movement disorder (tardive dyskinesia) in some users of antipsychotic, neuroleptic drugs[42] or worsen malignant melanoma.[7] Avoid phenylalanine if you have phenylketonuria or are pregnant—it may harm the fetus.

DL-PHENYLALANINE (DLPA) AND D-PHENYLALANINE (DPA)

RDA: None

Dosage: In studies from Germany and South America, depressives responded to 200–600 mg per day of DLPA or half as much DPA. American physicians generally prescribe more: 250 or 375 mg DLPA, three times a day.[43] On a protein-free stomach (see above), 200–600 mg per day still might do. Capsules of DLPA appear to be much better absorbed than tablets.[6]

Side effects, cautions and contradictions: Same as for L-phenylalanine.

SAM (S-ADENOSYLMETHIONINE) AND METHIONINE

Note: In 1994 SAM (*aka* ademetionine) was not yet on the market in North America.

RDA: The estimated requirement for methionine and cystine (a related amino acid) combined is 13 mg/kg body weight, or about 1 gram/day for a 150-pound person.

Dosage and precautions: Oral SAM: 600–1600 mg/day.[44,45] L-methionine: usually 1–2 grams/day;[6] DL-methionine may be effective at lower dosages.[6] For safe and efficient utilization of SAM and methionine, a generous intake of vitamin B6, folic acid, magnesium and calcium is essential.[6] A little extra tryptophan and (possibly) L-phenylalanine or tyrosine might also help.

Side effects: Typically mild and transient, SAM's side effects include dry mouth, thirst, nausea, vomiting, gas, urinary delay, blurred vision, headache, sweating, anxiety and restlessness.[6,44] SAM also appears to induce hypomania or mania—usually transient, but sometimes persisting even after discontinuing treatment—in about 10 to 15 percent of users,[44,45] mostly those with bipolar illness. Methionine's negligible side effects[6] probably mirror SAM's.

L-TRYPTOPHAN

Note: Tryptophan and 5-HTP (see below) have been off the market since 1989 due to unresolved safety concerns. They're available to doctors only as investigational new drugs by special application.

RDA: The estimated requirement is 3.5 mg/kg body weight, or about 250 mg/day for a 150-pound person.

Dosage: Usually 1.5–6 grams/day (slightly higher for bipolar depressions); up to twice the dosage for mania.[6,46] On a protein-free stomach, much lower doses of tryptophan may suffice—perhaps as low as one third, if also taken on a "carbohydrate-rich stomach" (carbohydrates indirectly increase tryptophan's passage into the brain).[7,47] Lower doses also are optimal when combined with cyclic antidepressants (Chapter 32).

To promote safe utilization of tryptophan and its conversion to serotonin, vitamins B6, B3 and C should also be taken; for every 500 mg of tryptophan, probably at least 10 mg of B6, 25 mg of B3 and 100 mg of C.[7,26,47,48] This may minimize side effects and contraindications.[7,26,48] Extra L-phenylalanine or L-tyrosine and (perhaps) methionine might also help, especially if tryptophan dosage is high.

Side effects:[7,46] Dose-dependent and transient drowsiness and lethargy have earned tryptophan its reputation as "nature's sleeping pill." With adjunctive vitamins, orthomolecular practitioners[7] rarely see other reported side effects: lightheadedness, headaches, nausea, vomiting, tremors, dry mouth, dizziness, blurred vision, agitation and sexual disinhibition.

Cautions and contraindications: As we saw in Chapter 11, a debilitating, sometimes deadly, eosinophilic-myalgic syndrome (EMS) occurred in many tryptophan users in the late 1980s. It was probably due to contamination, or (in rare cases) to concurrent vitamin deficiencies in biologically vulnerable individuals. Symptoms of EMS include severe muscle and joint pain, swollen arms or legs, skin rash, fever, weakness and elevated levels of eosinophils (a type of blood cell).

Animal experiments suggest certain metabolites of tryptophan can irritate the bladder or cause bladder tumors, but only if vitamin B6 and C are deficient.[26,48] This may also be true for EMS symptoms caused by uncontaminated tryptophan.

Tryptophan may aggravate asthma[47] and upset blood pressure in elderly people with hypertension.[7] In one study, newborns of hamsters fed extra tryptophan during pregnancy had a high mortality rate.[49] One very cautious expert feels tryptophan may be contraindicated for women on estrogens or oral contraceptives and for anyone with bladder irritation, overgrowth of gastrointestinal microorganisms or a history of cancer, diabetes or scleroderma-like conditions.[50]

Acute confusion or delirium, agitation, sweating, muscle jerking, dangerous body temperature elevations and other marked neurological reactions—*including two fatalities*[36]—have sometimes occurred when tryptophan has been combined with certain antidepressants (MAOIs,[51] lithium,[36] clomipramine,[52] fluoxetine [Prozac])[51] or with electroconvulsive therapy.[52]

L-5-HTP (L-5-HYDROXYTRYPTOPHAN)

Dosage: Usually 50–600 mg/day of enteric-coated L-5-HTP (oxitriptan), along with 150 mg of the drug carbidopa to discourage conversion of 5-HTP to serotonin outside the brain.[53] This substance has a narrow therapeutic window: "In some patients the effect of L-5-HTP hinges on 10–25 mg/day more or less."[53]

Side effects: "I have never in 20 years used an agent which . . . was so entirely without side effects," exults one psychiatrist. However he has seen hypomanic reactions in some patients on too high a dosage.[53] And there have been isolated cases of EMS[54] or EMS-like syndromes, eosinophilia and dermatitis.

NOTES

1. D. Bryce-Smith and R. I. D. Simpson, "Case of Anorexia Nervosa Responding to Zinc Sulphate," *Lancet* (Aug. 11, 1984):350.

. 2. S. E. Moller et al., "Relationship Between Plasma Ratio of Tryptophan to Competing Amino Acids and the Response to L-Tryptophan," *J Affect Dis* 2(March 1980):47–59.

3. S. E. Moller, "Plasma Amino Acid Profiles in Relation to Clinical Response to Moclobemide in Patients with Major Depression," *J Affect Dis* 27(April 1993):225–231.

4. J. M. Azorin et al., "L-Tyrosine and L-Tryptophan Membrane Transport in Erythrocytes and Antidepressant Drug Choice," *Biol Psychiatry* 27(April 1990):723–734.

5. H. M. Kravitz et al., "Dietary Supplements of Phenylalanine and Other Amino Acid Precursors of Brain Neuroamines in the Treatment of Depressive Disorders," *J Am Osteopath Org* 84(Suppl., September 1984):119–123.

6. Eric R. Braverman and Carl C. Pfeiffer, *The Healing Nutrients Within: Facts, Findings and New Research on Amino Acids* (New Canaan, Conn.: Keats Publishing, 1987).

7. Priscilla Slagle, *The Way Up from Down* (New York: Random House, 1987).

8. G. L. Faedda et al., "Outcome After Rapid vs Gradual Discontinuation of Lithium Treatment in Bipolar Disorders," *Arch Gen Psychiatry* 50(June 1993):448–455.

9. Patricia Hausman, *The Right Dose* (New York: Ballantine, 1987).

10. H. L. Newbold, *Mega-Nutrients for Your Nerves* (New York: Berkley Books, 1975).

11. Michael Lesser, *Nutrition and Vitamin Therapy* (New York: Grove Press, 1980).

12. Abram Hoffer, *Common Questions on Schizophrenia and Their Answers* (New Canaan, Conn.: Keats Publishing, 1987).

13. S. P. Lawrence, "Transient Focal Hepatic Defects Related to Sustained-Release Niacin," *J Clin Gastroenterol* 16(April 1993): 234–236.

14. D. R. Miller and K. C. Hayes, "Vitamin Excess and Toxicity." In John N. Hathcock, ed., *Nutritional Toxicology, Vol. 1* (New York: Academic Press, 1982), pp. 81–133.

15. M. L. Wahlqvist, "Effects on Plasma Cholesterol of Nicotinic Acid and Its Analogues." In Michael H. Briggs, ed., *Vitamins in Human Biology and Medicine* (Boca Raton, Fla.: CRC Press, 1981).

16. R. B. Colletti et al., "Niacin Treatment of Hypercholesterolemia in Children," *Pediatrics* 92(July 1993): 78–82.

17. M. L. Schwartz, "Severe Reversible Hyperglycemia as a Consequence of Niacin Therapy," *Arch Int Med* 13(September 1993):2050–2052.

18. James W. Long, *The Essential Guide to Prescription Drugs* (New York: Harper & Row, 1985).

19. K. H. Bassler, "Megavitamin Therapy With Pyridoxine," *Int J Vitam Nutr Res* 58(1, 1988):105–118.

20. M. G. Brush and M. Perry, "Pyridoxine and the Premenstrual Syndrome, *Lancet* (June 15, 1985):1399.

21. J. Mouret et al., "Treatment of Narcolepsy with L-Tyrosine, *Lancet* (December 24/31, 1988): 1458–1459.

22. R. Crellin et al., "Folates and Psychiatric Disorders: Clinical Potential," *Drugs* 45(May 1993):623–636.

23. R. Prakash and W. M. Petrie, "Psychiatric Changes Associated with an Excess of Folic Acid," *Clin Psychiatry* 139(September 1982): 1192–1193.

24. M. B. Zimmerman and B. Shane, "Supplemental Folic Acid," *Am J Clin Nutr* 58(August 1993):127–128.

25. G. M. Jaffe, "Vitamin C." In Lawrence J. Machlin, ed., *Handbook of Vitamins: Nutritional, Biochemical, and Clinical Aspects* (New York: Marcel Dekker, 1984), pp. 199–244.

26. Linus Pauling, *How to Live Longer and Feel Better* (New York: W. H. Freeman, 1986).

27. J. Costello, "Re: Ascorbic Acid Overdosing: A Risk Factor for Calcium Oxalate Nephrolithiasis" (letter), *J Urol* 149(May 1993):1146.

28. William H. Philpott and Dwight K. Kalita, *Brain Allergies: The Psychonutrient Connection,* rev. ed. (New Canaan, Conn.: Keats Publishing, 1987).

29. Sheldon Saul Hendler, *The Oxygen Breakthrough: Thirty Days to an Illness-Free Life* (New York: William Morrow, 1989).

30. A. Koppen et al., "Synergistic Effect of Nicotinamide and Choline Administration on Extracellular Choline Levels in the Brain," *J Pharmacol Exper Therapeutics* 266(August 1993):720–725.

31. N. Edwards, "Mental Disturbances Related to Metals." In Richard C. W. Hall, ed., *Psychiatric Presentations of Medical Illness* (Jamaica, N.Y.: Spectrum Publications, 1980), pp. 283–308.

32. B. P. Bourgoin et al., "Lead Content in 70 Brands of Dietary Calcium Supplements," *Am J Pub Health* 83(August 1993):1155–1160.

33. C. C. Pfeiffer and S. LaMola, "Zinc and Manganese in the Schizophrenias," *J Orthomolecular Psychiatry* 12(3, 1983):215–34.

34. M. B. Keller et al., "Subsyndromal Symptoms in Bipolar Disorder: A Comparison of Standard and Low Serum Levels of Lithium," *Arch Gen Psychiatry* 49(May 1992):371–376.

35. V. I. Reus, "Behavioral Aspects of Thyroid Disease in Women," *Psychiatric Clin North Am* 12(March 1989):153–165.

36. E. F. Staufenberg and D. Tantam, "Malignant Hyperpyrexia Syndrome in Combined Treatment" (letter), *Brit J Psychiatry* 154(April 1989):577–578.

37. D. F. Horrobin, "The Role of Essential Fatty Acids and Prostaglandins in the Premenstrual Syndrome," *J Reprod Med* 28(July 1983):465–468.

38. D. O. Rudin, "The Three Pellagras," *J Orthomolecular Psychiatry* 12(2, 1983): 91–110.

39. D. O. Rudin, "The Major Psychoses and Neuroses as Omega-3 Essential Fatty Acid Deficiency Syndrome: Substrate Pellagra," *Biol Psychiatry* 16(September 1981):837–850.

40. Donald O. Rudin and Clare Felix, *The Omega-3 Phenomenon: The Nutrition Breakthrough of the '80s* (New York: Rawson Associates, 1987).

41. M. E. Wolf and A. D. Mosnaim, "Phenylethylamine in Neuropsychiatric Disorders," *Gen Pharmacol* 14(4, 1983):385–390.

42. G. Gardos et al., "The Acute Effects of a Loading Dose of Phenylalanine in Unipolar Depressed Patients With and Without Tardive Dyskinesia," *Neuropsychopharmacology,* 6(June 1992):241–247.

43. Arnold Fox and Barry Fox, *DLPA to End Chronic Pain and Depression* (New York: Pocket Books, 1985).

44. J. F. Rosenbaum et al., "An Open-Label Pilot Study of Oral S-Adenosyl-L-Methionine in Major Depression: Interim Results," *Psychopharmacol Bull,* 24(1, 1988):189–194.

45. B. L. Kagan et al., "Oral *S*-Adenosylmethionine in Depression: A Randomized, Double-Blind, Placebo-Controlled Trial," *Am J Psychiatry,* 147(May 1990):591–595.

46. H. M. van Praag, "Management of Depression with Serotonin Precursors," *Biol Psychiatry,* 16(3, 1981):291–310.

47. Robert L. Pollock et al., *The Pain-Free Tryptophan Diet* (New York: Warner Books, 1986).

48. W. E. Catterall, "Tryptophan and Bladder Cancer" (letter), *Biol Psychiatry,* 24(October 1988):733–734.

49. A. H. Meir et al., "Tryptophan Feeding Adversely Influences Pregnancy," *Life Sciences,* 32(March 14, 1983):1193–1196.

50. T. L. Sourkes, "Toxicology of Serotonin Precursors," *Adv Biol Psychiatry*, 10(1983):160–175.

51. H. Sternbach, "The Serotonin Syndrome," *Am J Psychiatry*, 148(June 1991):705–713.

52. R. Persson, "Serotonergt Syndrom—En Fallbeskrivning" ["The Serotonin Syndrome—A Case Report"], *Nordisk Psykiatrisk Tidsskrift* 46(2, 1992): 117–119.

53. L. J. van Hiele, "*L*-5-Hydroxytryptophan in Depression: The First Substitution Therapy in Psychiatry?" *Neuropsychobiology* 6(4, 1980): 230–240.

54. MaryLynn D. Bryce, letter to author on behalf of David Kessler, M.D., Commissioner of the Food and Drug Administration, January 27, 1992.

THIRTEEN

Reactive Hypoglycemia: Emotional Havoc from the Wrong Kinds of Sweets and Starches

In the 1960s and 1970s, if you were into alternative medicine, you were almost certainly aware of reactive hypoglycemia. Self-help books by the dozen claimed that this disorder of blood sugar regulation lay lurking behind just about every mental disease and malaise, from clinical depression to criminal aggression. The cure? Just say no to refined carbohydrates (sugar, white flour, etc.), caffeine and booze.

Medical authorities balked. Reactive hypoglycemia is rare, they protested, and rarely if ever does it cause these myriad maladies. Although it may no longer be the self-help syndrome of the decade, the battle continues.

WILL THE REAL HYPOGLYCEMIA PLEASE STAND UP? _____

On some things orthodox physicians and proponents of the alternative view of reactive hypoglycemia (we'll call them "hypoglycemia doctors") agree.

Hypoglycemia means pathologically low (*hypo*) blood (*emia*) sugar (*glyc*).

Blood sugar is our major fuel source. It consists entirely of *glucose*, the simplest carbohydrate unit in most of the sugars and starches (complex carbohydrates) we eat. *Reactive* hypoglycemia typically happens like this: After eating or drinking something that sharply *raises* blood sugar—refined sugar or starch, alcohol or caffeine (these latter pull stored sugar from the liver)—the body over-reacts. It secretes so much insulin (the hormone that admits blood sugar into the cells) that, within a few hours, the blood sugar is too low for comfort. The brain especially feels the pinch, for it depends exclusively on blood sugar. Mental confusion, faintness, fatigue, dizziness, headache, spasms, yawning, blurred vision, cold spells or other symptoms may occur. Next, the adrenal glands may pour stress hormones into the blood to release sugar from the liver. This can mean more trouble, for these hormones can trigger nervousness, trembling, palpitations and other symptoms—*especially hunger.* Ironically, the hunger may drive the sufferer right back to the cookie jar.

Traditionally, reactive hypoglycemia has been diagnosed with the help of the *oral glucose tolerance test* (OGTT). On an empty stomach, the patient downs a few ounces of glucose in water. Over the next four or six hours his blood sugar is periodically measured. If it drops abnormally low (below 50 or 60 mg/dl), and if his symptoms flare up around then, reactive hypoglycemia may be diagnosed. Increasingly, however, experts are refusing to make the diagnosis unless they can measure low blood sugar levels during a *real life* symptomatic flare-up—and if a stiff dose of sugar brings relief.[1,2]

The hypoglycemia doctors (among whom are numbered most orthomolecular psychiatrists) use and interpret the OGTT much more flexibly. Even if the glucose nadir (the lowest blood sugar reading) is technically "normal," they will still diagnose reactive hypoglycemia if any of several other conditions are met:[3,4]

1. The blood sugar fails to rise substantially above the fasting level.
2. It falls sharply (i.e., by 50 mg/dl or more per hour) at any time.
3. The nadir is appreciably lower than the fasting blood sugar level.
4. The patient has any symptoms at any time during the test.

Predictably, studies in which the OGTT has been strictly interpreted have usually found reactive hypoglycemia in only a small proportion of people so diagnosed by hypoglycemia doctors.[1,2] But there have been significant exceptions. In studies from the National Institute of Mental Health (NIMH) and elsewhere, an extremely high incidence of reactive hypoglycemia has been documented in women with PMS, phobias and panic disorder,[5,6] and among impulsive, violent, suicidal or self-mutilating criminals.[7]

Other research has lent credence to the hypoglycemia doctors' liberal manner of interpreting the OGTT. Careful investigations have led authorities to concede that "normal" blood sugar nadirs—as high as 75 mg/dl—provoke symptoms in some sensitive hypoglycemics.[1,2] The *hypoglycemic index* (HI) is a measure of how sharply blood sugar falls during the 90 minutes before the nadir. Several research groups have shown that it's high in most people with symptoms of reactive hypoglycemia, *whether or not their glucose nadirs are low,* and that it's low in most people with no symptoms.[8,9] In one study from the University of British Columbia, subjects with high HIs experienced up to five times the psychological symptomatology before, during and after the nadir as subjects with low HIs.[9]

Other research supports, albeit in a left-handed way, the hypoglycemia doctors' willingness to diagnose reative hypoglycemia no matter when symptoms occur during the OGTT. Researchers at MIT and other centers have shown that people, women especially, tend to become lethargic and drowsy 30 minutes or two or three hours after eating a very sweet or starchy, low protein meal.[10] Ironically, these reactions have occurred while blood sugar is still *rising,* so the culprit must be something other than reactive hypoglycemia. The researchers believe it's soporifically high brain levels of *serotonin,* for insulin, which rises sharply after a carbohydrate meal, promotes the passage of serotonin's precursor, tryptophan, into the brain. Whatever the explanation, these findings confirm that *hyperglycemic* foods—sweets and starches that rapidly raise blood sugar—are a problem for some people. Even a typically skeptical authority maintains that people who think they have reactive hypoglycemia, but don't, do have some kind of problem handling refined carbohydrates and are best off without them.[11]

Yet depressives are more likely to see refined carbohydrates as a solution. Research from MIT,[12] NIMH,[13] and elsewhere has made it abundantly clear that many depressives—in particularly those who have winter depression, premenstrual depression, "atypical" depression or who are alcoholic—compulsively snack on hyperglycemic foods to feel better, to feel less fatigued, less tense, less confused—and less depressed.[12] To the MIT group, these carbohydrate fixes are benign "self-medication"—an instinctive attempt to raise depressingly low brain levels of serotonin (Chapter 11).[12] But to the hypoglycemia doctors, the sweet "fix" only perpetuates in the long run what it medicates for the moment. After all, carbohydrate-craving depressives remain depressed, despite the temporary relief they buy from food.[12] And their habit makes them prey to obesity, tooth decay, malnutrition and other health problems. But get them to give up their "drug" of choice, hypoglycemia doctors claim, and their symptoms gradually fade. Their depressions "disappear almost magically when hypoglycemia is corrected."[14]

So, perhaps, do any serotonin deficiencies they may have. High in unrefined complex carbohydrates, the most popular diet for reactive hypoglycemia would likely foster a steady, stable supply of serotonin in the brain. In contrast, the typical high protein, refined-carbohydrate-rich diet of modern Westerners provokes an unstable feast-and-famine serotonin situation in the brain.

Hypoglycemia doctors are not the only ones who vouch for antihypoglycemia diets. Mainstream internist Richard Podell reports: "About 40 percent of my patients whose history suggests a sugar-related problem improve after adopting an antihypoglycemia diet. Most continue to benefit for months or years. Thus I don't believe they are fooling themselves with a placebo effect."[15(p.33)]

For years, psychologists at Texas A & M University have been demonstrating that "a refined sucrose- and caffeine-free diet ameliorates depression and other symptoms such as anxiety and fatigue in selected individuals."[16] In one study, they prescribed an antihypoglycemia diet for four people with symptoms of reactive hypoglycemia or sugar/caffeine intolerance. All improved markedly. When they returned to their old diets two weeks later, they relapsed. Back on the antihypoglycemia diet they improved again. At least three had suffered from depression, including one fairly severe case which was turned off and on by each dietary switch. Later, three of the subjects were misinformed that sugar and caffeine weren't a problem for them after all. Greatly relieved, they returned to their old diets. They relapsed again.[17]

Most recently, at the annual meeting of the American Psychological Association, the Texas researchers and others reported their latest findings. In one study from Northern Arizona University, depressed subjects on a low sugar, high complex-carbohydrate diet were less fatigued than those on a high sugar, low complex-carbohydrate diet.[18]

DO YOU HAVE REACTIVE HYPOGLYCEMIA? _____

An OGTT, especially if interpreted by a hypoglycemia doctor, can help determine whether you have reactive hypoglycemia. The larger issue, however, is if refined carbohydrates are a problem for you—for whatever reason. If the timing of your symptoms or carbohydrate craving leads you to suspect they are, there's no harm in trying an antihypoglycemia diet on for size. Refined carbohydrates aren't good for you anyway.

TREATING REACTIVE HYPOGLYCEMIA _____

Two very different kinds of diets are recommended by hypoglycemia doctors (and conventional doctors) for reactive hypoglycemia. Both diets are in accord that sugar and sweets (including sucrose, glucose, dextrose, maltose, corn syrup and honey, but not necessarily fructose), caffeine, alcohol and tobacco should be eliminated; that refined complex carbohydrates (e.g., white bread) must be used very sparingly, if at all; and that non-starchy vegetables may be eaten freely. However, the traditional "Seale-Harris" anti-hypoglycemia diet severely restricts *all* carbohydrate-rich foods, including fresh fruits, whole grains and legumes, and heartily recommends large servings of fatty animal foods. This, of course, clashes with what most health authorities recommend today.

The other, more popular anti-hypoglycemia diet poses no such problems. The Airola diet[19] prescribes a low intake of meat and dairy foods and a high intake of whole, complex carbohydrate (high-fiber) foods: whole grains, legumes, nuts, seeds, vegetables and fresh fruits (provided they're not too sweet).

Still, some people reportedly fare better on the Seale-Harris diet.[15,20] If you're one of them, you can fashion a healthy version of it by selecting your fat and protein mainly from fish and seafood, wild game, fowl, low-fat dairy foods, nuts, seeds and (probably) beans.

Some hypoglycemia doctors claim that reactive hypoglycemia can also be allayed by certain foods and supplements: flaxseed, buckwheat, brewer's yeast, chromium, garlic and herbal bitters.[19-21] Bright light might also help. It reduces depression and carbohydrate craving in people with winter depression (Chapter 18).

Not everybody is sensitive to refined carbohydrates. Those who are may have other treatable conditions that make them so. Among these are allergies, digestive disorders, nutritional deficiencies, the Candida syndrome, endocrine disorders and emotional problems, including depression itself. These disorders can feed each other in a vicious circle. Treat one and you treat them all. Research suggests, for instance, that many depressed people with reactive hypoglycemia can be relieved of both conditions by taking serotonin-stimulating antidepressant drugs.[22] So a strict antihypoglycemia diet may not always be necessary when other antidepressant and health-promoting strategies are on the menu.

NOTES

1. F. D. Hofeldt, "Reactive Hypoglycemia," *Endocrinol Metabol Clin North Am* 18(March 1989):185–201.

2. J. Palardy et al., "Blood Glucose Measurements During Symptomatic Episodes in Patients With Suspected Postprandial Hypoglycemia," *N Eng J Med* 321(November 23, 1989):1421–1425.

3. H. L. Newbold, *Mega-Nutrients for Your Nerves* (New York: Berkley Books, 1975).

4. Carlton Fredericks, *Carlton Fredericks' New Low Blood Sugar and You* (New York: Putnam, 1985).

5. K. D. Denicoff et al., "Glucose Tolerance Testing in Women with Premenstrual Syndrome," *Am J Psychiatry* 147(April 1990):477–480.

6. T. W. Uhde et al., "Glucose Tolerance Testing in Panic Disorder," *Am J Psychiatry* 141(November 1984):1461–1463.

7. V. M. Linnoila and M. Virkkunen, "Aggression, Suicidality, and Serotonin," *J Clin Psychiatry* 53(Suppl., October 1992):46–51.

8. S. A. Chalew et al., "The Use of the Plasma Epinephrine Response in the Diagnosis of Idiopathic Postprandial Syndrome," *J Am Med Assoc* 251(February 3, 1984):612–615.

9. L. A. Taylor and S. J. Rachman, "The Effects of Blood Sugar Level Changes on Cognitive Function, Affective State, and Somatic Symptoms," *J Behav Med* 11(3, 1988):279–291.

10. B. Spring et al., "Psychobiological Effects of Carbohydrates," *J Clin Psychiatry* 50(Suppl., May 1989): 27–34.

11. J. B. Jaspan, "Hypoglycemia: Fact or Fiction?" *Hospital Practice—Office Edition* 24(March 30, 1989):11–12, 14.

12. R. J. Wurtman and J. J. Wurtman, "Carbohydrates and Depression," *Scientific American* (January, 1989):68–75.

13. E. Leibenluft et al., "Depressive Symptoms and the Self-Reported Use of Alcohol, Caffeine, and Carbohydrates in Normal Volunteers and Four Groups of Psychiatric Outpatients," *Am J Psychiatry* 150(February 1993):294–301.

14. Carlton Fredericks, *Carlton Fredericks' Nutrition Guide for the Prevention & Cure of Common Ailments & Diseases* (Simon and Schuster, 1982).

15. Richard N. Podell, *Doctor, Why Am I So Tired?* (New York: Pharos Books, 1987).

16. L. Christensen et al., "Dietary Alteration of Somatic Symptoms

and Regional Brain Electrical Activity," *Biol Psychiatry* 29(April 1, 1991):679–682.

17. L. Christensen et al., "Impact of a Dietary Change on Emotional Distress," *J Abnormal Psychol* 94(November 1985):565–579.

18. D. McDougall, "Coffee, Sugar a Tiring Medley," *Winnipeg Free Press,* 25 August 1993, p. B1.

19. Paavo Airola, *Hypoglycemia: A Better Approach* (Phoenix, Ariz.: Health Plus Publishers, 1977).

20. Patrick Quillin, *Healing Nutrients* (Chicago: Contemporary Books, 1987).

21. Simon Y. Mills, *The Dictionary of Modern Herbalism* (Rochester, Vt.: Healing Arts Press, 1988).

22. F. Lechin et al., "Doxepin Therapy for Postprandial Symptomatic Hypoglycaemic Patients," *Clin Sci* 80(April 1991):373–384.

FOURTEEN

Allergic Depression

Milk and all that comes from milk increases melancholy.
—ROBERT BURTON[1]

ALLERGIES just ain't what they used to be.

For many doctors and their patients, allergies have come to mean something much broader (and subtler) than sneezing, wheezing or itching whenever the immune system fires off its cannons at a peanut or a cat hair. These allergies needn't have anything to do with the immune system. And instead of making you scratchy, they can make you weepy—indeed, they can make you almost anything: achey, arthritic, psychotic, suicidal.

Ironically, these new-fangled allergies are just what doctors had in mind a century ago when they coined the term *allergy* to signify any altered or abnormal (*allos*) physiological reaction (*ergon*) to any material. Allergy simply meant "*x* doesn't agree with person *y*." Today, allergists who subscribe to this view call themselves *clinical ecologists.* They and like-minded practitioners, including most orthomolecular psychiatrists, reject the narrow, orthodox definition of allergy as a necessarily immunologic reaction, almost always triggered by a protein and confined to the superficial tissues of the body (the skin, the respiratory system, the digestive tract). Clinical ecologists maintain that any food, chemical or material is capable of triggering an adverse reaction in any organ of the body, with or without the help of the immune system. And they believe such allergies are a pervasive cause of human disease and distress.*

*Orthodox allergists and toxicologists also recognize the existence of nonimmunologic allergies, but they call them adverse food reactions, intolerances, or idiosyncratic toxic or pharmacologic reactions.[2,3] Unlike clinical ecologists,

They call those allergies that cause psychobehavioral or neurologic symptoms *cerebral* or *"brain" allergies*.

BRAIN ALLERGIES

Since early in this century medical journals have attested to the existence of what most doctors still regard as myth: allergies of the central nervous system, "brain allergies." "Allergies of the nervous system," stated one reviewer in 1976 in the academic journal of the American College of Allergists, *Annals of Allergy*, "cause diverse behavioral disturbances, including headaches, convulsions, learning disabilities, schizophrenia and depression."[4]

The case for brain allergies has been strengthened recently by a wave of double-blind, placebo-controlled trials. Judging by these studies, hidden food allergies are a common cause of migraine headaches[5] and hyperactivity,[6,7] and they may frequently be a factor in epilepsy,[6] schizophrenia[8] and depression.[9–11] While some authorities[12,13] have simply ignored these studies, dismissing brain allergies as "an epidemic of nonsense,"[12] other academics have been impressed, [14–17] even converted. When Dr. James C. Breneman, then chairman of the Food Allergy Committee of the American College of Allergists, revised his textbook on food allergy in 1984, he declared brain allergy to be a common cause of everything from poor concentration and neurosis to epilepsy and schizophrenia.[18]

ALLERGIC DEPRESSION

One of the most common symptoms of brain allergy is depression:

• Depression and allergy usually go together. "When one is relieved, so is the other," notes orthomolecular pioneer Abram Hof-

they consider such reactions—especially the psychobehavioral ones—to be rare. So they rarely look for them.

fer. "Treatment of the allergy will, in most cases, 'cure' the depression. I have seen this in several hundred patients over the past six years and can no longer doubt this conclusion."[19]

• At the Deaconess Hospital in St. Louis, psychiatrist George Ulett reports that severe, suicidal depression is one of "the myriad symptoms" he has found in food-allergic patients. "Such patients as these," he observes, "have improved markedly on diets eliminating those foods to which they reacted positively."[20]

Controlled research has tended to support these claims. Studies have consistently found an abnormally high rate of "atopic" (conventional immunologic) allergies among depressives.[16,17] In one study, depressed patients had four and a half times as many antibody reactions to 33 foods and inhalants as normal subjects. "Perhaps removing egg white, milk and cereal grains from their diets would prove to be an inexpensive way to initiate treatment for depressives," the researchers suggested.[21]

Why do depression and allergy go together? Psychologist Paul Marshall cites extensive evidence that the two conditions are both associated with a specific neurochemical imbalance (too much acetylcholine, not enough norepinephrine) and that by feeding this imbalance, each condition fuels the other.[17]

In a double-blind study, Dr. C. Keith Conners, a leading authority on hyperactivity, provoked mental and behavioral symptoms in nine out of ten adults with capsules of food they had tested allergic to. Placebo capsules had no effect.[10] In a similar study, David S. King of the University of California gave 30 psychiatric patients sublingual (under the tongue) extracts of foods to which they had been diagnosed allergic at a clinical ecology clinic. The patients had significantly more adverse psychological reactions—including severe depression—after the foods than after placebos. Later, those who complied with clinical ecological therapy fared better than those who didn't.[9]

In another double-blind study, 12 people—eight of them depressives—who claimed to have benefited from avoiding certain foods, proved significantly more reactive to those foods than to placebo.[17]

In a double-blind study from the University of Chicago Medical Center, psychiatrist John Crayton repeatedly challenged 23 psychiatric patients and 12 controls for eight days with sublingual drops of three common allergens—wheat, milk and chocolate—and placebo. "Only one of the normal subjects appeared to react to a food," Crayton reported, "while 16 of the 23 people who complained in the past of food sensitivity showed significant mood and behavior changes."[22] Most of the food-sensitive subjects, but not the controls, also showed immunologic signs of allergy.[11]

There have been very few negative studies[17,23] in which patients have reacted similarly to injections of allergens and placebo shots.

DO YOU HAVE ALLERGIC DEPRESSION? _____

Clinical ecologists find that certain factors increase the odds that your depression has an allergic cause.

• A history of atopic allergy (for example, hay fever, allergic asthma or eczema).

• Having symptoms highly suggestive of allergy: dark circles under the eyes ("allergic shiners"); large daily weight fluctuations due to water retention; fluctuating visual acuity. Also suggestive: fatigue and mental fogginess, especially in the morning; tension or irritability, possibly alternating with fatigue and depression (you may have outgrown this "tension-fatigue syndrome" in childhood and graduated to manic-depression); extreme sensitivity to noise, light, heat or cold; multiple aches and pains; spells of hyperarousal (e.g., palpitations, sweating, trembling).

• Addiction to foods or other substances. Clinical ecologists and mainstream researchers alike[22,24] have found that addictive behavior suggests allergy is afoot. The craved foods or drugs relieve for the moment the very symptoms they provoke in the long run. Addictive allergies to wheat, milk, chocolate and other commonly eaten foods are, in fact, said to account for most brain allergies. Interestingly, the proteins in some of these foods contain heroin-like peptides (protein breakdown products).[25]

DIAGNOSING ALLERGY

Clinical ecologists employ a variety of techniques to diagnose brain allergies. These include sublingual or intradermal (under-the-skin) provocation with suspected allergens, muscle testing, pulse testing, and lab tests (RAST, DIMSOFT, cytotoxic testing). (Traditional skin-patch testing is considered too insensitive.) Most of these techniques are controversial and unproven, but there is one that clinical ecologists and conventional allergists alike hold in high regard: *avoidance and provocation.*

Avoidance and Provocation

The principle is simple: If you avoid a food (or any other suspected allergen) for a few days or weeks and your symptoms improve, only to return when you eat the food again, you're probably allergic to it.

Because most allergic people prove to be intolerant of many foods, avoidance testing usually involves either going on an elimination diet (all common food allergens are eliminated), a hypoallergenic liquid diet such as Vivonex or a complete fast. (Suspected chemical allergens may also be avoided.)

During the first few days of avoidance, people with allergies typically go through a withdrawal phase, marked by cravings and symptomatic flare-ups. Some depressives become suicidal.[19] But after four to seven days (sometimes longer), most feel better, and some feel better than ever.

Foods can now be reintroduced, one per meal (sometimes, one per day). Because avoidance has cleared the person's system, his sensitivity to avoided allergens is dramatically exaggerated. A person who "never felt better" after abstaining from milk or eggs may find, when he eats them again, that he's "never felt worse."

(A stiff dose of baking soda, vitamin C and/or vitamin B6 can quell these exaggerated reactions, say clinical ecologists.)

TREATMENT

Avoiding the Enemy

The surest, simplest treatment for allergy is to avoid the enemy. Unfortunately, most people with brain allergies are at odds with a whole cupboardful of foods, most of them staples or favorites like wheat, milk, eggs, sugar, chocolate, tea, coffee and commonly used food additives. Familiarity, it seems, breeds allergy. (In Japan, rice allergy is rampant.) Fortunately, prolonged avoidance can breed renewed tolerance. After a few months, clinical ecologists report, people can usually reintroduce allergenic foods into their diets without ill effect—provided they don't get too familiar again. Enter "the rotary diversified diet." It prohibits you from eating any food more than once every four days or from eating members of the same food family (like potatoes and tomatoes) more than once every two days.[26,27]

Avoiding the enemy isn't the only way to cope with food allergies. You also can boost your ability to fight it.

Neutralization Therapy

Clinical ecologists report that just as they can turn allergic reactions on with sublingual drops or shots, they usually can turn them off with highly dilute doses of the very same allergens. When their patients take these diluted allergens regularly, clinical ecologists claim, their tolerance for the foods themselves is usually vastly improved. Some research casts serious doubt on these claims.[23] However, in a recent double-blind, placebo-controlled study, bimonthly injections of diluted allergens mixed with digestive enzyme enabled 16 out of 20 hyperactive children to tolerate their food allergens without relapse.[7]

Allergy-busting Supplements

In megadoses, certain nutrients can help prevent or relieve allergic reactions, including brain allergies, clinical ecologists claim.[27] The major ones are niacin, vitamin B6 and (especially) vitamin C, whose allergy-busting power has been experimentally verified.[18] Others include vitamin B5, methionine, calcium, free-form amino acids and lithium.[28] Interestingly, most of these nutrients seem to be antidepressants too.

Treating Underlying Disorders

Allergic reactivity is promoted by a variety of factors, many of them treatable.[3,18,26,27] An interesting example is "leaky gut," a type of malabsorption which gives allergenic food molecules easy access to the bloodstream. Leaky gut is promoted by emotional distress, certain drugs (alcohol, aspirin, methotrexate), celiac disease and intestinal overgrowth of gut-damaging microbes like *Candida* and *Giardia*. In one study, 11 of 32 chronic psychiatric inpatients were found to have this condition.[29] Other promoters of allergy include immunologic hyperactivity; indigestion and malabsorption; nutritional deficiencies; genetic flaws in handling certain food chemicals (as in lactose intolerance, celiac disease and phenylketonuria); alcohol abuse; diabetes; hypothyroidism; liver disease; febrile illnesses; emotional distress; and possibly mercury-amalgam dental fillings, menstruation, and fluorescent light.

It's interesting that a physical condition—allergy—that can promote mental upsets and disorders can also be promoted *by* them. But then, this kind of "reciprocausal relationship" (to coin a term) is typical in the mind-body domain. Emotional distress spreads its shock waves throughout the entire body. The digestive and immune systems, which handle allergenic foods and chemicals, are not spared. Just as we may be able to fight depression by avoiding provocative foods and chemicals, we may also be able to fight allergy by getting our mental house in order. Reportedly, some people who attribute their mental symptoms to allergy have responded to psychotherapy.[30] Through hypnotherapy,

FOOD ADDITIVES AND PESTICIDE RESIDUES

Not just foods, but food chemicals—additives, pesticide residues—may cause brain allergies in sensitive people.

The allergist Benjamin Feingold first brought this issue to public attention in the 1970s. His additive-free diet for hyperactive children was roundly condemned by medical authorities. But careful research has since led most to concede that some hyperactive children do react to additives in their food.[2,15,32] Notably, Feingold claimed that adults also react psychologically to artificial food colors.[33]

Clinical ecologists share Feingold's sentiments. They also implicate pesticide residues as the source of many people's brain allergies to fruits and vegetables. A patient of Theron Randolph's, for instance, "became depressed for days whenever she ate commercially available oranges." No such problem with organic oranges.[26]

In his book, *Diet for a Poisoned Planet,* David Steinman lists the pesticide residues in hundreds of foods and suggests ways that readers can devise a low-pesticide diet for themselves.[34] "Once you follow these instructions," advises EPA Senior Science Advisor William Marcus in his foreword, "feelings of tiredness and lack of clarity of thought will diminish and feelings of general well-being will return once again."[34]

others have deconditioned their trigger-happy psychoneuroimmunoallergic reflexes.[14,31] Living in fear of allergens may not be the only option.

GETTING HELP

The following organizations can help you find a qualified practitioner of clinical ecology:

Human Ecology Action League (HEAL)
P. O. Box 1369, Evanston, IL 60204
(312) 864–0995

American Academy of Environmental Medicine
P. O. Box 16106, Denver, CO 80216
(303) 662–9755

NOTES

1. Robert Burton, *The Anatomy of Melancholy*, 1621, various publishers.

2. B. Weiss, "Intersections of Psychiatry and Toxicology," *Int J Ment Health* 14(3, 1985):7–25.

3. American Academy of Allergy and Immunology Committee on Adverse Reactions to Foods, National Institute of Allergy and Infectious Diseases, *Adverse Reactions to Foods* (NIH Publication No. 84–2442, July 1984).

4. K. Hall, "Allergy of the Nervous System: A Review," *Ann Allergy* 36(January 1976):49–64.

5. L. E. Mansfield, "The Role of Food Allergy in Migraine: A Review," *Ann Allergy* 58(May 1987):313–317.

6. J. Egger et al., "Oligoantigenic Diet Treatment of Children with Epilepsy and Migraine," *J Pediatrics* 114(January 1989):51–58.

7. J. Egger et al., "Controlled Trial of Hyposensitisation in Children With Food-Induced Hyperkinetic Syndrome," *Lancet* 339(May 9, 1992):1150–1153.

8. D. N. Vlissides et al., "A Double-Blind Gluten-Free/Gluten-Load Controlled Trial in a Secure Ward Population," *Brit J Psychiatry* 148(April 1986):447–451.

9. D. S. King, "Can Allergic Exposure Provoke Psychological Symptoms? A Double-Blind Test," *Biol Psychiatry* 16(January 1981):3–19.

10. C. Keith Conners, *Food Additives and Hyperactive Children* (New York: Plenum Press, 1980).

11. J. W. Crayton, "Effects of Food Challenges on Complement Components in 'Food-Sensitive' Psychiatric Patients and Controls," *J Allergy Clin Immunol* 73(Suppl. 1, 1984):134.

12. S. Barrett, "Unproven 'Allergies': An Epidemic of Nonsense," *Nutr Today* (March/April 1989): 6–11.

13. A. I. Terr, "Clinical Ecology" (editorial), *J Allergy Clin Immunol* 79(March 1978):423–426.

14. Richard N. Podell, *Doctor, Why Am I So Tired?* (New York: Pharos Books, 1987).

15. M. A. Lipton and J. C. Wheless, "Diet as Therapy." In Sanford Miller, ed., *Nutrition & Behavior* (Philadelphia: Franklin Institute Press, 1981), pp. 213–233.

16. I. R. Bell, "Allergens, Physical Irritants, Depression, and Shyness," *J Appl Develop Psychol* 13(April–June 1992):125–133.

17. P. S. Marshall, "Allergy and Depression: A Neurochemical Threshold Model of the Relation Between the Illnesses," *Psychol Bull* 113(January 1993):23–43.

18. James C. Breneman, *Basics of Food Allergy,* second ed. (Springfield, Ill.: Charles C Thomas, 1984).

19. A. Hoffer, "Allergy, Depression and Tricyclic Antidepressants," *J Orthomolecular Psychiatry* 9(3, 1980):164–70.

20. G. Ulett, "Food Allergy—Cytotoxic Testing and the Central Nervous System," *Psychiatric J Univ Ottawa* 5(2, 1980):100–108.

21. A. A. Sugerman et al., "A Study of Antibody Levels in Alcoholic, Depressive and Schizophrenic Patients," *Ann Allergy* 48(March 1982):166–171.

22. G. Maleskey, "Find Your Food Foes and Discover Relief," *Prevention* 38(April 1986):97–112.

23. D. I. Jewett et al., "A Double-Blind Study of Symptom Provocation to Determine Food Sensitivity," *N England J Med* 323(August 16, 1990):429–433.

24. E. C. Hughes et al., "Migraine: A Diagnostic Test for Etiology of Food Sensitivity by a Nutritionally Supported Fast and Confirmed by Long Term Report," *Ann Allergy* 55(1985):28–32.

25. J. E. Morley, "Food Peptides: A New Class of Hormones?" *J Am Med Assoc* 247(May 7, 1982):2379–2380.

26. Theron G. Randolph and Ralph W. Moss, *An Alternative Approach to Allergies,* rev. ed. (New York: Harper & Row, 1989).

27. William H. Philpott and Dwight K. Kalita, *Brain Allergies: The Psychonutrient Connection* (New Canaan, Conn.: Keats Publishing, 1980, 1987).

28. Abram Hoffer and Morton Walker, *Orthomolecular Nutrition* (New Canaan, Conn.: Keats Publishing, 1978).

29. N. C. Wood et al., "Abnormal Intestinal Permeability: An Aetiological Factor in Chronic Psychiatric Disorders?" *Brit J Psychiatry* 150(1987):853–856.

30. D. E. Stewart "Psychiatric Assessment of Patients with '20th Century Disease' ('Total Allergy Syndrome')," *Can Med Assoc J* 133(1985):1001–1006.

31. Emmett E. Miller, *Software for the Mind: How to Program Your Own Mind for Optimum Health & Performance* (Berkeley, Calif.: Celestial Arts, 1987).

32. G. Kolata, "Consensus on Diets and Hyperactivity," *Science* 215(February 19, 1982):958.

33. Robert Buist, *Food Chemical Sensitivity: What It Is and How to Cope with It* (San Leandro, Calif.: Prism Press, 1986).

34. David Steinman, *Diet For a Poisoned Planet* (New York: Harmony Books, 1990).

FIFTEEN

Guidelines for a Healthy, Antidepressant Diet

IN the last few chapters on nutrition we've covered a lot of ground. In this chapter, I'd like to offer something simpler: a few very basic guidelines.

These guidelines are based on the best of what nutritional science and alternative medicine (including non-Western traditions) can tell us about eating for health in general, and for mental health in particular. It's not necessary to follow them to the letter. Just give them your serious consideration and take from them what you can or will.

1. *Favor whole foods over food* fractions. The foodstuffs that give us the most health problems are parts or fractions of food—sugar, sodium, fat, refined grains and so on—and the pseudo-foods made from them—junk pastries, "balloon bread," super fruit whizzy pops. Food fractions promote nutritional deficiencies and imbalances. Refined carbohydrates (sugar, white flour, white rice, etc.) and refined fats and oils have lost most of the nutrients we need to properly utilize them. It's no coincidence that eating too much "fractional" food and not enough whole food is a major cause of the diseases of civilization (cancer, heart disease . . . depression?).

2. *Minimize your consumption of foods and food products that have been* traumatically *processed or prepared.* Frying and other cooking methods that burn or brown food create billions of mu-tant chemicals that can be toxic or carcinogenic. Aggressive

commercial food processing—the refining of oils and grains, for example—typically devitalizes, contaminates, nutritionally depletes and chemically alters its wholesome starting materials.

3. *Look for food that's clean, pure and uncontaminated.* Steer away from commercial, additive-rich products. Wash foods thoroughly to remove chemical residues. Consider buying organic, unsprayed produce or avoiding the most pesticide-laden foods.[1]

4. *Eat a good balance of the different tissues and organs found in food—roots, seeds (including nuts, grains and legumes), leaves, flowers (e.g., broccoli), stalks, shoots, stems, fruits, (and if you eat meat) muscles, viscera (organ meats) and even bones and marrow (e.g., in soup stocks).* Because every tissue is rich in some nutrients, deficient in others, an "anatomically rounded" diet is a nutritionally well-balanced one, too.

5. *Maximize your consumption of fresh, "live" foods.* The nutritional value of food falls rapidly after harvesting or slaughter; decay immediately sets in, creating unwholesome new compounds. In contrast, raw foods may have special medicinal value. Raw nuts, seeds and cold-pressed oils, for instance, can reportedly raise low hormone levels.[2] As we saw in Chapter 5, this could be just what many depressives need.

6. *Beware of compulsive food preferences or of eating the same foods every day, all year around.* As we've seen in Chapter 14, eating any particular food too much or too often may promote addictive allergy.

7. *Respect your appetite.* Eating when you have no appetite— or eating what you have no appetite for—is a dubious practice. Pleasure in the smell and taste of food primes the digestive organs. If food is unappetizing, it's liable to go over poorly down below, provoking indigestion, malabsorption or allergy. Of course, if severe depression has eliminated your appetite, following it could eventually eliminate you. But then this might be the perfect

opportunity to undertake a medically-supervised fast to see if food allergies are getting you down.

8. *Consider eating in accordance with* who, what, when *and* where *you are—that is, eating* idiosyncratically, ancestrally, seasonally and geographically.

• Eating idiosyncratically (according to who you are) means listening to your body and respecting your appetites and preferences—within the context of a wholesome diet (your passion for jelly-fudge squares doesn't count here). It can also mean varying your diet to suit your constitutional type, as is the tradition in Eastern health systems like Ayurveda.

• Eating ancestrally is based on the idea that the diet that suited your ancestors' genes (assuming you know what they ate) probably suits yours too. When Northwest Coastal Indians return to their traditional, salmon-based diets, they reportedly become dramatically less prey to the suicidal depressions and other disorders that plague them on the modern Western diet.[3]

• Eating seasonally and geographically is based on the idea that different seasons and geographic/climatic conditions stress us in different ways. By eating creatures adapted to these conditions we can adapt better ourselves. This may be why the oils of cold-adapted fish and plants protect people in northern industrialized countries from the diseases of civilization while heat-adapted saturated fats do just the opposite.

Eating seasonally/geographically might be especially relevant to preventing seasonal/geographic mood disorders, such as winter and summer depression (Chapter 18).

NOTES

1. David Steinman, *Diet For a Poisoned Planet* (New York: Harmony Books, 1990).

2. H. L. Newbold, *Mega-Nutrients for Your Nerves* (New York: Berkley Books, 1975).

3. C. E. Bates, "Racially Determined Abnormal Essential Fatty Acid and Prostaglandin Metabolism and Food Allergies Linked to Autoimmune, Inflammatory, and Psychiatric Disorders among Coastal British Columbia Indians," *Medical Hypotheses* 25(1988):103–109.

SIXTEEN

Helpful Herbs

HERBALISM has always been the mainstay of world medicine. Even in the West today, one in every four drugs is herbal in origin.[1] Increasingly, research is affirming the benefits of herbs themselves: valerian for insomnia, feverfew for migraines, ginkgo biloba for dementia, garlic . . for everything!

That herbs can have powerful psychological effects is obvious from our experience with marijuana, cocaine (coca) and heroin (poppy). But herbalists claim there are milder herbal "nervines" that can medicate our mental ills more safely. For depression, the nervines of choice are called *nervous restoratives*.[2,3] Taken daily for weeks or months, herbalists maintain, these rejuvenative nervines bring "slow but real improvement" to depressed or debilitated users.[3(p. 78)]

Some nervous restoratives are relatively tranquilizing. These herbs, which include balm, lavender, licorice, marjoram, scullcap and vervain, are particularly good for depressives with insomnia, anxiety, or aches and pains.[1,3,4] Stimulating nervous restoratives—such as basil, ginseng, rosemary and sage—are better for fatigued or retarded depressives.[1,4,5]

Some nervines are *very* stimulating. These herbal stimulants—black tea, kava kava, kola (cola nut), damiana, green tea, safflower, saffron, yerba mate and yohimbe, among others[2-6]—can help depressives "reassert vitality and activity," says Simon Mills, a prominent British herbalist.[3(p. 197)] Indeed, yohimbine (derived from yohimbe) did just that for one depressive at Massachusetts General Hospital.[7]

Herbal stimulants must be used in moderation, Mills cautions, with support from nervous restoratives, good diet and nutritional supplements. Otherwise they can drain the brain's own stimulants.

Coffee is an example of the mixed blessings bestowed by strong herbal stimulants. Though it's touted as a mild antidepressant by some,[8] large doses of caffeine have been shown in controlled research to worsen many people's moods.[9] For some depressed java freaks, less coffee, not more, spells relief (see Chapter 13).[9]

SOME POPULAR HERBAL ANTIDEPRESSANTS ───────────

Balm (lemon balm, melissa): "Balm is sovereign for the brain, strengthening the memory, and powerfully chasing away melancholy,"[5(p.42)] a traditional herbalist, quite typically, wrote in extolling this gentle nervine. Modern herbalists still regard balm as a relaxing antidepressant, particularly agreeable to children.[1,3,10]

Damiana: Reputed to be an aphrodisiac,[3] damiana has testosterone-like properties which may also account for its reputation as a simulating antidepressant.[3,11,12]

Ginkgo biloba: Research suggests this pricey Indian herb can enhance mental performance, energy and mood, and even combat senile dementia.[13]

Ginseng: Ginseng—both the Asian *Panax* variety and the Siberian **Eleutherococcus** type (which, botanically, isn't actually a ginseng)—has a timeless reputation as an invigorating panacea for the frail, the weary and the senescent. It's also said to be useful for depression.[1–3,14,15]

Modern research lends credence to these claims.[14,15] In double-blind studies from Maudsley and St. Francis's hospitals in London, for instance, Korean ginseng boosted the performance of nurses and patients alike.[15] In a German study, it elevated the mood of 95 nursing home residents.[15]

AROMATHERAPY

"The way to health is to have an aromatic bath and scented massage every day," Hippocrates once said, apparently to his wife after a long, hard day at the clinic.[18(p.89)] As usual, Hippocrates had a nose for good medicine.

• At Duke University, pain has been relieved by the scent of peach.[19]

• In a study from the Rensselaer Polytechnic Institute, fragrant commercial air fresheners lightened office-workers' moods.[20]

• At Yale, the smell of apples and spices has been deeply relaxing, lavender mildly alerting and other scents have appeared to curb hunger, ease pain and relieve depression.[19,21]

• At the University of Vienna, caffeine-crazed rats have chilled out by whiffing lavender. Just like grandma's herbal pillows, the researchers exclaim.[22]

• In Italy, researchers have blown anxiety and depression away with a fine mist spray of essential plant oils.[23]

None of these findings have come as a surprise to aromatherapists. They've been freshening the air of sick rooms for millenia. For depression, they recommend the scents of the following essential plant oils (oils with an "r" also tend to relieve anxiety, anger, pain, and insomnia; oils with an "s" are stimulants; some oils are both):[24,25] Bergamot (r); clary sage (r); geranium (r; s in high doses); jasmine (r, s); lavender (r; s in high doses); marjoram (r); neroli (r; s in high doses); nutmeg (r); orange blossom (r); osmanthus (r); patchouli (r, s); rose (r); thyme (s) and ylang-ylang (r, s).

Here's how you can use essential oils:[19,24,25]

• A few drops can either be dabbed on a hot surface (a radiator, a bowl of hot water), dissolved in water and sprayed from a mister, sprinkled in your bath or placed in the medication well of a vaporizer.

- Five to 50 drops (depending on the oil) can be dissolved in 100 ml of massage oil.

- Some oils, like lavender and orange blossom, can be used as perfumes.

  For another kind of aromatherapy, try fresh flowers or incense.

Medicinally useful ginseng is never cheap. To avoid buying junk, buy only from a knowledgeable, reputable dealer.

Gotu kola: What ginseng is to Chinese herbalism, gotu kola is to Indian herbalism—a rejuvenant for the nervous and immune systems that supposedly increases intelligence, combats senility and relieves psychiatric ills, including depression.[2,3,11]

Oats: Once reputed to be an antidote for drug addiction,[8] oats and oatstraw still rank among herbalism's favorite nervous restoratives and antidepressants.[3,6,10,12]

St. John's Wort: St. John's Wort contains a chemical named hypericin which, like some antidepressant drugs, is an MAO inhibitor. In a small German study, the wort seemed to live up to its reputation as an antidepressant.[16]

Many other herbs are also reputed to have antidepressant effects. Among them are basil, bee pollen, borage, kola (cola nut), lavender, rosemary, thyme and vervain.[1-6,11,12]

USING HERBS _____

For medicinal purposes, dried herbs are usually steeped in boiled water to make a tea. If they're hard, they're gently boiled or simmered to make a decoction. Powdered, encapsulated herbs and herbal tinctures are also popular.

Therapeutic dosages of dried herbs usually range from 1 to 6 grams, two to four times a day.[1,3] Typically, the blander or sweeter tasting the herb, the higher the dosage.[2] Capsule dosages are usually half to a quarter as much.[2] Some herbs, like ginseng and gotu kola, may be prescribed in "courses": you take them for a few weeks, then pause for a week or two before repeating, if necessary.

Herbs may be contraindicated if you're pregnant (saffron, for instance, can cause miscarriage) or if you have certain medical conditions. Some can cause allergic reactions or side effects which can be annoying (such as rash, insomnia or headache) or, in rare cases, dangerous or fatal (liver damage, anaphylactic shock or heart failure).[17] So before using an herb, it's prudent to consult authoritative books or practitioners. Start with a low dosage and increase gradually, watching both for progress and adverse reactions.

NOTES

1. Gaea Weiss and Shandor Weiss, *Growing and Using Healing Herbs* (Emmaus, Penn.: Rodale Press, 1985).

2. Vasant Lad and David Frawley, *The Yoga of Herbs* (Santa Fe, N. M.: Lotus Press, 1986).

3. Simon Y. Mills, *The Dictionary of Modern Herbalism* (Rochester, Vt.: Healing Arts Press, 1988).

4. Jean Valnet, *The Practice of Aromatherapy* (Rochester, Vt.: Destiny Books, 1980).

5. W. T. Fernie, *Old-Fashioned Herbal Remedies* (Toronto: Coles, 1980).

6. F. Mitton and V. Mitton, *Mitton's Practical Modern Herbal* (New York: Arco, 1984).

7. M. H. Pollack and P. Hammerness, "Adjunctive Yohimbine for Treatment in Refractory Depression," *Biol Psychiatry* 33(February 1, 1993):220–221.

8. Jean Carper, *The Food Pharmacy* (New York: Bantam, 1988).

9. D. M. Veleber and D. I. Templer, "Effects of Caffeine on Anxiety and Depression," *J Abnormal Psych* 93(February 1984):120–122.

10. British Herbal Medicine Association, *British Herbal Pharmacopoeia 1972* (London: British Herbal Medicine Association, 1971).

11. Moshe Olshevsky et al., *The Manual of Natural Therapy* (New York: Facts on File, 1989).

12. Malcolm Stuart, ed., *The Encyclopedia of Herbs and Herbalism* (New York: Grosset & Dunlap, 1979).

13. J. Kleijnen and P. Knipschild, "Ginkgo Biloba for Cerebral Insufficiency," *Brit J Clin Pharmacol* 34(1992):352–358.

14. Frena Bloomfield, *Ginseng: "The Divine Herb"* (London: Century Hutchison, 1987).

15. Stephen Fulder, *Ginseng: The Magical Herb of the East* (Wellingborough, Northamptonshire: Thorsons, 1988).

16. Michael Castleman, *The Healing Herbs: The Ultimate Guide to the Curative Power of Nature's Medicines* (Emmaus, Penn.: Rodale Press, 1991).

17. P. F. D'Arcy, "Adverse Reactions and Interactions With Herbal Medicines. Part 1. Adverse Reactions," *Adverse Drug Reactions and Toxicological Reviews* 10(Winter 1991):189–208.

18. Michael van Straten, *The Complete Natural Health Consultant* (New York: Prentice Hall, 1987).

19. P. Weintraub, "Scentimental Journeys," *Omni* (April, 1986): 48–49, 52, 114, 116.

20. "Quirks and Quarks," CBC Radio, March 2, 1991.

21. J. Adolph, "Exploring Common Scents," *New Age Journal* 4(January/February 1988):9.

22. G. Buchbauer et al., ["Effects of Valerian Root Oil, Borneol, Isoborneol, Bornyl Acetate and Isobornyl Acetate on the Motility of Laboratory Animals (Mice) After Inhalation"], *Pharmazie* 47(August 1992):620–622.

23. Brian Inglis and Ruth West, *The Alternative Health Guide* (New York: Knopf, 1983).

24. David Hoffman, *The Herbal Handbook* (Rochester, Vt.: Healing Arts Press, 1988).

25. Valerie Ann Worwood, *The Complete Book of Essential Oils & Aromatherapy* (San Rafael, Calif.: New World Library, 1991).

SEVENTEEN

The Homeopathic Solution

THE brainchild of an iconoclastic German physician named Samuel Hahnemann who died 150 years ago, homeopathy is a most peculiar brand of medicine. The substances its remedies are made from give healthy persons the very symptoms the remedies are supposed to relieve. But that's okay. By the time these ingredients have been "potentized" (diluted) and "succussed" (shaken) into homeopathic form, there's little or nothing left of them anyway!

As fantastic as homeopathy may sound, few healing arts have inspired as much admiration from as many admirable devotees, including Goethe, William James, Mark Twain, Gandhi, Pope Pius X and Mother Teresa. In Britain, where nearly 50 percent of doctors sometimes refer patients to homeopathic colleagues, a survey suggests most patients are glad they did.[1]

THE CASE FOR HOMEOPATHY

At the turn of the century, one in every six doctors in the U.S. was a homeopath.[1] That homeopathy is not the flakey placebo most contemporary American doctors apparently think it is, is suggested by a surprisingly substantial body of evidence.

In placebo-controlled trials, homeopathic medications have lowered cholesterol in rabbits, prevented stillbirths in pigs, increased pain tolerance in rodents and dramatically protected mice against cancer, among other things.[1] Humans haven't fared too badly, either. When epidemiologists at the University of Limburg in the Netherlands set out to analyze the main body of controlled clinical trials, they found 105 of them, 75 double-blind. Homeopathy "worked" in 81 of these studies. In the 22 methodologically superior trials, homeopathy retained its edge in 15 against a variety of maladies.[2] However, a skeptic cites another review in which only 40 "acceptable" trials were found. Homeopathy fared no better than placebo overall, he claims.[3]

Only a handful of controlled trials of homeopathy have been undertaken for psychiatric conditions. Homeopathy has usually proven beneficial; it won its one match with depression.[2] Less formally, the British Homoeopathic Journal reports that of 120 "psychoneurotic" patients treated homeopathically, 79 percent improved after six months.[1] And at a New York county prison, the chief psychiatrist claims homeopathy dramatically improved the health and well-being of treated inmates. Suicides dwindled to zero.[1]

TREATING DEPRESSION HOMEOPATHICALLY

There are hundreds of homeopathic remedies. Each is an extreme dilution of a natural substance that causes a characteristic range of symptoms in sensitive, healthy persons. A dozen or so of these substances are so routinely depressing that they've become the remedies homeopaths usually prescribe to treat depression. The challenge of homeopathic prescription is to match the patient with the remedy that most closely mimics that individual's range of symptoms and idiosyncrasies—not just the depression, but any medical or personal quirks.

If you're mildly depressed, it may be feasible to select a homeopathic remedy yourself with the help of good reference books.[4] But if your depression is serious, it's best to consult a homeopath. Severe depression normally requires very potent (highly diluted) remedies which can trigger equally potent "heal-

BACH FLOWER REMEDIES

The Bach flower remedies are water extracts of the blossoms of 38 common flowers. Edward Bach (1886–1936), a mystically-minded English homeopathic physician, believed he had intuited the unique spiritual essence of each flower and its ability to counter one or another of the negative psychological qualities which (Bach also believed) lay at the root of all illnesses. Healing was simply a matter of matching a patient's negativity with the appropriate flower extract(s). All manner of ills, including depression, supposedly responded to this gentle approach.[5]

Today, Bach's remedies—and dozens of other flower essences developed by followers—are a popular, accessible alternative therapy available in most health food stores. Psychiatrist Herbert Fill, formerly New York City Commissioner of Mental Health, considers them an excellent substitute for psychotropic drugs.[6] Another psychiatrist reports that after three to six months, the remedies benefitted 32 out of 40 of his patients.[6] "Used wisely and with respect the remedies can be of inestimable value," avers yet another colleague.[5]

ing crises." These symptom flare-ups can be dangerous if you're suicidal.

Not just homeopaths, but over 1,000 medical doctors in the United States and Canada, as well as naturopaths, chiropractors, psychologists and other practitioners, practice homeopathy. A major mail-order supplier of homeopathic medications (including Bach flower remedies; see the box) and literature is Homeopathic Educational Services, 2124 Kittredge Street, Berkeley, CA 94704.

NOTES

1. Dana Ullman, *Homeopathy: Medicine for the 21st Century* (Berkeley, Calif.: North Atlantic Books, 1988).

2. J. Kleijnen et al., "Clinical Trials of Homeopathy," *Brit Med J* 302(February 9, 1991):316–323.

3. M. Baum, "Trials of Homeopathy" (letter), *Brit Med J* 302(March 2, 1991):529.

4. Trevor Smith, *Homeopathic Medicine for Mental Health* (Rochester, Vt.: Inner Traditions, 1989).

5. Nora Weeks, *The Medical Discoveries of Edward Bach, Physician* (New Canaan, Conn.: Keats Publishing, 1979).

6. Jane Heimlich, *What Your Doctor Won't Tell You* (New York: HarperCollins, 1990).

EIGHTEEN

Darkness and Light, Heat and Cold: The Elements and Depression

DARKNESS and light, heat and cold—the "elements" affect us physically and psychophysiologically. Yet only recently have scientists recognized how powerful the latter influence can be. For some of us, they have shown, the relationship between darkness and despair is more than metaphoric, and the kind of heat some of us can't stand really is measured with a thermometer.

SHEDDING LIGHT ON THE BLUES

In the early 1980s, psychiatrists at the National Institute of Mental Health (NIMH) rediscovered an old truth about depression and nature's flashiest stimulant, bright light. Every fall and winter when the days shorten and the cold shoos us indoors, some people fall into a torpor. Only with the light of spring do they recover (indeed, many become hyperactive or manic). But just set these people down in the dark of winter next to a sunny bank of bright lights for a few hours each day and soon most have snapped back to life.[1]

Dozens of studies have continued to shed light on this phenomenon of recurrent fall/winter depression—winter depression. for short.* It now seems that wherever the days get short in win-

*Recurrent fall/winter depression is also known as seasonal affective disorder, or SAD. But SAD can also mean spring/summer mania, summer depression, fall mania, or any other seasonal mood swing. We'll stay with *winter depression* here.

ter, most people experience at least some of the symptoms of winter depression, however mildly. The full-blown syndrome strikes 5 to 10 percent, depending on latitude. A milder syndrome afflicts three times as many.[1] Atypical depressives are especially hard hit, and many people prone to recurrent brief depressions are swamped by them in winter.

The major symptoms of winter depression are extreme lethargy, acute mental dullness and severe, sometimes suicidal, depression. Sufferers typically oversleep in the morning and pack on 5 to 10 or more pounds by indulging their craving for sweets and other carbohydrates, especially at night.

In clinical studies, phototherapy has usually entailed sitting for a few hours each day near a 2 x 4-foot light box containing six or eight 40-watt fluorescent tubes behind a plastic diffusing screen. In over two dozen controlled trials, phototherapy has rapidly brought improvement or recovery to between 60 and 75 percent of winter depressives.[1] Those with the most typical symptoms of the syndrome—oversleeping and sweet-craving—

DAWN SIMULATION

Some researchers are using an entirely different kind of light therapy to treat winter depression, with equal success.[6] Early every morning, around the time the sun begins to rise in the summer, a computer-controlled light comes on in the patient's bedroom. Gradually, as the patient still sleeps, the faint light brightens until, by wake-up time, the room is fully lit.[6]

"Dawn simulations" usually last 2 hours, though in one study a 10-minute version was nearly as effective.[6] Curiously, dawn simulations that peak at bright levels appear less effective (and less agreeable) than those that get no brighter than an average artificially lit room.[6]

"Dawn simulators" may be commercially available by the time you read this. If you're electronically adept you can make one yourself. A crude, untested alternative would be to time at least two or three low-wattage lights in your bedroom to come on sequentially.

PHOTOTHERAPY FOR *ORDINARY* DEPRESSION?

Being the stimulant it is, could bright light be a tonic for *any* kind of depression? Nearly a dozen studies have sought to answer that question. In these brief trials (never longer than two weeks), bright light has only been a weak antidepressant for the average nonseasonally depressed patient and a more potent mood-lifter for perhaps one in five, when compared to dim light or other control conditions.[7] Researchers wonder if longer trials would yield greater benefits.[7]

In the meantime, a few studies suggest bright light can be used, like thyroid hormone and lithium, to hasten response to slow-acting antidepressant drugs (and perhaps their natural counterparts) and to convert drug nonresponders into responders.[4,7]

Evidence so far suggests that people with nonseasonal depression who are most likely to benefit from light therapy a) are light-deprived, b) have a history of winter depression, and/or c) have winter-depressionlike symptoms.[4] While morning light therapy is the best bet for winter depression, evening light may often be preferable for nonseasonal depression.[4] The reason for that will become clear when we discuss light's effects on body rhythms in Chapter 20.

have responded best.[2,3] Discontinuing the extra light has quickly led to relapse.[1] Mild winter depression has also responded to phototherapy,[4] as has winter premenstrual syndrome.[5]

TAKING THE LIGHT CURE

Several considerations are involved in taking the light cure:

1. *What kind of light?* Research suggests any bright light source, fluorescent or incandescent, can be effective, though full-spectrum light (like the Duro-test "Vita-Lites" used in many studies) may have an edge.[8] Of course, the sun is the ultimate light

therapist. The snow on a sunny winter day vastly outshines any light box. And the cold could be an antidepressant in its own right (see below). The exercise you'd get outdoors certainly is (Chapter 22). Indoors, sitting next to a sunny window compares to sitting next to an NIMH-grade light box (available from The Sunbox Company, 1132 Taft St., Rockville, MD 20850, (301) 762–1786).

2. *How bright?* The most biologically active light suppresses the pineal gland's secretion of a neurochemical called melatonin. For most people, ordinary indoor light is too weak for this. Outdoor light, even on an overcast day, and the light within a few feet of a light box is bright enough. But so is the light from an ordinary shaded lamp or a brightly illuminated, light-colored surface, if your eyes are right next to it. Try burying your head in a book, for instance, with a powerful desk lamp right over it.

3. *How much light?* One to three hours a day of phototherapy has been the norm in clinical research. But as little as 15 to 40 minutes has sufficed in several trials, especially with very bright light (comparable to levels outdoors) in the morning, the earlier the better.[2,4]

4. *When?* The morning sleepiness of most winter depressives suggests that they have a "phase-delayed circadian rhythm" (I'll explain what that means in Chapter 20). Bright light in the morning is the remedy for that, and winter depressives respond to it best.[1,2,4]

SAFETY

Experts advise against trying phototherapy without medical supervision, because it's not without side effects. Some people become overactivated. A few become hyper-irritable, even manic. (Even mellow dawn simulation makes some people mildly manic.)[6] Headaches, eyestrain and nausea have also been reported. The side effects are probably dose-related. Bipolar persons especially—because they seem more sensitive to light[4]—may fare best on a "bright-light lite" regimen.

To minimize the risk of eye damage, experts recommend oph- thalmological screening and monitoring. Another concern is over- exposure to the magnetic fields of fluorescent lights. To address that, a shielded, full-spectrum light box is available from Tools For Exploration, 4460 Redwood Highway, Suite 2, San Rafael, CA 94903, 1–800–456–9887.

THE HOT AND THE COLD OF IT

The good temple priests of ancient Greece had a rough and ready remedy for people who clung too stubbornly to depression. They dumped them into cold water.[9] The Chinese have long been similarly inclined: "In . . . listless depressives, a brief moment of cold water bathing can revitalize mental spirits and enhance the mood."[10] And in Europe, no less an authority than Emil Kraepelin, a founder of modern psychiatry, advocated cold baths for depression.[11]

Cold therapy for depression might well have died with Kraepelin were it not for the same intrepid NIMH investigators who revived phototherapy. Some of their patients, they noticed, became depressed every summer, usually by May or June. Cool weather, trips north or the arrival of fall restored their spirits; in- deed, come the fall or winter and many would become manic or hypomanic (though a few would become depressed again in the winter).[8, 12]

One of their patients was struggling with her fifteenth consec- utive summer depression when the NIMH group came up with a bright idea. They confined her to an air-conditioned home and directed her to take cold showers a few times a day. Five days later her depression had all but vanished. They sent her back to her own un-air-conditioned home and she soon relapsed.[12]

The Chinese still think any depressive can benefit from a little cold.[10] Here's their prescription: Very gradually, expose yourself briefly every day to cooler and cooler air or water, but never so cold that you shiver, let alone freeze. Eventually you'll be able to enjoy a brief (as little as a few minutes), bracing cold-water swim, shower or bath (or a "cold air bath") every day.

NOTES

1. M. Blehar and N. E. Rosenthal, "Seasonal Affective Disorders and Phototherapy: Report of a National Institute of Mental Health-Sponsored Workshop," *Arch Gen Psych* 46(May 1989):469–474.

2. T. Partonen, "Effects of Morning Light Treatment on Subjective Sleepiness and Mood in Winter Depression," *Journal of Affective Disorders* 30(1994):47–56.

3. D. Stinson and C. Thompson, "Clinical Experience with Phototherapy," *Journal of Affective Disorders* 18(February 1990):129–135.

4. M. A. Hill, "Light, Circadian Rhythms, and Mood Disorders: A Review," *Ann Clin Psych* 4(June 1992):131–146.

5. B. L. Parry et al., "Treatment of a Patient with Seasonal Premenstrual Syndrome," *Am J Psychiatry* 144(June 1987):762–766.

6. D. H. Avery et al., "Dawn Simulation Treatment of Winter Depression: A Controlled Study," *Am J Psychiatry* 150(January 1993):113–117.

7. D. F. Kripke et al., "Controlled Trial of Bright Light for Nonseasonal Major Depressive Disorders," *Biol Psychiatry* 31(January 15, 1992):119–134.

8. T. A. Wehr and N. E. Rosenthal, "Seasonality and Affective Illness," *Am J Psychiatry* 146(July 1989):829–839.

9. A. Georgotas, "Evolution of the Concepts of Depression and Mania." In Anastasios Georgotas and Robert Cancro, eds., *Depression and Mania* (New York: Elsevier, 1988).

10. *Knocking at the Gate of Life and Other Healing Exercises From China: The Official Handbook of the People's Republic of China,* trans. Edward C. Chang (Emmaus, Penn.: Rodale Press, 1985).

11. T. A. Wehr, "Seasonal Affective Disorders: A Historical Overview." In Norman E. Rosenthal and Mary C. Blehar, eds., *Seasonal Affective Disorders and Phototherapy* (New York: Guilford Press, 1989), pp. 11–32.

12. T. A. Wehr et al., "Seasonal Affective Disorder with Summer Depression and Winter Hypomania," *Am J Psychiatry* 144(December 1987):1602–1603.

NINETEEN

Sleep Cures:
Sleep Therapy and
Sleep Deprivation

SHOW me a depressed person and I'll show you someone who, in all likelihood, has trouble in the sleep department, whether it be trouble falling asleep, trouble staying asleep, trouble getting up in the morning or trouble staying awake during the day.

Sleep problems can cause depression (sleep apnea is a graphic example), but usually they just seem to be part of the problem of being depressed. So who would think that sleeping "too much," not sleeping "enough" or (as we'll see in the next chapter) sleeping at the "wrong" times could also be part of the solution?

REST CURE, ANYONE? _____

When the world is too much upon them, some people know just what to do: they take a nap. And studies confirm that these pit stops from the daily grind do indeed freshen people's moods and perk up their performance.[1]

But what to do when you're so down and out, it seems like the kind of nap you need could last maybe a year? *Go for it.*

Sleep therapy is one of those intuitive techniques, like light therapy and cold therapy, that has always had a place in world psychiatry.[2] In India, traditional Ayurvedic psychiatrists prescribe "rest cures" of up to 15 hours a day. In Nigeria, medicine men treat their mentally disturbed patients to marathon, drug-induced sleep sessions. In the United States, the rest cure was championed a century ago by the distinguished neurologist Weir Mitchell.

In some parts of Europe and Asia—the former Soviet Union in particular—sleep therapy (ST) was still going strong as recently as 1960. That year, a Soviet psychiatrist named B. V. Andreev wrote a monograph on the subject.[3] ST, he noted, works best for patients who look and feel like they need it. Typically, Andreev observed, such persons can't stand "noise, bright light, and social intercourse"; they're foundering at work; they long for "peace, quiet, and solitude"; and they're very, very tired.[3(p. 33)] Those who benefit most from ST, Andreev and others found, are burned-out and depressed.

In a series of 87 patients Andreev reported the following results (the outcome for 12 depressives is in parentheses): 17 percent (16 percent) were "cured"; 37 percent (58 percent) considerably improved (back in action, but not fully recovered); 30 percent (8 percent) moderately improved; 13 percent (16 percent) slightly improved; and 3 percent (0 percent) unchanged.[3]

ST may be particularly beneficial for people whose depression and lethargy is a sequel to a toxic or infectious brain disease, research by Andreev and his contemporaries suggests.[3] Many such people would today be diagnosed as having chronic fatigue syndrome (CFS). Indeed, some people with CFS do find oversleeping helpful. At Charing Cross Hospital in London, a majority of 300 CFS patients responded well to ST (combined with measures to counteract their tendency to hyperventilate).[4]

Taking the Rest Cure

Catching some extra sleep at night or napping during the day could be all the sleep therapy you need. A full-blown rest cure is another matter.

At Charing Cross Hospital, the procedure, according to Dr. Stuart Rosen, is "to sleep the patient out for a few days, 15, 16, 17 hours a day . . . basically having several days where they just have nothing but their batteries recharged by a good sleep."[4] After that, ST continues on a more modest scale. Eventually patients return very gradually to a normal schedule.

In Andreev's clinic, patients would usually sate themselves on 11 to 17 hours of sleep a day for one or two weeks. Because they found very prolonged sleep disagreeable, they would get their extra sleep by napping from 10 AM to 2 PM and 3 PM to 7 PM. Bedtime was from 10 PM to 8 AM.

Quiet, peaceful surroundings are *de rigueur* for a rest cure. But for some depressives something completely different may be indicated.

"SLEEPLESS THERAPY"

It's one of psychiatry's most peculiar secrets. In some 60 studies conducted around the world since the 1970s, when depressed patients have been deprived of sleep for all or half of a night, better than half have felt markedly better—even sprightly or back to normal—the next day.[5,6]

There's a hitch though: What sleep deprivation (SD) giveth, sleep restoration taketh away. After a good night's sleep or two most have plunged down into the dumps again—very few have enjoyed lasting remission.

But all is not lost. Studies have shown that by *repeating* half a night or partial sleep deprivation (PSD), usually once a week or so, some depressives—perhaps one in every three or four—obtain relief that lasts.[6,7] Repeat PSD, suggests experts at the National Institute of Mental Health (NIMH), "might provide a clinically useful alternative treatment for depression, particularly in patients who cannot tolerate or do not respond to conventional antidepressant therapies."[8]

But there's more! Half a dozen controlled studies suggest SD can be combined synergistically with antidepressant drugs (or lithium) to produce rapid and sustained improvement or recovery from depression.[6,9] Most recently, psychiatrists at Vanderbilt University introduced antidepressant medication to 20 patients right after a night of total SD (TSD). Eleven responded immediately to the combination; the rest took a few weeks (the usual response time to drugs alone).[9]

SD has also converted antidepressant drug nonresponders into responders. The usual procedure has been to repeat TSD or PSD a few times for a week or two; then once a week (in the longer trials). In 14 trials involving over 400 patients, this has benefitted about 40 percent.[6,10]

SD's apparent ability to potentiate antidepressant drugs and lithium may extend to other natural antidepressants.

For people with very brief depressions, SD's transient benefits may not be a problem. Such people have sometimes been able to abort or prevent their depressions with SD.[6,11] Premenstrual depression is a case in point. In a study from NIMH, one full night of SD promptly relieved it in eight out of ten sufferers. So did two consecutive nights of PSD.[6]

Is Sleep Deprivation for You?

Studies have shown that if you have a relatively severe, typical form of depression, you have about a 67 percent chance of benefitting from SD.[5] If yours is an atypical depression, you have about a 45 percent chance.[5] Melancholic depression is especially responsive to SD,[12] and mild depression is least responsive.

How-To

Partial sleep deprivation seems to be as effective as total.[6] And *late* PSD—missing the *second half* of your night's sleep—has usually been more effective than early PSD (missing the first half).[6,8,10]

Here are some things you should know:

• Napping the next day can wipe out the effect of SD, especially if you nap early.[13]

• A small percentage of depressives—usually atypical ones—feel worse after SD;[7] and even some responders briefly feel worse than when they started after a night of recovery sleep.[7] SD can trigger mania in some bipolar or rapid cycling depressives and it may further worsen the thinking of schizophrenic or psychotic/delusional depressives.[7]

If you're a good candidate for SD, you're probably a good candidate for phase advancing your sleep-wake cycle too. That's our next subject.

NOTES

1. S. R. Daiss et al., "Napping Versus Resting: Effects on Performance and Mood," *Psychophysiology* 23(1, 1986):82.

2. Sudhir Kakar, *Shamans, Mystics & Doctors* (New York: Knopf, 1982).

3. B. V. Andreev, *Sleep Therapy in the Neuroses* (New York: Consultants Bureau, 1960).

4. "Quirks and Quarks," CBC Radio, Dec. 9, 1989.

5. D. A. Sack and T. A. Wehr, "Circadian Rhythms in Affective Disorders." In Anastasios Georgotas and Robert Cancro, eds., *Depression and Mania* (New York: Elsevier, 1988), pp. 312–331.

6. E. Leibenluft and T. A. Wehr, "Is Sleep Deprivation Useful in the Treatment of Depression?" *Am J Psychiatry* 149(February 1992):159–168.

7. J. C. Gillin et al., "Sleep and Affective Illness." In Robert M. Post and James C. Ballenger, eds., *Neurobiology of Mood Disorders* (Baltimore: Williams and Wilkins, 1984), pp. 157–189.

8. D. A. Sack et al., "The Timing and Duration of Sleep in Partial Sleep Deprivation Therapy of Depression," *Acta Psychiatr Scand* 77(February 1988):219–224.

9. R. C. Shelton and P. T. Loosen, "Sleep Deprivation Accelerates the Response to Nortriptyline," *Progress in Neuropsychopharmacol Biol Psychiatry* 17(January 1993):113–123.

10. E. Leibenluft et al., "A Clinical Trial of Sleep Deprivation in Combination with Antidepressant Medication," *Psychiatry Res* 46(March 1993):213–227.

11. C. M. Churchill and S. C. Dilsaver, "Partial Sleep Deprivation to Prevent 48-Hour Mood Cycles," *Acta Psychiatr Scand* 81(1990):398–399.

12. P. P. Roy-Byrne et al., "Antidepressant Effects of One Night's

Sleep Deprivation: Clinical and Theoretical Implications." In Post and Bal-lenger, *Neurobiology of Mood Disorders*, pp. 817–835.

13. M. Wiegand et al., "Effect of Morning and Afternoon Naps on Mood After Total Sleep Deprivation in Patients with Major Depression," *Biol Psychiatry* 33(March 15, 1993):467–476.

TWENTY

Healing Rhythms: Getting Your Body Clock Back in Sync

YOU'VE checked into the National Institute of Mental Health (NIMH) severely depressed. They poke you, they prod you, they shrink you, they medicate you, but nothing helps. So a research psychiatrist invites you to try something completely different: *go to bed and get up each morning six hours early*. After eyeballing him very carefully for signs of suppressed hysterical laughter, you shrug your shoulders and agree. A few days later you could kiss him.

To understand why you've responded so well to this phase advance of the sleep-wake cycle, as Thomas Wehr and his associates at NIMH would call it, we have to talk about *rhythm*.[1]

Nature is full of things that ebb and flow, expand and contract, revolve, rotate or fluctuate rhythmically in other ways. Everything from planets and stars to hearts and brain cells has rhythm. And it's largely through rhythm that the different parts of the natural world synchronize and coordinate with each other. The Earth's rhythmic revolution around the sun, for instance, creates the seasons, which set the pace of life on Earth. And Earth's daily rotation cues our own "circadian" (daily) body rhythms.

Which brings us back to depression. Scientists have found that many, perhaps most, seriously depressed persons have disturbed circadian rhythms. It's as if they were severely "jet lagged."[2] "Typical" depressives (page 5) usually appear to have flown west across five or six time zones. Their circadian rhythms are often five or six hours ahead of schedule—phase advanced five or six hours, in chronobiological parlance. This is probably why they wake up hours early each morning.

In the 1970s, Thomas Wehr and his associates at NIMH had an idea. If phase-advanced depressives would sleep when their body rhythms say they should, they would be more in sync internally, and perhaps this would ease their depression. Wehr and his colleagues enlisted a handful of bipolar depressed patients to be their guinea pigs. They had them go to bed and get up six hours early—a six-hour phase advance of their sleep-wake cycles. After two days, one recovered, two enjoyed partial improvement, and the fourth was so buoyed he became manic. But there was a snag. The recovered patient relapsed after two weeks, and though she responded again to another six-hour phase advance, she soon relapsed again. Subsequent phase advances no longer helped.[1]

Fleeting though it was, the antidepressant effect of phase advance of the sleep-wake cycle (PASWC) would later be confirmed in all but one of about half a dozen studies.[2,3] And as with its eccentric relative, sleep deprivation therapy, some of these studies would show that PASWC might have a future in combination with other antidepressant therapies. When Wehr's group added PASWC to the regimen of four depressed patients who weren't responding to antidepressant drugs, all recovered within a week and remained well up to a year later. They had gradually returned to a normal sleep schedule soon after recovery.[4] Other researchers gave 17 melancholic depressives who weren't responding to drugs a night of sleep deprivation followed by a six-hour PASWC. Over the next week the patients edged back to their old sleep schedules by an hour a day. Though six dropped out after the first night, half of the others responded immediately, the rest improving or recovering over the week. All 11 were discharged from the hospital a few weeks later.[3]

Like sleep deprivation, PASWC seems to be a useful way to jump-start the slower but steadier elements of an antidepressant regimen. It deserves special consideration, say authorities.[5]

The kind of jet lag other depressives have suggests they've been flying east, not west. They're phase *delayed*.[6] Typically young and not too severely depressed, they tend to be bushy-tailed at bedtime and dead tired in the morning. For them, going to bed and getting up hours later, not earlier (phase delaying their sleep-wake cycles) might be the ticket, some psychiatrists suggest.[6] Indeed, this has been shown to help in at least one study.[7] Similarly, a radical around-the-clock phase delay procedure for chronic night owls has usually relieved their depressiveness.[8] Unfortunately there's a prohibitive side effect to this procedure: some night owls' circadian rhythms become completely unhinged by it.[9]

Instead of changing your sleeping habits to match your circadian rhythms you can try something different: change your rhythms.

SHIFTING BODY RHYTHMS _____

Our circadian rhythms are programmable. The circadian clock—the master timepiece in our brains—takes its cue from the natural, social and behavioral rhythms in our lives. Researchers have found that by tightly scheduling these rhythms—in particular the powerful *chiaroscuro* of bright light and darkness—we can "reset" our circadian clocks to bring our body rhythms back into sync with our sleep-wake schedules.[10,11] This has worked for the night owls mentioned above,[12] and psychiatrists suspect it can help depressives too.[13]

The circadian clock is easiest to reset in the middle of the night, around 4:00 or 5:00 AM. Stimulate it (with bright light, exciting activities, etc.) earlier—i.e., as late at night as you can—and it'll think the night is still young and reset itself accordingly. Stimulate it instead not too long after 4:00 or 5:00 AM—early in the morning—and it'll start checking its watch for lunchtime. A few days of well-timed bright light can be all it takes to shift your phase-advanced or phase-delayed body rhythms "half way around the world," research shows.[11,12]

Here's how to do it. If you need to delay your circadian rhythms because they're phase-advanced (you're waking up early every morning), schedule stimulating activities and influences at night, especially late at night: high-protein meals, loud music, stimulating herbs and beverages, stimulating antidepressants like phenylalanine, tyrosine, methionine, thyroid hormone, exercise, and cold therapy—and bright light. For early in the day, schedule nonstimulating activities and influences: high-carbohydrate meals, nonstimulating antidepressants like tryptophan, vitamin C, calcium, magnesium, relaxation/meditation, and massage—and dim light or darkness. If you need to advance your body rhythms because they're phase-delayed (you're wakeful at night and sleepy in the morning), do the reverse. (Dawn simulation before you awaken in the morning [see Chapter 18] can also phase advance your rhythms, while "dusk simulation" [to coin a therapy] until 3:00 or 4:00 AM while you sleep might be an effective phase delayer.)

You'll know you've shifted your body rhythms far enough when your feelings of sleepiness and wakefulness are in sync with your sleep-wake schedule. To avoid shifting your rhythms any further, you'll need to moderate what you're doing, or quit.

NOTES

1. T. A. Wehr et al., "Phase Advance of the Circadian Sleep-Wake Cycle as an Antidepressant," *Science* 206(1979):710–13.

2. D. A. Sack and T. A. Wehr, "Circadian Rhythms in Affective Disorders." In Anastasios Georgotas and Robert Cancro, eds., *Depression and Mania* (New York: Elsevier, 1988), pp. 312–331.

3. J. Vollmann and M. Berger, "Sleep Deprivation with Consecutive Sleep-Phase Advance Therapy in Patients with Major Depression: A Pilot Study," *Biol Psychiatry* 33(1993):54–57.

4. D. A. Sack et al., "Potentiation of Antidepressant Medications by Phase Advance of the Sleep-Wake Cycle," *Am J Psychiatry* 142(May 1985):606–607.

5. R. M. A. Hirschfeld and F. K. Goodwin, "Mood Disorders." In John Talbott et al., eds., *The American Psychiatric Press Textbook of Psychiatry* (Washington: American Psychiatric Press, 1988), pp. 403–441.

6. A. J. Lewy et al., "Phase Delay and Hypersomnia" (letter), *Am J Psychiatry* 143(May 1986):679–680.

7. D. R. Hawkins et al., "Extended Sleep (Hypersomnia) in Young Depressed Patients," *Am J Psychiatry* 142(August 1985):905–910.

8. T. Ohta et al., "Daily Activity and Persistent Sleep-Wake Schedule Disorders," *Prog Neuropsychopharmacol Biol Psychiatry* 16 (July 1992): 529–537.

9. D. A. Oren and T. A. Wehr, "Hypernyctohemeral Syndrome After Chronotherapy for Delayed Sleep Phase Syndrome" (letter), *N Eng J Med* 327(December 10, 1992):1762.

10. A. J. Lewy et al., "Treating Phase Typed Chronobiologic Sleep and Mood Disorders Using Appropriately Timed Bright Artificial Light," *Psychopharmacol Bull* 21(3, 1985):368–372.

11. C. A. Czeisler et al., "Bright Light Induction of Strong (Type 0) Resetting of the Human Circadian Pacemaker," *Science* 244(June 16, 1989):1328–1333.

12. N. E. Rosenthal et al., "Phase-Shifting Effects of Bright Morning Light as Treatment for Delayed Sleep Phase Syndrome," *Sleep* 13(August 1990):354–361.

13. A. J. Lewy et al., "Winter Depression and the Phase-Shift Hypothesis for Bright Light's Therapeutic Effects." In Norman E. Rosenthal and Mary C. Blehar, eds., *Seasonal Affective Disorders and Phototherapy* (New York: Guilford Press, 1989), pp. 295–310.

TWENTY-ONE

Working Out: Exercising to Exorcise the Blues

*I think that I cannot preserve my health and spirits,
unless I spend four hours a day at least ... sauntering
through the woods and over the hills and fields,
absolutely free from all wordly engagements.*

—HENRY DAVID THOREAU[1]

*... [W]e recommend that any rational, safe, and effective
treatment regimen for depression should include a
prescription for vigorous exercise ...*

—ROBERT S. BROWN, PH.D.,

M.D., ET AL.[2]

WHEN *The Joy of Running*,[3] a seminal work on exercising your way to mental health, dashed onto the bestseller lists in 1976, it seemed as if the fitness craze had hit its wackiest stride. Visions of goateed psychoanalysts padding down running tracks in "Vienna U" track suits, their faithful patients in tow, rolled comically across the mind's eye.

But if there was ever any doubt back then about the legitimacy of exercising to exorcise your demons, there's little left now. Not only have the great masses discovered the feel-good benefits of exercise, so have the white-coated clinicians. In consensus statements, position papers and scholarly reviews, the National Institute of Mental Health, the International Society of Sport Psychology and other authorities have proclaimed the psychotherapeutic benefits of exercise.[4] The supporting evidence is substantial.

Dozens of studies have shown that sustained, vigorous physical activity—aerobic exercise—is like a bug repellant against negativity: fear, worry, anger, tension. Practiced regularly, exercise

"RUNNER'S HIGH"

Perhaps you're wondering if the antidepressant effect of exercise has anything to do with "runner's high." Runner's high is the euphoria that comes over many exercisers 30 to 45 minutes into an intense workout. It's also the serene, almost transcendental peace some enjoy if they push 20 to 45 minutes longer.[9] There is no evidence exercise has to get you high to get you up from depression. The modest workouts that relieve depression aren't even conducive to runner's high. But then, neither do they promote runner's high *addiction*, which can create problems of its own.[4]

brings improved self-image, greater self-confidence, less neuroticism, enhanced mental performance, greater composure under stress and less depression.[4] Indeed, aerobic exercise is as fit as any other antidepressant for mild to moderate depression, most of at least a dozen studies indicate.[4,5]

In one study,[6] aerobics was pitted against cognitive therapy, a short-term psychotherapy comparable in effect to antidepressant drugs (Chapter 25). The 54 mildly to moderately depressed subjects were mainly sedentary women. Those randomly assigned to walk/jog/run for 20 minutes, three times a week, in a supervised group, fared just as well as those assigned to weekly cognitive therapy. After four weeks, most of the 17 runners had recovered or improved. Only two had dropped out. At the end of the ten-week study, 11 were nearly or completely depression-free. Months later, most were still running to keep their blues at bay.

Exercise can even help relieve severe, major depression.[4,5,7] In one of several encouraging studies, both aerobic and nonaerobic exercise substantially reduced depression in hospitalized depressives.[5] In another, aerobics alone sufficed for many severely depressed women.[8]

GOING AEROBIC _____

What exactly is aerobic exercise? It's any activity that conditions your body to extract oxygen from the air (aerobic means "with oxygen") and distribute it to the working muscles. If it makes you breathe deeply and rapidly and gets your heart racing, it's an aerobic exercise. (If it makes you breathless, you've gone into "anaerobic" [without oxygen] metabolism.)

Exercise physiologists have a formula to gauge whether you're exercising aerobically at an optimal pace. First subtract your age from the number 220. This is your maximum heart rate. Now multiply this number by 60 percent and by 85 percent. If your pulse while exercising is anywhere between these two target heart rates (that is, between 60 percent and 85 percent of your maximum heart rate) you're in the aerobic target zone. (If you have heart disease or other medical conditions you might have to work out near the bottom of this zone.) Be physically active at this pace for at least 15 to 30 minutes a day, on average (the lower the heart rate, the longer the workout), and you'll soon be enjoying the many benefits—physical and psychological—of being aerobically fit.

But don't try to become an athlete overnight (if ever). Depressives in running programs normally spend most of their time walking. For weeks, they jog only in spurts. Yet "most . . . begin to feel better within a week and feel virtually well within three weeks."[10]

THE AEROBICS MENU _____

Any kind of aerobic (and perhaps nonaerobic—see box, *Nonaerobic Antidepressant?*) exercise can relieve depression, most experts assume, not just the walk/jog/running programs employed in most clinical studies.

Physiologically, the most efficient aerobic exercises include cross country skiing, running, jogging, aerobic power walking, uphill hiking, swimming, aerobic dancing, cycling, rowing, canoeing, boxing, skipping rope and running on the spot; digging, shoveling or other repetitive weight-moving activities, if sustained for more than a few minutes; squash, handball, racketball, lacrosse, soccer and basketball; and working out on a treadmill, trampoline, stationary bicycle or a rowing or skiing machine. Lighter activities like ice-skating and roller-skating, walking, gardening, lawnmowing with a hand mower and most popular dances are fine if you're not in great shape. Stop-and-start activities like volleyball, tennis, badminton, downhill skiing (short runs) and fencing must be performed longer for comparable aerobic benefits.

Different aerobic activities have different personalities, just like the people who are attracted to them. This could be related to the activities' psychotherapeutic benefits. Jogging, for instance, is very conducive to introspection or reverie. Dance is social, sensual and emotionally engaging. An absorbing competitive sport like racketball distracts you from your worries. When you select from the aerobics menu, consider these psychotherapeutic features:

- Many aerobic activities bring you together with other people in a spirit of camaraderie.
- Most allow you to get better and better at something, which can massage your ego.
- Many are playful. They can lighten you up, reconnect you with your "inner child."
- Many are conducive to emotional release or expression. You can, for example, exercise predator/prey instincts (chasing, fleeing), channel aggression (hitting, kicking), or move expressively (dancing).
- Some can be productive (gardening, housework), rewarding you with a sense of accomplishment.
- Many are monotonous (walking, jogging, rowing), leaving your mind free for inner work: meditation, suggestion, music therapy and the like.
- Many provide a diverting change of scenery: a walk in the park, a swim in the lake, a sightseeing bike ride.

NONAEROBIC ANTIDEPRESSANT?

Nonaerobic exercise is activity which is either too light to have an aerobic training effect (bowling, yoga) or too intense (anaerobic) to be sustained aerobically (weight lifting). It can build muscles (weight lifting), speed (sprinting), coordination (juggling), flexibility (yoga) or other specialized abilities. But it does little to condition the cardiovascular and respiratory systems, and it isn't thought to confer the major health benefits of aerobic exercise. Yet it does seem to confer the psychological benefits. Studies are few, but they consistently suggest that anaerobic exercise, and perhaps other nonaerobic activities, are comparable to aerobic exercise in antidepressant effect.[4,5,7] Still, for its other health benefits, aerobic activity should be at least part of any exercise program for depression.

SAFE EXERCISING _____

Exercise can be hazardous. It can be risky if you have certain medical conditions (such as cardiovascular disease, poorly controlled asthma and diabetes) or other risk factors (such as smoking or using certain drugs, including many antidepressants).* Intense exercise can even trigger panic attacks, if you're so inclined. No matter how healthy you are, if you're over 35 the American College of Sports Medicine recommends *consulting your doctor* before embarking on an exercise program.

The golden rule for exercising safely: *take it easy and don't overdo it.* Neglecting to spend a few minutes warming up and cooling down with light exercise before and after a workout is a prescription for aches, pains, muscle fatigue, nausea, dizziness, fainting, injuries, even life-threatening heart irregularities.[12] Plugging on despite suspicious symptoms, like chest pains, faintness or pallor, can endanger your life. Exercising too long, too hard

*An ample intake of magnesium may be key to preventing adverse cardiac reactions to exercise.[11]

and too often not only invites injuries, but ironically it "may lead to fatigue, anxiety, and depression."[4]

NOTES

1. Aaron Sussman and Ruth Goode, *The Magic of Walking* (New York: Simon and Schuster, 1967), p. 243.

2. R. S. Brown et al., "The Prescription of Exercise for Depression," *Physician and Sportsmedicine* 6(December 1978):34–45.

3. Thaddeus Kostrubala, *The Joy of Running* (New York: Lippincott, 1976).

4. International Society of Sport Psychology, "Physical Activity and Psychological Benefits: A Position Statement," *Sport Psychologist* 6(June 1992):199–203.

5. E. W. Martinsen et al., "Comparing Aerobic With Nonaerobic Forms of Exercise in the Treatment of Clinical Depression: A Randomized Trial," *Comprehensive Psychiatry* 4(July/August 1989):324–331.

6. J. Fremont and L. W. Craighead, "Aerobic Exercise and Cognitive Therapy in the Treatment of Dysphoric Moods," *Cognitive Ther Res* 11(2, 1987):241–251.

7. D. J. Ossip-Klein et al., "Effects of Running or Weight-Lifting on Self-Concept in Clinically Depressed Women," *J Consult Clin Psychol* 57(January 1989):158–161.

8. E. J. Doyne et al., "Aerobic Exercise as a Treatment for Depression in Women," *Behav Ther* 14(1983):434–440.

9. T. Kostrubala, "Running and Therapy." In Michael L. Sacks and Gary W. Buffone, eds., *Running as Therapy* (Lincoln: University of Nebraska Press, 1984), pp. 112–124.

10. R. R. Eischens and J. H. Greist, "Beginning and Continuing Running: Steps to Psychological Well-Being." In Sacks and Buffone, *Running as Therapy*, pp. 63–82.

11. A. J. Reyes et al., "Magnesium Supplementation in Hypertension Treated with Hydrochlorothiazide," *Curr Ther Res* 36(August 1984):332–340.

12. Kenneth H. Cooper, *The Aerobics Program for Total Well-Being* (New York: M. Evans and Company, 1982), p. 135.

TWENTY-TWO

Bodywork: Working the Body to Free the Mind

MASSAGE, therapeutic touch, *t'ai chi*, acupressure—there are a profusion of popular bodywork techniques out there. Some in particular can be helpful for depression.

MASSAGE

Subjectively, massage is soothing and revitalizing. Objectively, it relaxes muscles, reduces heart rate and blood pressure and improves circulation. Altogether, it evokes a deep, mind/body relaxation response. In clinical studies, even ordinary back rubs have modestly, but significantly, relieved pain, anxiety and depression in hospitalized patients.[1]

One psychotherapist sees massage as a natural antidote to "touch starvation." "[G]iven by a caring person massage can have a marked positive effect on the self-image and the body image," he notes.[2(p. 132)] When you're depressed and your self-image is as bleak as your mood, a massage by someone who cares can make a difference.

PSYCHOTHERAPEUTIC BODYWORK

Sometimes it's not just muscles that get loosened by massage. Sometimes powerful feelings or deep, disturbing memories are kneaded loose. Psychotherapeutically oriented bodyworkers welcome these eruptions. Indeed, they invite them.

Most forms of psychotherapeutic bodywork derive from the work of a few pioneers: Wilhelm Reich, Alexander Lowen and Ida Rolf.

From Reich to Bioenergetics

Early in his career the psychoanalyst Wilhelm Reich (1897–1957) made a painful discovery. Try as he might to connect with his patients, he kept butting up against a brick wall of "character armor." Clenched jaws, stiff necks, braced shoulders, rigid pelvises—these and other defensive body habits prevented his patients from even acknowledging, let alone expressing many of their deepest feelings. To breach this wall, Reich rolled up his sleeves and began chipping away with his bare hands. Soon he evolved a method of digging into one rigid musculoskeletal "band" of character armor after another, from head down to pelvis. As he poked away, Reich would bid his patients to groan, kick, hit, scream—do whatever their unleashed inner selves dictated. As they came alive with emotion and buzzed with long-buried memories, Reich the psychoanalyst helped them put body and soul back together again.

Reich's most influential student, the American psychiatrist Alexander Lowen, has introduced explicit spirituality and Eastern mysticism into Reich's system. He invites depressives to swing towels and kick pillows with Reichian abandon, but, with a nod to *t'ai chi* (see below) and other Taoist practices, he also prescribes an assortment of gentler "bioenergetic" exercises. These are meant to ground and center depressed people in the vital, energetic bodies they've cut themselves off from.[3]

Rolfing

Bad posture, the biochemist Ida Rolf concluded, is the root of much evil. Her solution—"structural integration," or "Rolfing"—is to dig into the connective tissue surrounding every muscle and work it like putty until the body can assume its ideal posture: poised, balanced and erect.

A painful process that lasts months, Rolfing typically unleashes gales of psychic baggage which many Rolfers help their clients "work through." The successfully Rolfed body is commonly experienced as a tower of free-flowing energy (often taller by an inch or two!) and incredible lightness of being.[4]

The Alexander Technique

F. M. Alexander (1869–1955) was an actor who, like Reich, Lowen and Rolf, believed something was seriously wrong with how people used their bodies. But instead of attacking the problem with his hands, Alexander taught his clients to solve it with their minds. He taught them to sense and use their bodies with unique self-awareness and sensitivity.

In his classic on the Alexander Technique, physician Wilfred Barlow expounds on its role in promoting mental health.[5] If a person slouches, Barlow argues, his posture is fertile soil for depression. To illustrate, Barlow shows "before and after" pictures of a depressed woman. Collapsed posturally and psychologically in the first shot, she stands erect and emotionally uplifted a few weeks later in the second, a successful student of the Alexander Technique.

HATHA YOGA _____

More than just an exotic stretching system, *hatha* (physical) *yoga* is, in significant ways, a forerunner to the bodywork systems of Reich, Rolf and Alexander. What Reich called character armor resembles what yogis call *kleshas*: chronic, maladaptive psychological tendencies that distort posture and disturb body function.[6] The purpose of hatha yoga is to bend, stretch, and twist these kleshas out of our systems. Research suggests hatha yoga does indeed confer broad psychologic benefits (including lowered depression) on its practitioners.[7]

There are two major types of klesha, each a departure in one or another direction from the ideal or *sattvic* posture. A sattvic person has the gracefully erect bearing of someone who has been Rolfed or has mastered the Alexander Technique. A person with the *rajasic* klesha has the bearing of a drill sergeant. Back over-arched, chest and butt pushed out, muscles stiff and tight, she's inclined to rigidity, compulsiveness and emotional insensitivity. In contrast, the *tamasic* type has the slack, downcast bearing of the meek or depressed. Droopy head, rounded shoulders, sunken chest, she's afraid to embrace life and "gives up easily and tends towards self-pity, carrying the burdens of the world on the shoulders."[6] The rajasic person tightens or explodes under stress; the tamasic slackens or implodes.

Whichever klesha you're inclined to, *asanas* (yogic postures) which bend or stretch your body in the opposite direction are the cure.[6] For the hunched tamasic, the backward-bending rajasic asanas arch the back, puff out the chest and flatten the shoulders. To adopt these postures (the cobra, locust, bow and dancer, for instance) is to feel the outgoingness of rajasic energy—assertiveness training, yoga style.

For the rajasic person, forward-bending asanas, like the sitting forward-bend, in which you slowly fold yourself up like a closed book, are the ticket. With their navel-gazing self-intimacy, these asanas can gently bring the stoical raja face to face with his soft underbelly, with his suppressed grief or shame. And while they may intensify the tamasic's passivity and introversion, in small doses they may simply soothe and relax him.

BREATHING AND BREATHWORK

Eastern bodyworkers have always said so, and now Western bodyworkers and some scientists concur: *most of us don't breathe right*. We breathe shallowly from the top of the chest when we should be letting our bellies bulge like babies so the bottoms of our lungs, where the blood-flow is greatest, can breathe too. Deprived of *prana*, the "life force" in the air, we are less vital and alert, say the yogis. Starved for oxygen, the scientists point out, and stuffed with unexpired carbon dioxide, we weaken our immune systems, lower our energy and are prey to anxiety and depression.[8] Just look how depressed people with clinical breathing disorders are![9] But "do it [breathe] right," promises physician and biochemist Sheldon Hendler, "and you may inherit more than the wind; you're also likely to acquire high energy, improved metabolism, good health, endurance, and longevity.[8 (p. 95)]

When you inhale the "right" way, your belly balloons out to let the muscle layer at the bottom of the chest cavity, the diaphragm, drop a few inches and give your lungs more breathing room. To get the idea, Hendler suggests resting your hands on your belly just under the rib cage and feeling it balloon all the way out as you inhale and contract as you exhale. (The *complete breathing* exercise of hatha yoga goes even further than this.) Doing this just a few minutes each day, Hendler promises, can greatly boost your vitality and well-being.

T'AI CHI CHUAN

Kung Fu on Valium, meditation in motion—in China, where exercise is a favorite form of psychotherapy, the immensely popular discipline of *t'ai chi chuan* is the exercise of choice for depression.[10] Here in the West, where t'ai chi is also catching on, research suggests it has the stress-relieving effects of moderate exercise.[11] The long form, which usually takes 45 minutes, is preferable to the short form for treating depression, according to physician and t'ai chi Grand Master S. C. Man.[12]

ACUPUNCTURE

If depression has given you a craving for punishment, the prickly art of acupuncture might seem like just the medicine for you.

In China, acupuncture (especially electroacupuncture—in

which mild electrical current is passed through the needles) is a popular prescription for nervous exhaustion and depression.[13] In Russia, psychiatrists are confirming the antidepressant effect.[14] And in the United States, psychiatrist Louise Wensel of the Washington Acupuncture Center in Washington, D.C. has (at last count) treated 872 depressives with a combined acupuncture and orthomolecular regimen.[15] Of those, 686 (79 percent) have enjoyed "significant" improvement, 183 (21 percent) "slight" improvement, and for just three, no improvement. Wensel's patients have typically begun to feel better after the very first of six to ten daily acupuncture treatments. Maintenance sessions have then come every week or two, or every few months.

Harder evidence comes from J. S. Han of Beijing Medical University.[16] Han cites research showing that acupuncture can stimulate major mood-regulating neurochemicals like norepinephrine, serotonin, and the endorphins. In a controlled study at Han's university, five weeks of daily electroacupuncture brought complete or near-complete relief to most of 47 severely depressed patients. Because there were no side effects, Han rated electroacupuncture superior to its competition, a popular antidepressant drug.

THERAPEUTIC TOUCH

Something miraculous is happening to the nursing profession. Thousands of nurses are learning to heal by laying on of hands. And many are learning it at *school*. Some are even learning *therapeutic touch* at New York University from the nursing professor there who "discovered" it.[17]

Therapeutic touch is a modern revival of healing through goodwill—through channeling TLC from one person's "energy field" to another's. A hit among nurses and patients in many clinics and hospitals, its most conspicuous benefits are subjective: it makes people feel better. Over a dozen studies attest to that.[18]

SAFE BODYWORKING

If there are any hazards to bodywork (assuming a competent practitioner), they're mostly psychological. Bodywork, particularly the aggressive, psychotherapeutically oriented kind, can unleash people's demons. If client and therapist aren't up to handling them, depression can get worse, not better.

Finding a Bodyworker

Reputation, training and certification are a bodywork therapist or instructor's best qualifications. Training for bodywork disciplines can involve hundreds, sometimes thousands, of hours of supervised study and practice prior to certification. Practitioners who have little training—a weekend workshop, a mail-order diploma—are less likely to measure up.

NOTES

1. T. Field et al., "Massage Reduces Anxiety in Child and Adolescent Psychiatric Patients," *J Am Acad Child Adolescent Psychiatry* 31(January 1992): 125–131.

2. H. A. Otto, "Toward a Wholistic Psychotherapy, Counseling, and Social Work Treatment Program." In Herbert A. Otto and James W. Knight, eds., *Dimensions in Holistic Healing* (Chicago: Nelson Hall, 1979), pp. 125–140.

3. Alexander Lowen, *Depression and the Body: The Biological Basis of Faith and Reality* (Harmondsworth, Middlesex, England: Penguin Books, 1973).

4. Sherry Suib Cohen, *The Magic of Touch* (New York: Harper & Row, 1987).

5. Winfred Barlow, *The Alexander Principle*, rev. ed. (London: Gollancz, 1990).

6. M. Lockhart, "The Teacher's Role in the Therapeutic Process." In M. L. Gharote and Maureen Lockhart, eds., *The Art of Survival: A Guide to Yoga Therapy* (London: Unwin Paperbacks, 1987), pp. 37–65.

7. International Society of Sport Psychology, "Physical Activity and Psychological Benefits: A Position Statement," *Sport Psychologist* 6(June 1992):199–203.

8. Sheldon Saul Hendler, *The Oxygen Breakthrough: 30 Days to an Illness-Free Life* (New York: William Morrow, 1989).

9. R. Kellner et al., "Dyspnea, Anxiety, and Depression in Chronic Respiratory Impairment," *Gen Hosp Psychiatry* 14(January 1992):20–28.

10. *Knocking at the Gate of Life and Other Healing Exercises From China: The Official Handbook of the People's Republic of China*, trans. Edward C. Chang (Emmaus, Penn.: Rodale Press, 1985).

11. P. Jin, "Efficacy of Tai Chi, Brisk Walking, Meditation, and Reading in Reducing Mental and Emotional Stress," *J Psychosom Res* 36(May 1992):361–370.

12. S. C. Man, personal communication, 1988.

13. W. Chang, "Electroacupuncture and ECT" (letter), *Biol Psychiatry* 19(August 1984):1271–1272.

14. K. I. Dudaeva et al., [Neurophysiologic Changes During the Treatment of Endogenous Depression by Reflexotherapy], *Zhurnal Nevropatologii I Psikhiatrii Imeni S. S. Korsakova* 90(4, 1990):99–103.

15. Louise O. Wensel, *Acupuncture in Medical Practice* (Reston, Va.: Reston Publishing, 1980).

16. J. S. Han, "Electroacupuncture: An Alternative to Antidepressants for Treating Affective Diseases?" *Int J Neurosc* 29:79–92, 1986.

17. Delores Krieger, *Accepting Your Power to Heal: The Personal Practice of Therapeutic Touch* (San Francisco: Bear and Co., 1993).

18. J. F. Quinn and A. J. Strelkauskas, "Psychoimmunologic Effects of Therapeutic Touch on Practitioners and Recently Bereaved Recipients: A Pilot Study," *Adv Nurs Sci* 15(June 1993):13–26.

TWENTY-THREE

Journeys Out of Stress: Relaxation and Meditation

THERE is a dizzying variety of antidotes in the self-improvement marketplace to that most formidable health foe, stress. Yet nearly all of these tools and techniques feature the same active ingredient: relaxation.

It's no surprise. Relaxation is the opposite of the tense, "fight-or-flight" state provoked by stress. What stress perturbs in our bodies and minds, relaxation restores. Teach people to relax or meditate, studies show, and their health tends to improve: their need for potentially depressing medications (for epilepsy, hypertension, migraine, anxiety, insomnia) diminishes or disappears: their spirits rise.[1-10] They even seem to live longer![8]

RELAXATION FOR DEPRESSION

It might seem odd to suggest we need to relax when we're depressed. Aren't we "relaxed" enough as it is?

Well, not exactly. Passive on the outside, underneath we're apt to be seething with tension, our autonomic nervous systems on overdrive.[11] We may be still, but we're not serene. We're stuck. Stuck with problems we can't resolve, struggling with them one moment, collapsing in despair the next. Real relaxation can help us get off this treadmill in a variety of ways:

• When we relax, we relax the high-strung sympathetic side of our autonomic nervous systems. The parasympathetic side, which facilitates recovery from the effects of stress, takes over. The deeper we relax, the deeper the healing that can take place.

• Deep relaxation facilitates inner work. We can read and know our own minds more clearly (Chapter 25), paint richer healing imagery (Chapter 27) and absorb therapeutic suggestions at deeper levels (Chapter 26). As we approach the still center of our being, we come to know ourselves and our true needs more intimately. We may even have moments in which we seem to transcend our worldly identities and come home to something more fundamental, something ineffably secure and satisfying.

By itself, relaxation seems to be only a mild antidepressant[12] (meditation is stronger stuff). But used as the basis for other psychotherapeutic practices (suggestion, music therapy, and the like) or as part of a broader antidepressant program, it's likely to be a worthwhile investment.

HOW TO RELAX

Relaxing doesn't mean collapsing into your favorite easy chair to watch the six o'clock news through gritted teeth.

To really relax it's not enough just to sit still. We also have to let go of the tensions in our bodies and minds. Our muscles and wills are always grabbing at things—or resisting them. To relax, we have to cool this striving and straining down. Many tools and techniques can help us. Some work mainly through the body, some through the mind, but all ultimately relax the *mind/body* as a whole. Here are some of the most popular and effective ones.

Progressive Muscle Relaxation

A relaxed body begets a relaxed mind. This is the premise of *progressive muscle relaxation* (PMR), probably the most commonly prescribed of relaxation techniques. In PMR you sit or lie back, close your eyes and progressively relax each of your muscle groups, from head down to toe (or vice versa).

It helps to first exaggerate the tension. Before trying to relax your jaw, for instance, clench it for a few seconds. Then let it go for 20 to 30 seconds. After you've done this a few times your jaw might still feel like a battering ram, but if you keep practicing your PMR scales twice a day (as recommended) it should soon begin to soften.[13] After a few weeks or months you should be able to demilitarize your entire body in just minutes or seconds.[13]

Suggestion and Imagery

A powerful way to get your mind/body to relax is to ask it to. As you inhale, mentally say "I am ..." As you exhale, say "... re-laxed," feeling the tension drain out of you.[14]

Images can speak louder than words. Saying "relax, relax, relax already!" to your stiff neck may not get you far. But if you picture your neck as a thick, wire cable and then patiently imagine the strands unwinding, your neck may take the hint. Or perhaps it's more like a poker that needs melting. Or a steel beam. . . . The point is, *your* imagery is the best imagery.

Here's a powerful technique from my own arsenal. Close your eyes and let your attention go to any tense or uncomfortable part of your body. Now ask yourself what you can apply to that spot to make it feel better (light, warmth, fluid, touch, etc.). Do it in your imagination and then move on to the next uncomfortable spot.

Here are a few "stock" relaxation images:[15]

Lie down and imagine you're in a peaceful place, then . . .

Imagine you're a marionette, your head and limbs sprawled loosely in all directions.

Imagine your body parts are made of concrete, sinking, sinking, sinking . . .

Imagine they're balloons. Let the air out, one balloon at a time.

Relaxing Clenched Attitudes

Another way to relax is to release the tension in mental muscles taut with anger, worry, shame, resentment, craving or dread. You can loosen their grip just by acknowledging them.

While mentally repeating the words *I accept* (or *I recognize* or *I understand*), let some inner tension fill your consciousness until you can recognize and name it. (I accept . . . I accept . . . *I accept that I wish I weren't growing old*.) Keep repeating the process. Every time you recognize and name an inner tension, you relax a little more.*

MEDITATION _____

Every day millions of North Americans take time off to meditate. Often it's on the advice of their doctors, for research suggests meditation is a stress-relief tool *par excellence*, good for whatever ails you and then some.[1,2,4–8,10] Psychologically, meditators tend to become less tense, less neurotic, less addictive,[4,6,10,17] more empathic, loving, flexible, intelligent, creative and productive.[2,6] And less depressed.

Meditation, some therapists report, can be very helpful for people who suffer chronically from mild depression.[18] Controlled studies have generally concurred.[4,10] In a well-designed trial from Princeton University, most of 76 mildly depressed, "stressed out" subjects improved markedly within six weeks of learning to meditate. Nonmeditating controls improved only slightly.[1]

Meditation's value for major depression is less certain. One research group found transcendental meditation (TM) unhelpful for severely depressed patients who were very slowed down, but highly effective for those who were agitated.[19] Curiously, therapists have reported that severely depressed patients often have to be coaxed to keep meditating, especially when they start to feel *better*![18–20] "I had my own feelings back again," is how one tough

*This exercise is inspired by a powerful self-help technique called "focusing."[16]

customer—referring to her depressive feelings—described the benefits of not meditating anymore to Princeton psychologist Patricia Carrington.[18] Adjunctive psychotherapy can make meditation more agreeable to depressives, just as meditation, according to the American Psychiatric Association, can make psychotherapy more effective.[7]

HOW TO MEDITATE

The common denominator in the many different forms of meditation is *focus*. The common goal: to shift the meditator's attention from the frenetic periphery of his being to the peaceful center. (The health benefits are extra.) The most popular forms of meditation are mantra meditation and mindfulness/insight meditation.

Mantra Meditation

In the East, mantras are regarded as sacred sounds which convey Divine Grace to the meditator. Gurus carefully pick an appropriate mantra for each student. TM also provides each meditator with his or her own sacred Sanskrit mantra, but according to ex-TM teachers it's selected by formula from a very limited stock. Most Western meditation experts advise people to pick any traditional Eastern or Western mantra they like—or to invent their own, reflecting their personal values and preferences.[3,18,21] Research suggests that this is an effective approach.[1,3,18] After you've settled on a mantra, traditionalists recommend sticking with it.

Some popular mantras:

Hindu: *Ram* (rohm). *Rama* (*roh*-ma). *Om mani padme hum. Om namah Shivaya.*

Christian: *God is Love. My God and my all. Jesus. Lord Jesus Christ, have mercy upon me.* (This Prayer of the Heart may make a better mantra if shortened, e.g., *Lord have mercy*, or simply, *Mercy*.) *Hail Mary. The Lord is my Shepherd. Kyrie eleison.*

Judaic/Hebrew: *Shalom* (shah-*lom*—peace). *Adonai* (uh-doh-*nie*—God). *Elohim* (eh-loh-*heem*—God). *Adonai Elohenu, Adonai Ehad* (The Lord our God, the Lord is One).

Muslim: *Allah* (God). *La ilaha illa llah* (There is no God but God).

Secular: *Peace. Love. Hope. Faith.*

Others: *In God (All, One) are we all. God (All) and I are one. God be my guide.*

Affirmations (Chapter 26) can also be used or adapted as mantras.

A SIMPLE GUIDE TO MANTRA MEDITATION:

Pick a time when you're alert. Sit (preferably with your back straight), close your eyes, relax for a moment and when it feels right, begin thinking your mantra. Allow the pace, volume, intonation and any other qualities of the mantra to vary if they will. Whenever your mind wanders, gently return to the mantra.

As you follow the mantra, your stream of consciousness will continue as usual. But the contents will come from deeper or subtler levels and may be more vivid and compelling. If anything comes up that disturbs or engrosses you, let it flow without getting carried away by it. Spontaneous nervous activity such as twitches or vocalizations may also occur. When you can, refocus on the mantra. If your associations or reactions are too disturbing, don't meditate without professional guidance.

Don't strive for spiritual effects during meditation. Meditation is about being, not doing; letting, not willing. Efforts to stage-manage things inhibit the spontaneity of the process.[3,20]

After ten or 20 minutes, stop thinking the mantra and take a minute or two to gently "surface" by slowly stretching, rubbing your eyes, and so forth.

Mindfulness Meditation

Zen "sitting meditation" (*shikan-taza*) and the *vipissana* mindfulness-insight meditation of Therevadan Buddhism are major examples of a type of meditation that focuses nonselectively on the spectacle of consciousness, on everything that crosses the mind. To get a taste of what it's like, close your eyes and simply witness whatever is happening in your mind—each passing thought, sensation, emotion or impulse—*without getting swallowed up and carried away*, without losing yourself in the passing show. Whenever you catch yourself getting caught up (or drifting or daydreaming), witness *that,* too.

Mindfulness meditation gradually weans us from our hyponotic identification with the contents of our consciousness. It nurtures true inner freedom. At the University of Massachusetts Medical Center, Dr. Jon Kabat-Zinn and his associates teach it to patients. Their research suggests that it greatly reduces their tension, anxiety and depression.[10,22]

HOW MUCH MEDITATION?

Spiritual aspirants sometimes meditate all day, every day. But for ordinary "householders," the usual prescription is two 15– to 30–minute sessions a day. Adverse reactions to meditation (see below) are "dose-related." Even a few minutes a day can make some depressives feel worse, which is why Patricia Carrington recommends they meditate very briefly until they're sure meditation agrees with them. It's also prudent to have access to a therapist in case overly disturbing material comes up.[18]

Sometimes meditation produces instant euphoria, but that soon passes. The lasting benefits of meditation unfold subtly over weeks, months and years.

TECHNO-RELAXATION

If you're one of those people who likes to relax with gadgets and gizmos, you'll be glad to know there are gadgets and gizmos out there that can help you relax.

Floating

In most major cities there is a health club, a tanning salon or a flotation center where you can park your body for a spell in a flotation tank: a lightless, soundless, womb-temperature chamber where you float in peace on a dead sea of mineral water. With sensory stimulation pared to a minimum, it's not uncommon for floaters to drift into a state of blissful disembodiment. So disencumbered, research suggests, they can more readily tackle personal problems, lick bad habits, find relief from pain or mild depression or enjoy other benefits.[23,24]

Biofeedback

Portable and affordable, electronic biofeedback devices allow you to eavesdrop on your body's subtlest tension signals—sweating, muscle tension, brain waves. This feedback can guide you to exceptionally deep levels of relaxation.

"Mind Machines" and Psychoacoustic Tapes

When we relax, our brain waves "relax" too, becoming slower and steadier. Light and sound pulsing forcefully at these same low frequencies can also "relax" our brain waves. The rest of us follows suit, which is the way "mind machines" work.

The simplest mind machines, which are about as small and cheap as a good Walkman, come with earphones and/or goggles to convey the relaxing frequencies to your brain. But some psychoacoustic self-help tapes and CDs do the trick for a fraction of the cost. Typically, these recordings are overlaid with New Age sound effects—Tibetan bells, whale songs and the like—and mellow New Age or classical music. Many also feature suggestions (often subliminal), affirmations, guided imagery or other therapeutic talk.

Electrostimulation Devices

The healing power of electricity may sound like something out of 19th-century fringe medicine, but it's hard at work today in most hospital pain clinics in the guise of *transcutaneous electrical nerve stimulation* (TENS). Portable TENS devices usually help relieve chronic pain by delivering weak electric currents to the site of the pain or to relevant acupuncture points. Similar devices (traditionally known as "electrosleep") have also been used for many years to relieve neuropsychiatric disorders. Most controlled studies suggest these *cranial electrical stimulation devices* can be helpful for anxiety, insomnia, chronic pain, dementia, drug dependency and perhaps depression.[25] Consumer versions such as the "Alpha-Stim" are catching on as mind machines.[26]

The Mind/Body Tech Marketplace

Mind/body tools and toys can be purchased from self-improvement stores and mail-order companies. A major mail-order retailer is Tools For Exploration, 4460 Redwood Highway, Suite 2, San Rafael, CA 94903, 1–800–456–9887. In some cities you can buy time on a mind machine at a "brain spa" or a "mind gym."

OTHER WAYS TO RELAX

Several other relaxation aids are discussed elsewhere in the book: most forms of bodywork (e.g., massage, yoga, therapeutic touch), relaxing music and tranquilizing herbs and scents. There's more on relaxing suggestions in Chapter 27 and on relaxing imagery in Chapter 28.

Of course, you can use more than one relaxation tool or technique at a time.

IS IT SAFE TO RELAX?

Ironically, relaxation and meditation can themselves be stressful. The loosening of chronic tensions can create shock waves—aches, pains, tics, twitches, crying, screaming—and temporarily worsen health problems, including depression. Some people are disturbed—even panicked or driven temporarily psychotic[27]—when threatening psychic material works its way out of the unconscious like a splinter. Others are dislocated by the changes in self-image and consciousness that meditation (especially if practiced intensively) can induce.[27] For many people, it seems, the benefits of long-term meditation are marred by at least one or two negative effects: psychological or psychosomatic symptoms (e.g., anxiety, depression, depersonalization), interpersonal conflicts or "addiction" to meditation.[27] People who meditate the most and the longest seem particularly prone to these mixed reactions to meditation,[27] perhaps because they're more disturbed to begin with. Clearly, deep relaxation and meditation techniques are "psychoactive drugs" that must be used with some caution and, for most people, in moderation.

NOTES

1. P. Carrington et al., "The Use of Meditation-Relaxation Techniques for the Management of Stress in a Working Population," *J Occup Med* 22(April 1980):221–231.

2. P. Carrington, "Meditation Techniques in Clinical Practice." In Lawrence Edwin Abt and Irving R. Stuart, eds., *The Newer Therapies: A Sourcebook* (New York: Van Nostrand Reinhold, 1982), pp. 60–78.

3. Herbert Benson with William Proctor, *Beyond the Relaxation Response* (New York: Times Books, 1984).

4. M. M. Delmonte, "Psychometric Scores and Meditation Practice: A Literature Review," *Person Individ Diff* 5(5, 1984):559–563.

5. C. Patel et al., "Trial of Relaxation in Reducing Coronary Risk," *Brit Med J* 290(April 13, 1985):1103–1106.

6. Robert Roth, *Maharishi Mahesh Yogi's Transcendental Meditation* (New York: Donald I. Fine, 1987).

7. J. L. Craven, "Meditation and Psychotherapy," *Can J Psychiatry* 34(October 1989):648–653.

8. C. N. Alexander et al., "Transcendental Meditation, Mindfulness, and Longevity: An Experimental Study With the Elderly," *J Person Soc Psychol* 57(December 1989):950–964.

9. C. A. Puskarich et al., "Controlled Examination of Effects of Progressive Relaxation Training on Seizure Reduction," *Epilepsia* 33(July-August 1992):675–680.

10. J. Kabat-Zinn et al., "Effectiveness of a Meditation-Based Stress Reduction Program in the Treatment of Anxiety Disorders," *Am J Psychiatry* 149(July 1992):936–943.

11. K. Achte et al., eds., *Psychopathology of Depression* (Helsinki: Psychiatrica Finnica Supplementum, 1980).

12. I. L. McCann and D. S. Holmes, "Influence of Aerobic Exercise on Depression," *J Person Soc Psychol* 46(5, 1984):1142–1147.

13. Martha Davis et al., *The Relaxation & Stress Reduction Workbook*, 3rd ed. (Oakland, Calif.: New Harbinger Publications, 1988).

14. C. N. Shealy, "Self-Health: From Pain to Health Maintenance." In Leslie J. Kaslof, ed., *Wholistic Dimensions in Healing* (Garden City, NY: Doubleday, 1978), pp. 176–178.

15. Maxwell Maltz, *Psycho-Cybernetics* (New York: Pocket Books, 1966).

16. Eugene T. Gendlin, *Focusing* (New York: Bantam, 1978, 1981).

17. K. R. Eppley et al., "Differential Effects of Relaxation Techniques on Trait Anxiety: A Meta-Analysis," *J Clin Psychol* 45(November 1989):957–974.

18. Patricia Carrington, *Freedom in Meditation* (Garden City, N. Y.: Anchor Press, 1977).

19. B. C. Glueck and C. F. Stroebel, "Biofeedback and Meditation in the Treatment of Psychiatric Illnesses," *Compr Psychiatry* 16(July/August 1975):303–321.

20. Harold H. Bloomfield et al., *TM: Discovering Inner Energy and Overcoming Stress* (New York: Dell, 1975).

21. Daniel Goleman, *The Meditative Mind* (Los Angeles: Tarcher, 1988).

22. Jon Kabat-Zinn, *Full Catastrophe Living* (New York: Delta, 1991).

23. Michael Hutchison, *The Book of Floating* (New York: William Morrow, 1984).

24. A. Barabasz and M. Barabasz, eds., *Clinical and Experimental Restricted Environmental Stimulation* (New York: Springer, 1993).

25. See for example: E. M. Krupitsky et al., "The Administration of Transcranial Electric Treatment for Affective Disturbances Therapy in Alcoholic Patients," *Drug and Alcohol Dependence* 27(January 1991):1–6.

26. Michael Hutchison, *Megabrain: New Tools and Techniques for Brain Growth and Mind Expansion* (New York: William Morrow, 1986).

27. D. H. Shapiro, "Adverse Effects of Meditation: A Preliminary Investigation of Long-Term Meditators," *Int J Psychosom* 39(1–4, 1992):62–67.

Thinking, feeling, expressing, communicating, taking action . . . These are some of the ways we spontaneously try and cope with the problems that depress us—and with depression itself. But anything we do naturally can also be nurtured. We can learn specific psychotherapeutic techniques and strategies; we can benefit from the experience of psychotherapists and others who have trod the path to recovery or illumined it; we can, in other words, learn to cope better.

As we'll see in the next seven chapters; this can be as powerful a means as any to overcome depression.

TWENTY-FOUR

Being More Active to Become Less Depressed

When we're psychologically depressed, we're *behaviorally* depressed. Life no longer sweeps us up so easily into its swirl of activities. On the contrary, expecting more pain than gain, we retreat. But the more we pull back, the more convinced we become we really *are* unfit for life. And that depresses us even more.

There's a very direct and simple (on the face of it simplistic) antidote to this vicious cycle: *Be more active.*

This, of course, is easier said than done. Cognitive-behavioral therapists (perhaps the majority of clinical psychologists today) are the experts in teaching depressives how. They're convinced from clinical experience and dozens of studies (e.g., of cognitive therapy [Chapter 25]) that "the most powerful antidepressant is successful performance"[1] and that "virtually *any* meaningful activity has a decent chance of brightening your mood."[2] (p.86)

THE ART OF BEING MORE ACTIVE TO BECOME LESS DEPRESSED

Cognitive-behavioral self-help books all teach the art of being more active to become less depressed.[2,3,4] Here are the basics.

Developing an Inventory of Activities

The first thing you have to do is come up with an "inventory" of activities you can schedule. A good method is to get relaxed and then "brainstorm" on the possibilities, recording them on paper or computer. To brainstorm means going for quantity, variety and originality of ideas, without worrying about being "right." It means erring on the side of too much rather than too little, happily recording even the "silliest" notions. These silly ones can speak volumes about your real feelings. And later they often can be adapted to the real world. "I feel like flying to the moon" can amount to buying a telescope or taking a course in astronomy.

Here are some brainstorming aids:

• Try some sentence completions. Keep repeating the opening words to trigger deeper, richer associations. Every sentence begins with "I would like to" or "I want to" and continues with:

know . . . learn . . . understand . . . make . . . build . . . design . . . find . . . discover . . . invent . . . go . . . play . . . be with . . . talk to . . . see . . . hear . . . feel . . . smell . . . taste . . . tell . . . say . . . show . . . explain . . . fix . . . clean . . . improve . . . get . . . buy . . . give . . . help . . . be able to . . .

Or just try: I would like to _____.

Also try:

God (my Higher Self, the Universe, Jesus) would like me to (wants me to) _____.

I should (ought to, need to, have to) _____. This sentence completion is mainly intended to get some of the ghosts of guilt out of your head. You'll probably feel better for it. As to whether you act on any of these "shoulds," the next chapter on cognitive therapy will help you decide how compulsory they really "should" be.

**Visualize your "depressed self." Ask: "What can he *do* to help himself?" Consider asking any of your "benign inner figures" what they think (for more on them, see page 233).

Now that you have a list of activities, you can get your critical faculties back in gear. You'll need them to convert this raw material into an inventory of doable, schedulable activities. Bear in mind that activities are most likely to relieve depression if:

They're inherently pleasurable or uplifting for you. (Or used to be, before you got depressed.)

They engross you and distract you from your worries.

They enhance your self-esteem; they make you feel decent, lovable, capable, admirable.

They bring approval from "significant others."

They help you achieve personal goals, fulfill wishes.

They help resolve the very problem(s) you're depressed about. (Chapter 26 is all about that.)

They further the treatment of your depression or are antidepressants themselves (e.g., planning and implementing an antidepressant program for yourself [Chapter 33]).

You *have* to do them, and so doing them lightens your guilt load.

Scheduling Activities

Now that you have an inventory of activities, the best way to ensure some actually get done is to *schedule* them. Cognitive-behavioral therapists recommend scheduling activities a week at a time, for every hour of the day. Include routine activities (washing, eating), obligatory activities (work, school), relatively passive ones (napping, watching television), blocks of free time, and, of course, time to work on the schedule itself. Feel free to schedule on more or less than a weekly basis, if that suits you, and to make your schedule more or less structured (e.g., to schedule alternative activities for the same time periods). It's important not to feel daunted by the schedule. Think of it as a guideline you can alter as you go along, not a rule book. "Accomplishing even a part of your scheduled activities," promises cognitive therapist David Burns, "will in all probability give you some satisfaction and will combat your depression."[2(p.87)]

Finally, every day try to record how much pleasure or discomfort you got from each activity on a scale of -5 to +5. On a separate scale record how good you felt for *having done* it. High scoring activities can be repeated more often.

WORKING ON YOUR RESISTANCES _____

Having trouble following your schedule? Having trouble *drafting* a schedule? It's hard work defying depressive inertia, with its nihilism and self-doubt. In the next chapter we'll explore some of the cognitive solutions recommended by cognitive-behavioral therapists. Here you might like to try a powerful sentence completion my friend Anna Olson teaches in her creative writing workshops: "I want (would like) to [name the activity you're having trouble doing], but I can't because———." Complete the sentence, on paper, with whatever comes into your head (and heart) at least a dozen times. It often takes that long to get to the bottom of things.

MAKING IT EASY FOR YOURSELF _____

Here are some other things you can do to make it easier "to be more active to become less depressed."

• Always *reward yourself* for performing scheduled activities, especially the hard ones. Rewards can be *money, time* (to indulge in idle pleasures), *points* (redeemable in dollars or time), and/or simply patting yourself on the back for triumphing over your inertia. (Patting yourself on the back at every turn—learning to schmooze with yourself, big time—is the essence of a very effective cognitive-behavioral therapy for depression.[5]) It can also help greatly if loved ones cheer you on.

• Break large or complex activities down into bite-size, schedulable steps or subactivities. Reward yourself for each step, even if you don't make it to the finish line.

• Schedule activities "on time," not "by the job." In other words, for 9:00 to 9:30 AM, don't schedule "fix the ozone layer" or "write that novel"; schedule *"work on* fixing the ozone layer" or "sharpen pencils." When you schedule "on time" you always win just by showing up; and at this point winning is more important, clinically, than necessarily getting anything done.

• Don't be dismayed if activities aren't as fun or facile as they used to be. You're like an injured athlete, easing back into training. It'll be a while before you can play again with your old verve.

• Don't beat yourself for breaking your schedule. Depression being the dead weight it is, much of the time you'll deserve top honors just for following your feet out of bed in the morning. Just try to modify your schedule to keep it within reach.

• Regard your "failures" as opportunities to become more aware of, and to work on, the mental stuff that got in the way. Which brings us to our next chapter.

NOTES

1. P. McLean, "Behavioral Therapy: Theory and Research." In John A. Rush, ed., *Short-Term Psychotherapies for Depression* (New York: The Guilford Press, 1982), pp. 19–49.

2. David D. Burns, *Feeling Good: The New Mood Therapy* (New York: William Morrow, 1980).

3. Peter M. Lewinsohn et al., *Control Your Depression* (Englewood Cliffs, N. J.: Prentice-Hall, 1978).

4. Gary Emery, *A New Beginning: How You Can Change Your Life Through Cognitive Therapy* (New York: Simon and Schuster, 1981).

5. L. P. Rehm et al., "Cognitive and Behavioral Targets in a Self-Control Therapy Program for Depression," *J Consult Clin Psychol* 55(1, 1987):60–67.

TWENTY-FIVE

Reasoning with Yourself: The Cognitive Approach to Depression

As a man thinketh in his heart, so is he.

—THE BIBLE

There is nothing either good or bad but thinking makes it so.

—HAMLET

DEPRESSED people are notoriously, stubbornly, negative. Try telling them life isn't really *that* bleak, that they aren't *really* such horrible persons, that their fate *isn't* sealed, that they *will* get better and what do you get? Disbelief. "That may be true for other people, but not for me. . . . You don't know how rotten I really am. . . . My situation is hopeless—I know it with every fiber of my being."

Aaron Beck was well aware of this airtight negativity of depression. As a psychiatrist who had written a minor classic on depression, he had been fencing with it for years. Yet he still believed that if you could just *reason* with depressives persistently enough—or, better yet, get them to reason that way with themselves—you might be able to free them from the stranglehold of their negative thinking—and from depression itself.

He was right! The program for reasoning your way out of depression that Beck developed in the 1960s and 1970s at the University of Philadelphia is probably the most intensively investigated of all psychotherapies. In well over two dozen controlled clinical trials, Beck's *cognitive therapy* (CT) has almost always brought relief or recovery to a majority of major depressives within weeks. Typically, by the end of a 12- to 20-week course of

CT, one hour a week, the average patient has enjoyed a greater than 70-percent reduction in depression, equalling or bettering control patients' response to antidepressant drugs.[1,2] CT has even proven irresistible to some of the most severely depressed inpatients.[3] Once recovered, CT alumni seem to hold up as well as depressives maintained on drugs.[3]

The Greek Stoic philosopher Epictetus, a hero of cognitive therapists, summed up their philosophy long ago: "Men are disturbed not by things, but by the view which they take of them." The cognitive prescription for depression, therefore, is to change your point of view. To that end, cognitive therapy invites us to become more critically aware of the thoughts and attitudes that depress us. It teaches us to systematically challenge their validity and replace them with more reasonable, more positive, alternatives. By persisting, we can gradually lift ourselves out of depression.

That's not the whole prescription, however. Cognitive therapy is actually a cognitive-*behavioral* therapy. Its clinical success depends, in part, on its "behavioral" emphasis on helping depressives be more active to become less depressed (Chapter 24).

Cognitive therapists have penned a number of excellent self-help books[4,5] which they claim can be used successfully by anyone who is mildly depressed and neither suicidal nor delusional. At least one clinical study suggests they're right.[6] Cognitive approaches are also featured in the self-help books of respected psychologists such as Albert Ellis[7] and Martin Seligman.[8]

If you're severely depressed, you may find it's just too hard to be calmly reasonable the cognitive way without professional help. Many clinical psychologists (and some psychiatrists) can provide that.

Here's how cognitive therapy works.

GETTING IN TOUCH WITH YOUR DEPRESSING "AUTOMATIC THOUGHTS"

Between what happens to us at point A and our depressive reaction to it at point B, cognitive therapists observe, there always are *thoughts*, in words or images, that get us there. Typically, these thoughts flash through our minds and leave their mark on us with little or no conscious scrutiny on our part. So hypnotized are we by these *automatic thoughts* (as cognitive therapists call them) that we barely realize we've just called ourselves some soul-withering name, accused ourselves of some unpardonable sin, swallowed uncritically some vision of doom and gloom or thought ourselves into a depressive corner in some other way.

The first order of business in cognitive therapy is to become more consciously aware of these depressing thoughts, to yank them out of the shadows and expose them to the light of reason. We can do this at any time, not just when the thoughts are occurring. Whenever we like, we can reflect on some depressing circumstance or situation and recall or recreate (or *anticipate*, if it's a downer we're dreading) the automatic thoughts associated with it.

Here's one way to do it. Close your eyes, relax and imagine a depressing problem or situation in your life. What is (are) the thought(s) that pass through your mind when you start to get down? *Write down* as many as you can think of. If they're hazy or ill defined, take time to bring them into focus. If they're nonverbal—visual images or sensations, for instance—verbalize them.

WORKING ON YOUR DEPRESSING AUTOMATIC THOUGHTS

Now you're ready to "talk back" to these automatic thoughts, one at a time—to challenge their truthfulness, reasonableness and just plain fairness and see if you can't replace them with kinder, gentler, more constructive alternatives. It's best to do this *on paper*. "Negative ideas are so powerful," cognitive therapists warn, "that if you try to answer them in your head, they'll immediately erase the answers."[5(p.65)]

Here are some things to consider as you challenge each automatic thought:

What evidence do I really have to support this thought?

Are there any other ways I could view this situation? How would other people see it? How would a fly on the wall, an extraterrestrial, a personal hero of mine, or God see it? Am I taking this too personally?

Am I overgeneralizing? Jumping to conclusions? Exaggerating or "catastrophizing"[7]—making a mountain out of a molehill, an abyss out of a pot-hole?

Am I wearing blinders? Am I screening out the positive—looking for "the cloud behind every silver lining"?

Am I thinking in rigid, all-or-nothing, black-or-white terms?

Am I guilty of what Albert Ellis calls "musturbatory thinking," of dogmatically and self-frustratingly insisting things *must* or *should* be a certain way?[7] Am I crippling myself with perfectionism?

Am I tyrannizing myself? Would I treat another person this way? Shouldn't I be kind to myself too?

Is this line of thought helping me or hindering me on my life's path? Can I come up with constructive alternatives that won't be so stifling?

Even if I *am* correct in my negative view, is the situation really *that bad*? Am I underestimating my ability to solve or cope with the problem? Am I forgetting that "this too shall pass"?

Is there some way I can test the validity of this thought—something I can do, someone I can ask?

ROOTING OUT THE MALADAPTIVE ASSUMPTIONS THAT UNDERLY YOUR AUTOMATIC THOUGHTS _____

Why do we have such depressing automatic thoughts in the first place? Why do we say such dispiriting things to ourselves? According to cognitive therapists it's because, deep down, we subscribe to equally negative or self-destructive beliefs. Our automatic thoughts are just a reflection of these maladaptive assumptions, which are even more deeply ingrained and unconscious. Typically we've absorbed these maladaptive "tapes," "programs" or unwritten "rule books" for living in our most impressionable formative years, and often under duress. We implicitly believe that (select the ones that apply):

I can't be happy unless everybody likes me.

If I fail at _____, I'm a failure as a person.

It's shameful to show weakness.

I have to be outstanding to be acceptable.

If I'm good to people, they must be good to me.

There's no way I can cope with disaster.

I'm nobody if/unless _____.

I *have* to love and be kind to *everyone*. (Worthy as an ideal; maladaptive as an assumption.)

Becoming aware of your maladaptive assumptions (the ones above are just a few examples), challenging them and replacing them with more adaptive ones is a major goal of cognitive therapy. And well it should be, for research indicates that if we recover from depression, yet continue to harbor many maladaptive assumptions, we are that much more likely to get depressed again.[9] Our unchallenged assumptions, it seems, always lie in wait, ready to trigger more depressing automatic thoughts the next time they're rubbed the wrong way by circumstances.

There are several ways you can recognize your maladaptive assumptions.

One powerful method is described by cognitive therapist David Burns.[4] Pick one of your depressing automatic thoughts and, for the sake of argument, assume it's *true*. Now, ask yourself: "Why would that be so bad?" When you've answered, ask: "Why would *that* be so bad?" Repeat until you can go no further. Each answer uncovers a more basic assumption.

Another powerful tool for identifying maladaptive assumptions is sentence completions. Try these:

I can't (don't deserve to) be happy (content, pleased with myself) unless _____.

I'm not lovable (likable, respectable, a good person) unless_____.

I deserve to be depressed because (if) _____.

While thinking of something that's depressing you, repeatedly complete the following sentences: I should _____. I shouldn't _____.

The assumptions you identify through these techniques should be taken to task, as you did your automatic thoughts. When you question and weigh them in the balance, can you make them more "adaptive"? Can you reject or reformulate them so that they sit well with your conscious values while allowing you to live and breathe?

Adaptively revised assumptions can become *affirmations*. More on those in Chapter 27.

NOTES

1. K. S. Dobson, "A Meta-Analysis of the Efficacy of Cognitive Therapy for Depression," *J Consult Clin Psychol* 57(March 1989):414–419.

2. J. H. Wright and M. E. Thase, "Cognitive and Biological Therapies: A Synthesis," *Psych Ann* 22(September 1992):451–458.

3. C. J. Robins and A. M. Hayes, "An Appraisal of Cognitive Therapy," *J Consult Clin Psychol* 61(April 1993):205–214.

4. David D. Burns, *Feeling Good: The New Mood Therapy* (New York: William Morrow, 1980).

5. Gary Emery, *A New Beginning: How You Can Change Your Life Through Cognitive Therapy* (New York: Simon and Schuster, 1981).

6. F. Scogin et al., "Comparative Efficacy of Cognitive and Behavioral Bibliotherapy for Mildly and Moderately Depressed Older Adults," *J Consult Clin Psychol* 57(March 1989):403–407.

7. Albert Ellis, *How to Stubbornly Refuse to Make Yourself Miserable About Anything—Yes, Anything* (New York: Carol Publishing, 1988).

8. Martin Seligman, *Learned Optimism* (New York: Random House, 1990).

9. A. D. Simons et al., "Cognitive Therapy and Pharmacotherapy for Depression," *Arch Gen Psychiatry* 43(January 1986):43–48.

TWENTY-SIX

Creative Problem-Solving for the Causes of Your Depression

As I've suggested in Chapter 2, whenever we become depressed we become depressed *about something*—something in our lives we find intolerable: a problem we feel *must* be solved. The problem may be sharp and focused—divorce, unemployment, the death of a loved one—or vague and diffuse—"I can't get anything done," "I can't seem to enjoy myself anymore." Its causes may be psychosocial, biophysical or both. But the problem is the reason we are depressed, and an obvious way to get undepressed is to resolve it. There's an art to that—and it can be learned.

For decades, psychologists have been teaching people how to solve their practical and professional problems the way an Einstein, an Edison or a Da Vinci might have. Recently, they've brought their problem-solving courses to the clinic. They've begun teaching people how to apply these creative problem-solving techniques to their *personal* problems—the problems that make them anxious, depressed, addictive, violent. Preliminary research suggests that this may be as effective a treatment for depression as any other.[1-3] In two studies,[2,3] a regimen of eight or ten weeks of "problem-solving therapy," one to one-and-a-half hours a week in small groups, has brought recovery or marked improvement to 23 out of 25 moderately to severely depressed persons. Only four out of 26 control-group subjects have fared this well. Months later, the clinical response has persisted.

Problem-solving therapy is usually taught by clinical psychologists, one-on-one or in groups. A typical course consists of 14 to 16 weekly two-hour sessions.[1] The dropout rate in clinical studies has been close to zero.

There don't seem to be any self-help books on problem-solving therapy. Academic books on the subject by Thomas D'Zurilla[1] and Arthur Nezu and associates[4] can be useful substitutes. So can self-help books on creative problem-solving in general, such as the classics by Sidney Parnes and associates.[5]

PROBLEM-SOLVING TOOLS AND TECHNIQUES _____

There are many things you can do to facilitate the creative problem-solving process:

Get into a creativity-enhancing state. Relaxation and meditation techniques and tools will get you there.

"Brainstorm." The basis of creative problem-solving is coming up with new ideas, lots of them. Enter *brainstorming*. More an attitude than a technique, brainstorming simply means tying and gagging the inner censor/critic and opening the floodgates. It's the opposite of getting all squinched up mentally, worrying about finding the one and only, RIGHT ANSWER. Often, right answers come dressed in the "wrong" clothing. They look impossible, irrelevant or silly, at first glance. But later, with a little creative tailoring they can look like a million bucks. When you brainstorm, every strange and motley idea—"the wilder the idea the better"[1 (p.125)]—is eagerly welcomed and duly recorded.

Externalize. You'll be working with lots of ideas. To avoid losing any—and to keep your head clear for new ones—"externalize" them as they come up by writing them on paper or computer.

Go with the creative flow. Our minds tend to bring forth their ideas and insights nonlinearly. Their tendency is to hop from *a* to *g* to *b* to *x* to *c* and then to *34*. And like spirals, they keep wanting to circle back over old ground to deposit fresh insights. We can get a lot further faster if we accept this tendency rather than resist it—if we stop trying to make progress in a straight line. So, *leave lots of white space* between and around all of your externalizations.

Use your imagination. Don't just think in words. *Imagine*—in as much detail as possible and from more than one point of view.

Translate the general to the specific, the abstract to the concrete and vice versa. Whenever you find yourself using an abstract or general concept (self-esteem, jealousy, success), translate it into specific, concrete examples. These are much easier to work with and act on. On the other hand, whenever you find yourself immersed in concrete specifics, see if you can infer the abstract principles they represent. There's power in knowing where the different spokes of the wheel converge.

THE STEPS IN CREATIVE PROBLEM-SOLVING _____

Creative problem-solving evolves in steps and stages, although considerable backtracking and leapfrogging normally take place (remember, we've gone nonlinear here!).

Getting in the Problem-Solving Mood

Perhaps the most critical step, especially when we're depressed, is the first one: overcoming our fear of trying, our pessimism, self-doubt and inertia. When this step was deliberately omitted in one clinical study, the antidepressant effect of problem-solving therapy was cut in half.[3]

So how do you get into the problem-solving mood?

• Try thinking of your problems not as *threats*, but as challenges or opportunities. If you're haunted by visions of failure, close your eyes, relax and imagine what it would be like to succeed. Promise yourself that even if you don't "succeed," you'll probably learn a useful thing or two in the process and that no sincere efforts are really wasted.

• Aim low. Don't think in terms of "Now I'm going to solve all of my problems." Just schedule a reasonable amount of time—say half an hour or an hour—to work on solving *a* problem. As long as you log the time, you've succeeded. Then collect a fat reward and, if you like, schedule another problem-solving session.

• Many of the antidepressant strategies discussed elsewhere in this book can help allay the apprehension, fatigue or other negativities you may be bringing to this exercise. They include cognitive therapy, relaxation, meditation, exercise, bodywork, suggestion and imagery work, art therapies, improved nutrition and nutritional and herbal supplements.

Taking Stock of Your Problems

Before you choose a problem to work on, it's a good idea to take stock of the whole range you have on your plate. Where are you hurting? Where is your life failing? That's where your problems are. Try describing or classifying each problem in more than one way, from more than one angle. Different descriptions will later suggest different solutions.

One problem often results from another, and many little problems can result from the same big one. To identify these underlying problems, ask "Why?" Why did my business fail? Why am I tired all the time? Why can't I get along with _____?

Selecting a Problem to Work On

In deciding which problem(s) to work on, it can help to rate the contenders according to criteria such as these:

How responsible for your depression does the problem seem to be?

How solvable do you think it is?

How much would settling it improve your life in general?

How bad would it be for you *not* to resolve it?

Clarifying Your Problem

Now that you've chosen a problem, your next challenge is to examine it much more closely than you probably have until now. *Is it really what you think it is?* Use the "cognitive" approach to find out. Subject the problem to the same kinds of questions you would ask of an automatic thought—"What evidence do I have that this is true?", "Am I jumping to conclusions?", and so on (see page 212). Do "research" if necessary: for example, observe your problem in action, read about it, ask other people's advice.

Now that you have a clearer take on your problem, the next step is to formulate one or, better yet, several goal statements for its solution "How can I [goal]?" "What can I do to _____?" The more of these goal statements you can come up with (each to tackle the problem from a different angle), the more alternative solutions you'll be able to come up with later.

It's not too late to identify deeper, perhaps more significant problems. Ask *Why?* of each goal statement. *Why* do you want to _____ anyway?

Coming Up with Alternative Solutions

Now it's time to brainstorm in high gear, to generate as many wild and crazy alternative solutions for your goal statements as you can.

A potent technique for generating original ideas is metaphorical or analagous thinking. Say your goal statement is "How can I meet a mate?" Metaphorically, you might redefine it as "how does a flower attract bees?" Analagously: "How would I find new clients for my business?" The most productive metaphors and analogies derive from things you know well. If you're a gardener you might ask, "How would I find new flowers for my garden?"

Another strategy is to think of other people. "How would Joe meet prospective partners?" Or do sentence completions: "To meet prospective partners I could _____."

Choosing Solutions

Now you can ungag your inner critic. He can help you evaluate your alternative solutions. Do any of the crazy ones contain a kernel of inspired lunacy that can be converted into something useful? Which ones can be rejected at a glance?

It helps to rehearse would-be solutions in your imagination or even with real people.

When you've amassed a group of contenders, rate them according to criteria such as *potential effectiveness, difficulty, fringe benefits* and *costs/risks*.

Perhaps you can't come up with any viable solutions, even after going back to the well or reconsidering and redefining your problem. In that case, just pick another problem to work on.

Implementing Your Solution Plan

Unless your problem is really simple, you'll probably want to go after it with more than one solution, concurrently or consecutively. And each solution will probably have to be broken down into small steps—*steps you can schedule (on paper) and reward yourself for doing*. As we saw in Chapter 24, this alone can help lift your depression.

When you try to implement your solutions, internal obstacles—automatic thoughts, cold feet, white-knuckle panics, may rear their ugly heads. You can deal with them using the same kinds of strategies recommended earlier for getting in the problem-solving mood. You can even treat them as problems to be solved in their own right. (How can I overcome my fear of _____? How can I stop procrastinating?)

One of the best ways to keep yourself on track is to let at least one other person in on what you're doing, someone supportive who can cheer you on. Or find a "buddy" who has a problem or two they'd like to solve themselves.

Evaluating Your Efforts

Well, is it working? It helps to keep a "before and after" record or score sheet of any problem-related variables that can tell you that. Take some time to figure out what those should be and how you could rate them.

If your strategy isn't working, go back to the drawing board and try again. If you keep getting nowhere, just choose another problem to work on.

TRYING IS WHAT COUNTS _____

In the end, actually solving your depressing problems may not be all that critical to relieving your depression. Often it's not any problem in particular, but the overwhelming *mass* of unsolved problems in our lives that depresses us. Simply reengaging ourselves in the *effort* to solve them, and seeing that we can at least solve a few minor ones—win a few battles, if not the war—is remoralizing and empowering enough to restore our faith in ourselves. And that may be all the antidepressant we need.

NOTES _____

1. Thomas J. D'Zurilla, *Problem-Solving Therapy* (New York: Springer, 1986).

2. A. M. Nezu, "Efficacy of a Social Problem-Solving Therapy Approach for Unipolar Depression," *J Consult Clin Psychol* 54(4, 1986):196–202.

3. A. M. Nezu and M. G. Perri, "Social Problem-Solving Therapy for Unipolar Depression: An Initial Dismantling Investigation," *J Consult Clin Psychol* 57(3, 1989):408–413.

4. Arthur Nezu et al., *Problem-Solving Therapy for Depression* (New York: Wiley, 1989).

5. Sidney Parnes et al., *Guide to Creative Action* (New York: Scribner's, 1977).

TWENTY-SEVEN

Word Medicine: Suggestions for Self-Help

WHEN a hypnotist says "Your eyelids are getting heavy," she is giving you a "suggestion." But as she would be the first to admit, *anything* you hear, see or read is a suggestion that can influence you for better or worse. And that includes the suggestions you give yourself.

When we're depressed, our autosuggestions (including our automatic thoughts) are overwhelmingly negative. Positive suggestions (auto- or otherwise) we're inclined to discount, negative ones we welcome like old friends.

There are two ways we can put our suggestions on a more positive keel: (1) We can attempt to soften up and revise the negative ones, *à la* cognitive therapy. (2) We can determinedly love-bomb our desolate psyches with positive suggestions. Cognitive therapy has demonstrated the effectiveness of the first approach. But what of the second?

THE ANTIDEPRESSANT POWER OF SUGGESTION _____

Hypnotherapy could be defined as the art of imparting positive suggestions to a relaxed, receptive mind. A century ago the eminent French neurologist Hippolyte Bernheim claimed hypnosis could heal "depression of the spirit."[1(p.25)] Hypnotherapists today still consider their art an effective antidote to the blues, though usually with help from other therapies if the depression is more than mild.[2,3] Supporting research is surprisingly hard to find, though. In one study, 16 of 17 emotionally disturbed patients improved significantly after three weeks of relaxation with hypnotic suggestion. Their depression dropped by nearly 40 percent,[4] a better outcome than relaxation alone usually produces.

Ironically, the hardest evidence for the antidepressant effect of suggestion comes from a field viewed by many skeptical academics with the same disdain they once reserved for hypnosis itself: *subliminal suggestion.*

Subliminal suggestions or messages are too faint or fleeting to register consciously, but just strong enough to make their presence felt "unconsciously." Most clinical studies of subliminal suggestion have explored the unconscious impact of a Freudian, loaded message: "Mommy and I are one." The theory, rooted in psychoanalysis, is that this message, when perceived subliminally, can evoke "symbiotic fantasies" of being reunited with "the good mother" of infancy. And that's supposed to be good for you.

Recently, a researcher analyzed nearly 60 placebo-controlled clinical trials of the subliminal symbiotic prescription.[5] There were some 2,500 subjects in the studies, including 110 depressives. "Mommy and I are one"—and, to a lesser extent, other subliminal symbiotic suggestions like "Daddy and I are one"—tended to be very beneficial indeed. Among other things, they significantly relieved depression and anxiety, improved academic performance in students and soothed schizophrenics. Remarkably, in most of these studies, the "Mommy message" was flashed before the subjects' eyes less than a dozen times over a few weeks—less than a tenth of a second's worth of subliminal psychotherapy!

Evidence that subliminal auditory suggestions—the kind found on self-help tapes—can influence us is much more limited.[6] In one double-blind study, depressed patients in psychotherapy improved more with real subliminal tapes than with "placebo" ones.[6] But in studies involving other conditions (such as overweight and drug dependency), placebo tapes have sometimes equalled subliminals.[7]

WORKING WITH SUGGESTIONS _____

Probably the best time to work with suggestions is when we're deeply relaxed. (This is all a hypnotic trance usually amounts to these days.) In our ordinary waking state, our minds tend to be preoccupied with externals, and suggestions may penetrate no deeper. But if we close our eyes, relax and focus inward, suggestions can reach us "where we live," where our beliefs and values are rooted. When we're relaxed it's also easier to calmly contemplate our negative autosuggestions.

The twilight state when we haven't quite fallen asleep at night or fully awakened in the morning is also considered a good time for working with suggestions. It may even be possible to soak up good suggestions or affirmations while we're sleeping. Even people undergoing major surgery have done so in some (but not all) studies.[8]

WORKING WITH YOUR DEPRESSING AUTOSUGGESTIONS ____

Here are some exercises you can try:

• Focus on a depressing trouble-spot in your life. Immerse yourself in the feelings and sensations associated with it and then allow "the whole thing" to verbalize itself. Fine-tune the language until it feels just right. Allow more images and feelings to emerge and verbalize those too. Continue the process, welcoming any *positive* images, feelings and "suggestions" that may emerge.*

Think of this exercise as an opportunity to shed light on and nourish some of the darker places in your psyche. Record any significant positive suggestions you come up with. You can use them as affirmations later.

*This exercise is inspired by Eugene Gendlin's "Focusing" technique (*Focusing* [Toronto: Bantam, 1981]).

• Try some sentence completions. Use the unfinished sentences like probes to awaken feelings and images. Then complete the sentence. (I can't. . . . I can't. . . . I can't *stand this loneliness*.) Repeat them to pull new endings out of your subconscious.

I can't _____. I won't _____. I can't accept _____. I must _____. I'm sorry (I regret) _____. I admit (confess) _____. I'm afraid _____. I resent _____. I'm mad (angry) _____. I dread _____. I don't care _____.

See if you can temper the negativity of some of these sentences by reflecting on them or "cognitively" challenging them as in Chapter 25. Some of these negative suggestions can be converted into very personal affirmations just by changing a word or two ("I *can* stand this loneliness").

• Many negative autosuggestions are actually internalizations of other people's criticisms or harsh values. You may have swallowed these whole in childhood. The next time you catch yourself replaying one of these old tapes, ask yourself: "Who wants me to believe_____?" If you can identify the culprit(s)—or imagine someone who would fit the bill—you can mentally confront them. You can argue or reason with them; exhort them to be fair and kind; ask them why they're picking on you. You can get inside *their* skin for a change and disarm them with kindness and concern.

WORKING WITH POSITIVE SUGGESTIONS _____

Sentence completions can also be used to come up with positive autosuggestions when you're depressed. At first you may draw a blank, but if you keep at it the words will gradually kindle a positive response, however modest (I'm glad. . . . I'm glad. . . . *I'm glad I have all my limbs*). It's OK to be "sick" or sarcastic to get the bile out of your system. Gradually the sentences will become more and more truly positive, and so will your mood. The best ones can become personal affirmations.

I'm glad _____. I forgive _____. I apologize _____. I thank _____. I can _____. I will _____. I look forward to _____. I like _____. I love _____. I believe _____. I revere _____. I admire _____. I respect _____. I'm a good (fine, lovable, likable, respectable, admirable) person because _____. God (Jesus, the Universe) loves me because _____.

AFFIRMATIONS

Affirmations are inspiring, life-enhancing sayings. "Mommy and I are one" is an affirmation of sorts. So is French hypnotherapist Emil Coue's famous autosuggestion: "Every day in every way, I am getting better and better." Many great sayings, prayers and mantras (see page 195) can be affirmations, sometimes with a little modification: *The kingdom of God is within. To myself I am true.* Some of the best affirmations are the ones you invent yourself.

Probably the best way to work with affirmations is to repeat or contemplate them in your mind, flowing with the imagery they provoke, changing the words, perhaps, to suit your sensibility and opening all your pores to their benign influence.

Here are some examples:

The essence of me is goodness. (Essence is good.)

Love surrounds me and fills me.

God is All; All is God.

In the arms of God (Jesus, my beloved) I rest.

God's (my beloved's) caress consoles me.

I am renewed (restored, reborn).

I breathe universal love.

All is forgiven.

I forgive and am forgiven.[9]

I bless and release all those who have caused me pain.[10]

God (Jesus, Mary, my Creator) and I are one.

God be my guide.

I let go and let God.[9]

God grant me the serenity to accept the things I cannot change, the courage to change the things I can, and the wisdom to know the difference. (This is the beloved "serenity prayer" of Alcoholics Anonymous and the Twelve-Step movement.)

My broken heart is an open heart.[9]

I release the past and embrace the now.

I will be happy.

NOTES

1. George J. Pratt et al., eds., *A Clinical Hypnosis Primer* (New York: Wiley, 1988).

2. Ursula Markham, *Hypnosis* (London: MacDonald & Co., 1987).

3. J. J. Thomas, "Psychotherapy." In Pratt et al., *Clinical Hypnosis Primer*, pp. 217–32.

4. R. C. Gould and V. E. Krynicki, "Comparative Effectiveness of Hypnotherapy on Different Psychological Symptoms," *Am J Clin Hypnosis* 32(October 1989):110–117.

5. R. A. Hardaway, "Subliminally Activated Symbiotic Fantasies: Facts and Artifacts," *Psychol Bull* 107(March 1990):177–195.

6. M. J. Urban, "Auditory Subliminal Stimulation: A Re-examination," *Perceptual and Motor Skills* 74(April 1992):515–541.

7. P. M. Merikle and H. E. Skanes, "Subliminal Self-Help Audiotapes: A Search for Placebo Effects," *J Appl Psych* 77(October 1992):772–776.

8. W. H. Liu et al., "Therapeutic Suggestions During General Anaesthesia in Patients Undergoing Hysterectomy," *Brit J Anaesth* 68(March 1992):277–281.

9. Adapted from Douglas Bloch, *Words That Heal: Affirmations & Meditations for Daily Living* (New York: Bantam, 1988).

10. Bloch, *Words That Heal*.

TWENTY-EIGHT

Imaginary Healing: Therapeutic Imagery for the Blues

To the self, images speak as loudly as, if not louder than, words. After all, words would be meaningless without the images they evoke.

More than just a movie screen upon which are projected our inner fantasies and realities, the imagination is also a drawing board upon which we can shape those materials. It is (arguably) the primary language of hypnotherapy. In clinical psychology, it is the medium for two of the most effective treatments for fears and phobias (systematic desensitization and implosive therapy) and a frequently called-upon ally in cognitive-behavioral therapies. Transpersonal psychotherapists, Jungian analysts and New Age-type therapists all enlist the power of their clients' imaginations for healing.

Experimentally, in at least half a dozen controlled trials therapeutic imagery has consistently brought some acute relief from depression; in some studies, it has been associated with long-term relief as well.[1] In one remarkable study experiment, winter depressives were hypnotized and told to *imagine* bright light for three hours every morning. Their depression scores plummeted.[2]

Therapeutic imagery probably can at least be somewhat helpful if you're severely or chronically depressed. If you only have a touch of the blues, it could be the cure.

WORKING WITH IMAGERY _____

Often called visualization, therapeutic imagery can actually involve *any* of the senses, and language as well. Words help both to evoke imagery and to integrate it with the conceptual side of our minds. Therapeutic imagery also involves emotions—sometimes very strong ones. Psychotherapists from Freud on have observed that giving these feelings vent is integral to healing with imagery.[3]

It's easiest to work with imagery when you're relaxed (Chapter 23). Even a few minutes a day can be effective, according to some experts.[4] Too much imagery, however, may be disorienting. If you have any problems keeping a hold on reality, it's best not to get into imagery at all without professional guidance. Here are some exercises you can try.

Imagining Your Depression

Whenever he uncovered the images "concealed" within his troubled feelings, the great psychoanalyst Carl Jung observed, he became "inwardly calmed and reassured."[3(p.185)] "Start[ing] with your point of trouble,"[4(p.208)] as Jung did, is a time-honored method in therapeutic imagery.

Start by letting your depression engulf you: really feel it. Then let a mental image of it take shape—a place, an object, a soundscape, a tactile image, an image of yourself (perhaps exaggerated in some way). If you're blank, keep saying "I feel like. . . ." Take time to develop and refine the image until it seems to fit your depression like a glove.

Now, *be with the image* and either allow it to change of its own accord (this is a movie, not a snapshot) or actively nudge it along yourself. The goal is for the image to develop organically from negative to positive.

Say your image is of a desert. To actively work on it, you might roll in some clouds and let it rain. Then imagine vegetation springing up, transforming the desert into a fertile plain. If you let the image unfold of its own accord, it might follow a less predictable course. Perhaps the sun would grow hotter and hotter, literally incinerating or vaporizing the desert, leaving you suspended in a cool, dark vacuum. Then, drops of heavenly rain would condense, showering you with a wonderfully vitalizing torrent, while, down below, a lush valley would spring to life.

Imaginary Activities

In our imaginations we can *do* anything—including psychotherapeutic things: going on a Godzilla rampage to vent anger; seeking comfort at the breast (or in the womb) of a giant Earth Mother; performing cathartic acts of self-destruction and renewal. Here are some possibilities (adjust them to taste):

Imagine something dirty, fouled, broken, or dilapidated. Clean and/or repair it.

Imagine yourself dirty, fouled, broken or dilapidated. Imagine a spring or a brook filled with a magically cleansing/healing fluid. Bathe in it.

Imagine yourself encrusted in an incredibly thick and dry old skin. Feel it flake or peel off, revealing a new skin underneath.

Imagine a wounded, suffering creature. Tend to it.

Working with Inner Selves, Healers and Other Figures

A very popular imagery technique is to get in touch with inner figures—inner healers, spirit guides, power animals, inner children, actual people you know or other entities, real or imaginary. Interacting with these archetypes, alter-egos or projections may be a way to channel love and wisdom to our conscious selves from unconscious (or other) sources.

Popular inner figures are the benign ones: deities and spiritual heroes; moral or intellectual heroes; inner healers; archetypal sages, tricksters and power animals; wise extraterrestrials, and so on.

Other inner figures are our "subselves." Historical subselves include wounded inner children whom we can "re-parent"; bright-eyed, idealistic youths who can refresh us with their passion and idealism; aged, deathbed selves who can bring a philosophic, bird's-eye view to our present concerns. There also are grotesque shadow selves chained in the cellar who need light and kindness. There are depressed and dysfunctional selves who need attention and advice. There are healthy, functional selves who can share their gifts with the rest of us. There are ideal and idealized selves in need of mature reevaluation.

In our imaginations, we can also have heart-to-heart encounters with real people we know, alive or dead.

A spontaneous way to contact inner figures is to relax, focus inward and either wait for one to appear or search one out. You can increase the likelihood of conjuring a relevant inner figure if you imagine you're somewhere related to how you're feeling (or how you would like to feel). To attract a specific kind of inner figure, imagine yourself in an appropriate setting—a childhood haunt or home for an inner child, a natural setting for a power animal, a sacred place for a spiritual figure.

Don't "give your power" to inner figures. "They" are fallible like everyone else, and their influence should be filtered through the rest of your sensibilities.

EMOTIONAL IMAGES AND MEMORIES FROM THE PAST _____

Psychiatrists have long known that when someone relives a traumatic experience with full emotional intensity, she's likely to experience a therapeutic release or catharsis.[3] This was how many shell-shocked soldiers were rehabilitated during the Second World War. Today some therapists use hypnotic age regression to return people to the scene of past traumas. These regressions sometimes seem to go back as far as infancy, birth, life in the womb or life before the womb (past lives!). Real or imaginary, they are intense, personal psychodramas that can help "heal the past" or resolve current psychological problems (usually in a gradual way after many regressions).[5]

USING WORDS AS A TRIGGER _____

Words, through the feelings and images they evoke, can be like consciousness-altering drugs—if you keep repeating them. Some words to dispel depression include: faith, trust, hope, love, courage, patience, confidence, acceptance, serenity, cheerfulness, enthusiasm, and joy.

NOTES _____

1. K. D. Schultz, "The Use of Imagery in Alleviating Depression." In Anees A. Sheikh, ed., *Imagination and Healing* (Farmingdale, N.Y.: Baywood Publishing, 1984), pp. 129–158.

2. P. Richter et al., "Imaginary Versus Real Light for Winter Depression," *Biol Psychiatry* 31(March 1992):534–536.

3. Mike Samuels and Nancy Samuels, *Seeing with the Mind's Eye* (New York: Random House, 1975).

4. Gerald Epstein, *Healing Visualizations* (New York: Bantam, 1989).

5. Hellmut W. A. Karle, *Hypnosis and Hypnotherapy: A Patient's Guide* (Wellingborough, Northamptonshire, England: Thorson's, 1988).

TWENTY-NINE

Interpersonal Healing: The Social Dimension of Depression and Its Treatment

FEW things have as much bearing on how happy or unhappy we are as our relationships. Not having any is one of the more potent promoters of depression, disease and even premature death.[1] Having the wrong kind of relationship may be even more depressing.[2] But should you have a good one or two—a close confidante, a supportive spouse—you're that much less likely to be easy prey for depression.[2]

Not surprisingly, relationships are a focus of most psychotherapies for depression—the major focus of some.

MARITAL THERAPY

Of all the interpersonal problems that can depress us, none, it seems, is so commonly to blame as marital problems.[3,4] And no matter why you're depressed, if your partner is unsympathetic or unsupportive you'll have a harder time recovering—and an easier time relapsing later.[2,3] But a supportive partner will have just the opposite effect.[2,5]

It's enough to make you think some sort of therapy that would help depressives and their problematic partners get along better—that would teach them to communicate better, resolve their conflicts more effectively, be intimate more supportively—would be a capital treatment for depression. It is. In three studies, cognitive-behavioral marital therapy has been as effective for maritally distressed depressives as cognitive therapy, and produced greater long-term marital satisfaction.[3-5]

ASSERTIVENESS TRAINING AND SOCIAL SKILLS TRAINING ____

Social ease and aplomb do not go together with depression. Whether it's a cause of depression, a symptom or both, depressives typically are withdrawn, uncommunicative, unassertive and at a loss to enjoy themselves socially.[6] Fixing these behavior patterns can be a key to recovery, cognitive-behavioral therapists maintain. "[W]hen patients learn to ask for what they want, resist unwelcome requests or exploitation from others, initiate conversations, and develop more intimate relationships, therapeutic gains are impressive," one expert notes.[7] The "training" program is commonly called assertiveness training (AT) or social skills training (SST).

AT/SST has shown its clinical effectiveness in most controlled trials.[8,9] In one 12-week study involving 125 moderately to severely depressed women, a comprehensive SST program outperformed both antidepressant medication and psychoanalytic-style therapy.[8] In another study, when SST was added to the regimen of about a dozen hospitalized depressives and continued for 20 weeks after discharge, they fared "strikingly" better than routinely treated controls.[10]

AT/SST is like being coached in acting or a sport. Commonly, it begins with you, the "student," describing a problem area in your social life and then acting it out, with the therapist, or other members of an AT/SST group, playing the other parts. Next, the therapist or a group member plays or "models" *your part*, only closer to the way you'd like to be able to play it. With that as your inspiration, you try again, and (usually) again and again. This is all done in a relaxed, even playful way, with lots of gentle, constructive advice and praise for every baby step. If internal resistance (automatic thoughts and the like) gets in the way, cognitive advice on dealing with it is usually forthcoming.

TALKING TO SOMEONE

Many experts believe there is one common ingredient that accounts more than anything else for the success of widely different types of psychotherapy: the personal qualities of the therapist.[8,11] So potent is the therapeutic influence of a compassionate and understanding listener that even nontherapists who possess that quality, one study suggests, can do clients as much good as professionals.[12] So if you know someone who fits the bill, confiding in him or her could really help.

INTERPERSONAL PSYCHOTHERAPY

One type of psychotherapy goes out of its way to provide depressives with a sympathetic, supportive confidante. Developed by two prominent authorities on depression, interpersonal psychotherapy (IPT) posits that depression is always fuelled (if not necessarily caused) by interpersonal problems—conflicts, losses, role problems or social skills deficits. IPT therapists help clients single out one or two such problems they can potentially resolve in a few months. Therapy involves not just talking, but freely expressing your feelings; not just understanding the problem(s), but taking action to solve them.

Several studies suggest IPT may be as effective as drugs and other major psychotherapies (including cognitive therapy) for mild to moderate depression.[13] In recovered depressives, monthly IPT has significantly helped prevent relapse.[14]

STRENGTH IN NUMBERS

If talking to one sympathetic listener can be helpful, talking to several may be even better. Group therapy, encounter groups and support groups provide some unique psychotherapeutic opportunities:

• Mutual self-disclosure, of a kind seldom found elsewhere, is the norm in such groups. This social unmasking satisfies a deep hunger to be known and accepted for who you really are.

• Groups tend to be egalitarian—people helping people. To some, this can be more inviting and empowering than one-on-one psychotherapy where, typically, self-disclosure is one-sided and the therapist may be perceived as an authority figure rather than an equal.

• Groups are workshops in social skills training, rife with opportunities for enhancing your interpersonal sensitivities and skills.

• In groups where people share the same problem or condition, *empathy* and *understanding*—two great healers—are available in abundant supply.

Support Groups

By far the most popular and accessible therapeutic groups are support groups. Dozens, even hundreds, can be found in any large city. Many are networked into larger umbrella organizations. For people with depression there are two prominent ones:

• The National Manic Depressive and Depressive Association (NMDDA) provides information and support to people with mood disorders and their families. Although the NMDDA encourages medical treatment, members value most (according to a recent survey) the emotional support and acceptance they get through the association's "rap groups," public meetings, lectures and telephone assistance.[15]

• Recovery, Inc. sponsors cognitively oriented support groups. At meetings, members describe their distressing feelings or experiences and everyone pitches in to "spot" the underlying maladaptive attitudes.[16] The longer people stick with Recovery, Inc., one survey suggests, the better they feel and the less professional help they seek.[16]

The granddaddy of all support groups is Alcoholics Anonymous (AA). Today there are AA-style "Twelve-Step" groups for virtually every compulsive antisocial or self-destructive behavior (Overeaters Anonymous, Gamblers Anonymous) and the victims of these behaviors (Adult Children of Alcoholics, Incest Survivors Anonymous). Emotions Anonymous attracts many people whose primary problem is depression.

In Twelve-Step meetings, people share their stories and help each other apply "the Twelve Steps." The Twelve Steps are directions for a moral and spiritual path to recovery. They begin with an admission of helplessness and a decision to seek Divine guidance. This is followed by "a searching and fearless moral inventory" of yourself, the admission to God (or any "Higher Power" you believe in) and another person of "the exact nature of [your] wrongs," and the making of "amends . . . wherever possible." The Steps culminate with the resolution to "[seek] through prayer and meditation" to understand and follow God's will for you and "to carry the [Twelve-Step] message" to others in need.

Bill W., the co-founder of AA, acknowledged that the Twelve Steps couldn't cure him of his own depressiveness. Support is indisputably beneficial, but it isn't always enough.

FIDO RX

Our fellow humans are not the only warm souls that can comfort us in our times of need. So can our pets. Their presence can shield us with "a protective armor against much of the pain of living . . . that few human beings can give with such unvarying constancy," pet therapy enthusiasts say.[17(p.10)] "[K]nowing that at least one other entity depends on you for its needs and survival can make the difference between apathy and surrender and participation in life," others argue.[18(p.38)] Pet-pushing psychiatrist Michael McCulloch claims the pet cure helps distract his depressed patients from their worries and relieves their loneliness.[17] Even research suggests that pets can help prevent depression in bereaved, socially isolated seniors and perhaps even prolong life in heart-attack survivors.[19] Now that's the kind of medicine it's worth cleaning up after.

NOTES

1. P. L. Morris et al., "Association of Depression with 10-Year Poststroke Mortality," *Am J Psychiatry* 150(January 1993):124–129.

2. N. S. Jacobson et al., "Couple Therapy as a Treatment for Depression: II. The Effects of Relationship Quality and Therapy on Depressive Relapse," *J Consult Clin Psychol* 61(June 1993):516–519.

3. N. S. Jacobson et al., "Marital Therapy and Spouse Involvement in the Treatment of Depression, Agoraphobia, and Alcoholism," *J Consult Clin Psychol* 57(January 1989):5–10.

4. K. D. O'Leary and S. R. H. Beach, "Marital Therapy: A Viable Treatment for Depression and Marital Discord," *Am J Psychiatry* 147(February 1990):183–186.

5. N. S. Jacobson et al., "Marital Therapy as a Treatment for Depression," *J Consult Clin Psychol* 59(April 1991):547–557.

6. P. M. Lewinsohn and H. M. Hoberman, "Depression." In Alan S. Bellack et al., eds., *International Handbook of Behavior Modification and Therapy* (New York: Plenum, 1982), pp. 397–431.

7. A. A. Lazarus, "The Multimodal Approach to the Treatment of Minor Depression," *Am J Psychother* 46(January 1992):50–57.

8. A. S. Bellack, "Psychotherapy Research in Depression: An Overview." In E. Edward Beckham and William R. Leber, eds., *Handbook of Depression* (Homewood, Ill.: Dorsey Press, 1985) pp. 204–219.

9. S. S. Rude, "Relative Benefits of Assertion or Cognitive Self-Control Treatment for Depression as a Function of Proficiency in Each Domain," *J Consult Clin Psychol* 54(June 1986):390–394.

10. I. W. Miller et al., "Cognitive-Behavioral Treatment of Depressed Inpatients: Six- and Twelve-Month Follow-Up," *Am J Psychiatry* 146(October 1989):1274–1279.

11. E. Fuller Torrey, *Witchdoctors and Psychiatrists: The Common Roots of Psychotherapy and Its Future* (New York: Harper & Row, 1986).

12. H. H. Strupp and S. W. Hadley, "Specific vs Nonspecific Factors in Psychotherapy," *Arch Gen Psychiatry* 36(1979):1125–1136.

13. See for example: J. C. Markowitz et al., "Interpersonal Psycho-

therapy of Depressed HIV-Positive Outpatients," *Hosp Commun Psychiatry* 43(September 1992):885–890.

14. E. Frank et al., "Three-Year Outcomes for Maintenance Therapies in Recurrent Depression," *Arch Gen Psychiatry*, 47(December 1990):1093–1099.

15. L. F. Kurtz, "Mutual Aid for Affective Disorders: the Manic Depressive and Depressive Association," *Am J Orthopsychiatry* 58(January 1988):152–155.

16. M. Galanter, "Zealous Self-Help Groups as Adjuncts to Psychiatric Treatment: A Study of Recovery, Inc.," *Am J Psychiatry* 145(October 1988):1248–1253.

17. Alan Beck and Aaron Katcher, *Between Pets and People: The Importance of Animal Companionship* (New York: Putnam, 1983).

18. Odean Cusack and Elaine Smith, *Pets and the Elderly: The Therapeutic Bond* (New York: Haworth Press, 1984).

19. Barbara J. Culliton, "Take Two Pets and Call Me in the Morning," *Science* 237(September 1987):1560–1561.

THIRTY

The Healing Arts

ART is "soulstuff" made tangible, the artist's essence given shape and form. And art, in turn, shapes, forms and sometimes *heals* the souls of those who make or partake of it.

When we're depressed, art—whether it is a painting in a gallery or a movie from a video store—can help heal us in a number of ways:

- It can be a pleasant diversion when we're too worried for our own good.
- Creating it can uplift us, helping us feel creative and productive again.
- It can reach into our hearts and touch or transform our troubled feelings.
- It can reveal ourselves to ourselves and to each other, combatting our loneliness and alienation.
- It can provoke two of our healthiest coping responses: laughter and crying.[1]

The arts are so diverse that, as long as you give yourself permission, you should have no trouble finding an artistic outlet when you're depressed. Here are just a few suggestions.

MUSIC THERAPY

Music's ability to heal the soul is the stuff of legend in every culture. In hospitals and institutions today, music is still used to lift people's moods, ease pain and tension and break through walls of isolation.

Modern research, though scant, has tended to confirm music's psychotherapeutic benefits.[2,3] In one interesting study, people with animal phobias were exposed (from a distance) to the animals they feared—a standard behavioral therapy. Those who simultaneously listened to music they liked got over their phobias more readily than those who sweated it out in silence.[4]

Bright, cheerful music—Mozart, Vivaldi, bluegrass, polka, Klezmer, Salsa, reggae—is the most obvious prescription for the blues. But when depression runs deeper in the bone, music that resonates *with it* may be more persuasive. As one melancholic music lover puts it: "When I hear sad music composed by a man who suffered, as did Chopin, Beethoven and Tchaikovsky, I feel that I am 'seconded,' and in feeling the beauty of that music I forget I am not well."[5(p.254)]

For great music to second your sadness, try Fauré (*Pelleas et Mellisande*);* Ravel ("Pavane for a Dead Princess"); Rachmaninoff ("Vocalise"; *Second Symphony*: Adagio); Dvorak (*New World Symphony*: Largo); Chopin; Barber (Adagio for Strings) or your favorite sad ballads or blues songs. Bring your emotional turmoil in for a more rugged workout to the great romantic composers: Beethoven, Brahms, Tchaikovsky (*Sixth Symphony*), Mahler. If you're more adventurous, more modern, dissonant music can second your feelings of confusion, angst, alienation or despair.

Music that brims with faith, hope, love, courage or strength can be inspiring and empowering. Beethoven's exuberant "Ode to Joy" chorus (*Ninth Symphony*) is a classic example. Other standouts include the music of Bach, Handel (*Messiah*), Schubert ("Ave Maria"), Verdi (the Triumphal March from *Aïda*), Puccini (*Turandot*), Wagner, Dvorak (*New World Symphony*), Vaughan Wil-

*Examples are in parentheses.

liams ("Lark Ascending"; *Pastoral Symphony*: Lento) and much folk, "world beat" and pop/rock music.

Music can, of course, be great for relaxation or reverie. Try Baroque slow movements (Pachelbel's Canon in D, Bach's "Air on the G String"); Fauré ("Pavane"); Debussy ("Prélude à l'Après-midi d'un Faune," "Clair de Lune"); Satie ("Gymnopédies"); Vaughan Williams (*Pastoral Symphony*: Molto Moderato); Delius; "cool" jazz and New Age music.

Finally, let's not overlook music as a stimulant. Try Mozart, Prokofiev, march music, Zydeco, Dixieland, Klezmer, bluegrass, Gypsy music, Salsa, Indian and Near Eastern music, rock and pop.

WRITING AS THERAPY

For some people, writing is a tool to probe their darkest thoughts and feelings, and feel better for it. Some psychotherapists even prescribe writing as therapy.[5-7] At Southern Methodist University, James Pennebaker and associates are demonstrating how good a thing that prescription can be.[6,7]

In one of their studies, university students poured their most painful secrets into private journals, 15 minutes a day for four days. Immersing themselves in memories of abuse, neglect, failure or humiliation was at first disturbing. But later the students felt lighter, happier, more in touch with themselves. Their visits to the student health center dropped by half! Other students who had been told to write about superficial matters or to dryly recount the details of their problems enjoyed no such benefits. Neither did students who were told to write out their feelings without thought or reflection. A second study not only replicated these findings, it showed that confessional writing (as Pennebaker calls it) literally boosts the immune system.[6,7]

Therapeutic writing should be done informally, without worrying about literary quality. It's the process that counts.

Here are some exercises.

Writing Your Hurts Out

This is Pennebaker's "confessional writing" approach. Pick a personal subject or issue that's so hot you may have trouble just thinking about it. Write about it for at least 15 minutes *with your heart and your head*, feeling and thinking your way through.

Letters from the Edge

Here's your chance to speak your mind to a significant other, to loosen that long-bitten tongue, in a letter you'll never send. The significant other can even be *you*—or anyone else, real or imaginary, whose ear you'd like to bend.

Writing workshop leader Anna Olson recommends a powerful technique for working through your ambivalences. Clear the decks with a vituperative "angry letter," then follow it with an appreciative "love letter."

Points of View

Select an important personal issue you're confused or conflicted about. Write about it from the point of view of the conflicting persons or parts of yourself. Can you think of anyone who might have something more to contribute? Write about it from their point of view.

VISUAL ART

Art therapist Janie Rhyne describes a client, a chronically depressed psychiatric social worker, who for years had been sitting atop a volcano of rage and despair. She urged him to paint his feelings out on a large sheet of paper. He attacked it with red and black paint, muttering about "blood and guts" and "horror, terror, fury, nothingness." Then he covered another—and another, and another. . . . As he vented his long pent-up feelings, his palette softened and his images became less and less chaotic. He later told Rhyne that in that single session he had expressed more of himself than he had in a year of psychotherapy.[8]

Here are a few ways you can make art psychotherapeutically rewarding.

Connecting with the World

Pick a subject you feel drawn to. It doesn't have to be fancy: the corner of a room, a patch of grass, a hand or an eye will do. Observe your subject, *connect with it* and sketch it with simple materials like pencil and paper.

You can explore your subject in a series of rough sketches or studies. Then, if you wish, use more sophisticated media, like colored pencils or pens, pastels or paints.

Drawing on Your Imagination

The subject here can be anything that's before your eyes or in your mind's eye. Bend appearances to suit your fancy. Drawing on your memory and imagination, create a picture of your problems, obsessions, hopes, dreams, fears, wishes—the more personal and subjective the better.

Alternatively, clip images from magazines, newspapers or other sources and build a collage.

An Abstract Language

The story here is told in abstract shapes, colors, patterns and textures. Fluid media—brush and ink, paints, oil pastels, computer paint programs—serve best for speaking your mind with lines, strokes, splatters, smudges, blobs and other subjective marks and forms.

Anything goes. In a very black and alienated mood, a student of Rhyne's set out to paint an entire sheet of paper *black*. "Painting in black and giving in to my feelings seemed to have a very liberating effect on my black mood," she commented. "In a sense,

I painted my way out of the corner and as my mood brightened, my colors brightened."[8(p.60)]

Creating a Microcosm

The world of geometric forms and patterns is one of order, calm, stability. To enter it all you need is a compass—the kind you make circles with. Here's an exercise to get you started:

Set the radius of your compass to about ½ to 1 inch. Draw a circle (circle A) in the center of your paper. Next, put the point of the compass at the top of the circle and draw another circle (circle B). Then put the compass point on each of the points where circle B intersected circle A and draw new circles. Now draw circles at each of the new intersection points. Finally draw a circle at the last intersection point. Now see what forms take shape when you connect the intersection points on circle A in different ways. Now extend the drawing by continuing to draw circles with their centers at the intersection points outside of circle A. (Keep the radius of the compass constant.) Continue exploring for different forms and patterns by connecting intersection points with straight lines. Depending on how you shade or color the different facets of these line patterns, dramatically different drawings or paintings will emerge.

NOTES

1. R. A. Martin and J. P. Dobbin, "Sense of Humor, Hassles, and Immunoglobulin A: Evidence for a Stress-Moderating Effect of Humor," *Int J Psychiatry Med* 18(1, 1988):93–105.

2. S. L. Curtis, "The Effect of Music on Pain Relief and Relaxation of the Terminally Ill," *J Music Ther* 23(1, 1986):10–24.

3. V. N. Stratton and A. H. Zalanowski, "The Effects of Music and Paintings on Mood," *J Music Ther* 26(1, 1989):30–41.

4. G. H. Eifert et al., "Affect Modification Through Evaluative Conditioning with Music," *Behav Res Ther* 26(4, 1988):321–330.

5. Roberto Assagioli, *Psychosynthesis* (Harmondsworth, Middlesex, England: Penguin, 1976).

6. James W. Pennebaker, *Opening Up: The Healing Power of Confiding in Others* (New York: William Morrow, 1990).

7. D. S. Berry and J. W. Pennebaker, "Nonverbal and Verbal Emotional Expression and Health," *Psychother Psychosom* 59(1, 1993):11–19.

8. Janie Rhyne, *The Gestalt Art Experience* (Monterey, Calif.: Brooks/Cole Publishing, 1973).

THIRTY-ONE

Seeking Formal Psychotherapy

THERE are over two hundred different kinds of psychotherapy out there. And while most, if not all, purport to relieve depression, very few have been formally put to the test. Here's what the research does tell us:

• Psychoanalysis and other traditional insight-oriented therapies seem to be of little acute benefit for depression.[1,2] Whether these approaches can, very gradually, bring about deep personality changes that reduce depressiveness in the long run (as proponents usually claim) is still an open question.

• Traditional behavior therapies, which pay little attention to thoughts and feelings and focus on manipulating behavior alone, are relatively weak antidepressants.[2]

• Cognitive-behavioral therapies (like cognitive therapy [Chapter 25], problem-solving therapy [Chapter 26], self-control therapy, interpersonal therapy, social skills training [Chapter 24] and cognitive-behavioral marital therapy [Chapter 29]), which work simultaneously on thoughts, attitudes and behaviors, are powerful antidepressants.

• Interpersonal psychotherapy (Chapter 29)—a brief, focused therapy that combines insight, catharsis, emotional support, problem-solving and cognitive-behavioral counseling—appears to be a useful treatment for depression. It's probably as effective as antidepressant drugs for mildly to moderately depressed persons.

• Interpersonal psychotherapy and cognitive-behavioral therapies are "well tolerated." Usually only 5 to 15 percent of patients drop out during a typical three- to four-month course—about half to one-third the dropout rate for antidepressant drugs. These psychotherapies typically bring major improvements within two to four weeks and complete recovery by the end of treatment to over half of all patients with major depression.[3] Even those with what many would pigeonhole as a biological or endogenous depression—severe, recurrent major depression, with many physical symptoms—commonly improve or recover.[3] However people with chronic, mild depression (dysthymia) appear less responsive to short-term psychotherapy.[4]

• There is little, if any, research into psychotherapy for melancholic (page 5), psychotic/delusional or bipolar depression. This is mainly because psychiatrists are pessimistic that psychotherapy can have much impact on these kinds of depression.

WHICH THERAPIST?

No less important a consideration than the kind of psychotherapy is the kind of psychotherapist. The most effective psychotherapist, research indicates, is warm, compassionate, sincere, understanding and (perhaps most importantly) someone you can get along with. If the chemistry is bad, it doesn't augur well, and you'd best look for someone else.[5]

Psychotherapy is practiced mainly by psychiatrists, clinical psychologists, clinical social workers and various unlicensed (and often untrained) therapists.

SAFETY

Psychotherapy can be hazardous to your mental health. Although the established psychotherapies for depression appear relatively innocuous and without reports of treatment casualties, there are inherent risks in psychotherapy in general and in some therapies (and therapists) in particular:

• Some psychotherapies/ists take an aggressive, confrontational approach to the client and his problems. This can push some people over the edge.

• Even with a gentle approach, the excavation of emotionally loaded unconscious material—taboo feelings and impulses, memories of abuse or trauma—can bring temporary pain or clinical deterioration.

• A therapist can foist ideas or values on a client that violate the client's integrity. Psychoanalysts, for instance, have traditionally, as a matter of dogma, pressured incest survivors to interpret their memories as "wish-fulfillment fantasies."

• Clients can become childishly dependent on or awed by their therapists, converting them into surrogate parents, gurus or demigods. Some therapists seize this opportunity to seduce or exploit their clients. Typically this erodes the clients' self-esteem and mental health even more.

• Even the most innocuous psychotherapy can be dangerous if the therapist is incompetent, irresponsible or unscrupulous. To some extent, a therapist's competence can be ensured by choosing one who is well trained and certified, registered or licensed. Her integrity can be checked by contacting her professional association or disciplinary body (if she has one) and asking if there have been any complaints or legal actions against her.

NOTES

1. H. H. Strupp et al., "Psychodynamic Therapy: Theory and Research." In A. John Rush, ed., *Short-Term Psychotherapies for Depression* (New York: The Guilford Press, 1982), pp. 215–250.

2. A. T. Beck et al., "Treatment of Depression with Cognitive Therapy and Amitriptyline," *Arch Gen Psychiatry* 42(February 1985):142–148.

3. M. E. Thase et al., "Severity of Depression and Response to Cognitive Behavior Therapy," *Am J Psychiatry* 148(June 1991):784–789.

4. L. R. Gonzales et al., "Longitudinal Follow-Up of Unipolar Depressives: An Investigation of Predictors of Relapse," *J Consult Clin Psychol* 53(August 1985):461–469.

5. E. Fuller Torrey, *Witchdoctors and Psychiatrists: The Common Roots of Psychotherapy and Its Future* (New York: Harper & Row, 1986).

THIRTY-TWO

"Unnatural" Antidepressants: Antidepressant Drugs and Electroconvulsive Therapy

LIKE it or not, the treatment of choice for major depression in most doctors' books is antidepressant drugs. When drugs, with or without psychotherapy or other natural adjuncts like lithium and thyroid hormone, don't work, many psychiatrists will turn to electroconvulsive ("shock") therapy (ECT).

The major advantage antidepressant drugs have over natural treatments is economic: much more money has gone into establishing their efficacy in controlled research and selling them to doctors. The disadvantage is that they're artificial substances, designed for profit by drug companies, not for biological purposes by nature. Usually they produce many annoying side effects; sometimes very serious or (rarely) fatal ones.[1]

Yet the side effects of being severely depressed are pretty serious themselves. Natural treatments can't be counted on to work all of the time, or to always work fast enough or conveniently enough. Drugs, and even ECT, sometimes need to be considered as alternatives or adjuncts.

DRUGS FOR DEPRESSION

Most of the 20-odd antidepressant drugs belong to two families: the cyclic (tricyclic, bicyclic and so forth) antidepressants and the monoamine oxidase inhibitors (MAO inhibitors or MAOIs). A handful of newer antidepressants, including Prozac, are known as selective serotonin reuptake inhibitors, or SSRIs.

The first cyclic and MAOI antidepressants were developed in the 1950s. Since then a dozen or so "copycat" drugs have been developed in their image, as well as a few genuinely novel antidepressants, notably the SSRIs. None of these drugs, however, has proven significantly more effective than the originals—*for the average depressive*. But for individuals, some antidepressants clearly work better than others.

How effective are these drugs?

• In clinical studies, usually 15 to 40 percent of patients with major depression quit because of side effects or lack of improvement. Of the remainder, about 65 to 75 percent "respond" (improve considerably or recover) within four to eight weeks, improvement usually beginning after two to three weeks. When nonresponders are given much higher than normal dosages or switched to a different antidepressant drug, about 50 percent respond. Even more tend to respond when their antidepressant is augmented by lithium, thyroid hormone or tryptophan.

• Antidepressant drugs are strikingly superior to placebos for major depression—when it's severe. But the more mild the depression, the smaller the advantage, and in the mildest depressions, a placebo will usually do just as well.

• Recovered depressives must continue taking their antidepressant—preferably at full dosage—for several months to minimize the risk of relapse or indefinitely to forestall recurrences.[2]

• Some research suggests the effectiveness of antidepressant drugs has been systematically exaggerated in clinical studies. According to one analysis of the literature, the conspicuous side effects of antidepressant drugs interfere with the "blindness" of researchers in clinical studies, allowing them to rate the drugs as much more effective than they really are. Under more truly "blind" conditions, the advantage of antidepressant drugs over placebo shrinks significantly and all but disappears in patients' own ratings.[3]

There are many subtleties to the art of prescribing antidepressant drugs successfully. Psychiatrists—particularly those who work in mood disorder clinics—are the best experts.

I can't discuss antidepressant drugs in detail here. *The Essential Guide to Psychiatric Drugs* (New York: St. Martin's Press, 1990) by psychiatrist Jack M. Gorman is a good reference. For an exhaustive (and exhausting) summary of the side effects, cautions, contraindications and the like of antidepressant drugs, consult the hefty drug reference books in your library. What I would like to do is highlight some important facts about antidepressant drugs that don't always get the "airplay" they deserve.

• Cyclic antidepressants seldom work for atypical depressions (see page 5), but MAOIs very often do. The newer reversible MAOIs (e.g., deprenyl) aren't as risky to use as the older ones (phenelzine and tranylcypromine).

• Cyclic antidepressants sometimes are disastrous for people with a personal or family history of bipolar disorder, worsening and prolonging their depression or provoking a severe, rapid-cycling bipolar disorder.

• Don't be eager to try a new drug. In recent years two new antidepressants (zimelidine and nomifensine) had to be withdrawn when very serious side effects not evident in clinical trials became apparent.[1]

• Extreme drowsiness and many of the other annoying side effects of cyclic antidepressants that cause some people to flush their prescription down the toilet usually subside after the first few weeks.

• Impaired sexual function (impotence, inability to reach orgasm) is a very common (and persistent) side effect of antidepressant drugs.[4]

• Elderly persons are more susceptible to adverse antidepressant drug effects such as heart attacks and strokes, falling after getting up suddenly and delirious or psychotic reactions.

• Amoxapine (Asendin) sometimes causes a grotesque and persistent movement disorder called *tardive dyskinesia* (TD). Antipsychotic drugs (which often are prescribed for psychotically depressed or manic persons) frequently cause TD. (Supplements of manganese, vitamin E and vitamin B3 may prevent or treat TD.)

• Alprazolam (Xanax), like other benzodiazepines (Valium, Halcion), can become a habit that's extremely hard to break.

• Despite its reputation as a revolutionary wonder-drug, research suggests Prozac (fluoxetine) and other expensive new SSRIs are no more effective for the average depressive than older, much cheaper antidepressants—and not necessarily easier to tolerate.[5]

• Most depressives become less suicidal on antidepressants, but some become more suicidal or suicidal for the first time, and a few become homicidal, obsessive, unbearably agitated or psychiatrically worsened in other ways. Prozac may be the worst offender, but almost any antidepressant drug (and theoretically some of their natural surrogates) can have this effect.[6] If this happens to you, it's important to get psychiatric help immediately. A timely change in treatment could save your life.

• Quitting an antidepressant drug should be done very gradually, over a period of months. If you hurry, you may experience withdrawal symptoms or a sudden relapse.[2]

ELECTROCONVULSIVE THERAPY

A barbaric procedure for shocking incorrigible mental patients into vegetablelike compliance—that's the popular image of electroconvulsive therapy (ECT). Yet in responsible hands, ECT is one of the most effective and, arguably, *safest* treatments for severe depression. More potent, it seems, than antidepressant drugs, ECT works about as rapidly for antidepressant nonresponders (its usual clients))—and perhaps more often—than thyroid hormone or lithium.[7,8] Most importantly, for some people nothing else seems to work. Even some orthomolecular psychiatrists use it;[9,10] and more than one psychiatrist has told me that if he were severely depressed ECT would be his own treatment of choice.

Yet ECT continues to be controversial. Although it is safe

enough for most elderly people who can't handle antidepressant drugs, it is, nonetheless, dogged by a reputation for causing permanent memory loss, even brain damage. Proponents of ECT insist that, at its worst, ECT only erases memories for the time around which it was administered—a small price to pay. But some people swear it's robbed them of precious older memories. Although controlled studies have yet to corroborate these complaints, even proponents admit that insensitive research methodology may be to blame.[7]

If you do have to resort to ECT, research suggests memory problems can be minimized without compromising clinical efficacy if (1) ECT is administered bifrontally;[11] (2) a moderate dose of anesthetic is used and concomitant psychotropic drugs are avoided;[7,8] (3) the lowest "dose" of *brief pulse* current necessary to provoke an adequate seizure is used (not all ECT clinics are equipped to do this);[7,8] (4) ECT is given no more than two or three times a week;[7] and (5) the patient spends a few hours resting in a dark, quiet room after coming to.[12] Anecdotally, psychiatrist Abram Hoffer claims that megadoses of vitamin B3 can also prevent ECT-induced memory loss.[9]

NOTES

1. J. Cookson, "Side Effects of Antidepressants," *Brit J Psychiatry* 163(Suppl. 20, 1993):20–24.

2. E. Richelson, "Treatment of Acute Depression," *Psychiat Clin North Am* 16(September 1993):461–478.

3. R. P. Greenberg et al., "A Meta-analysis of Antidepressant Outcome Under 'Blinder' Conditions," *J Consult Clin Psychol* 60(October 1992):664–669.

4. R. Balon et al., "Sexual Dysfunction During Antidepressant Treatment," *J Clin Psychiatry* 54(June 1993):209–212.

5. F. Song et al., "Selective Serotonin Reuptake Inhibitors: Meta-analysis of Efficacy and Acceptability," *Brit Med J* 306(March 13, 1993):683–687.

6. M. H. Teicher et al., "Antidepressant Drugs and the Emergence of Suicidal Tendencies," *Drug Safety* 8(March 1993):186–212.

7. M. W. Enns and J. P. Reiss, "Electroconvulsive Therapy," *Can J Psychiatry* 37(December 1992):671–678.

8. A. Khan et al., "Electroconvulsive Therapy," *Psychiat Clin North Am* 16(September 1993):497–513.

9. Abram Hoffer, *Common Questions on Schizophrenia and Their Answers* (New Canaan, Conn.: Keats Publishing, 1987).

10. Harvey M. Ross, *Fighting Depression* (New Canaan, Conn.: Keats Publishing, 1992).

11. F. J. Letemendia et al., "Therapeutic Advantage of Bifrontal Electrode Placement in ECT," *Psychol Med* 23(May 1993):349–360.

12. P. Suedfeld et al., "Reduction of Post-ECT Memory Complaints Through Brief, Partial Restricted Environmental Stimulation (REST)," *Prog Neuro-Psychopharmacol Biol Psychiatry* 13(1989):693–700.

THIRTY-THREE

Putting It All Together: Planning and Implementing a Depression Recovery Program for Yourself

WE'VE come a long way and covered a lot of ground. Is your head spinning? Mine sure is. You've only had to read this book—I've had to *write* the darned thing!

Where to start? How to choose from among so many treatment possibilities? How to devise a program for recovery?

I say *program* because unless there is an obvious primary cause for your depression with a "magic bullet" treatment to match, it would be imprudent to pin your hopes on just one—or perhaps even two or three—antidepressant therapies. Better to avail yourself of a range of them.[1]

You may already have a clear idea of which ones you'd like to try, based, perhaps, on the evidence in their favor, their suitability or appeal to you as an individual, their ease, safety, convenience or other criteria. More likely, your mind isn't made up. May I suggest you thumb through the book one more time to review the options and, if you haven't done so already, rate the contenders.

In selecting antidepressant strategies, consider aiming for a "balanced diet."[1] You might try, for instance, to include approaches from each of these diverse categories:

- *Physical/physiological approaches*, like hypotoxic living, improved nutrition and using supplements.
- *Body approaches*, like exercise, sleep deprivation and bodywork.

- *Behavioral approaches*, like being more active and problem-solving.
- *Emotional and social/interpersonal approaches*, like art therapy, talking to someone and social skills training.
- *Cognitive mental approaches*, like cognitive therapy, suggestion and meditation.

Note that some antidepressant strategies encompass more than one category. Exercise, for instance, can be body-oriented, social, emotional (expressive dancing) and/or mental (meditating while you walk).

Here are some more suggestions:

- Schedule time to plan your program and to periodically review and revise it.

- Review Chapter 24 on being more active to become less depressed and Chapter 26 on creative problem-solving. Most of the ideas in these chapters on planning and scheduling activities, rewarding yourself and other matters are applicable here, too.

- Get other people to help, if you can. It's hard when you're depressed to pull yourself up by your own bootstraps—to find the energy and staying power to make appointments, procure antidepressant products, assert yourself with health professionals, stick to your regimens, and so on. Other people, at least those that understand the trials of depression, can provide moral support and practical help.

- Be patient. When you've been depressed for a long time, recovery is usually a slow and bumpy process—two steps forward, one step back. The backward steps can be bitterly disheartening if you think they're permanent. They rarely are, though an adjustment in therapy is called for if your recovery really stalls. Similarly, if you only obtain a partial recovery after a few weeks or months, it's important to try alternatives to make it complete. Partial recovery can rather easily slide back down into relapse.[2]

- Be flexible. If something doesn't seem to be working for you after you've given it a good try, try something else.

• After you've recovered, continue following your program for at least a few months. This is to prevent relapse. Then, if you like, you can take a month or two to scale down to a lighter, maintenance program to help prevent future recurrences. Continuing full-strength, however, will afford the most protection, especially if you have a history of recurrent depression (this puts you at high risk).[3]

• If you don't feel up to planning any fancy "depression recovery program," don't bother, at least for now. Just do whatever you can, and perhaps see a professional.

That's it! We've finally arrived at the end of our journey together. It's been a pleasure having you along for the ride. From here on in, the journey should keep getting better and better. No matter how hard it may be for you to believe that, the odds are in your favor.

NOTES

1. A. A. Lazarus, "The Multimodal Approach to the Treatment of Minor Depression," *Am J Psychother* 46(January 1992):50–57.

2. M. E. Thase et al., "Relapse After Cognitive Behavior Therapy of Depression," *Am J Psychiatry* 8(August 1992):1046–1052.

3. D. J. Kupfer, "Management of Recurrent Depression," *J Clin Psychiatry* 54(February Supplement, 1993):29–33.

Index